Transforming Learning

Instructional and Assessment Strategies for Leadership Education

A Volume in
Contemporary Perspectives on Leadership Learning

Series Editor:
Kathy L. Guthrie,
Florida State University

Transforming Learning

Instructional and Assessment Strategies for Leadership Education

By

Kathy L. Guthrie, Daniel M. Jenkins, and Associates

Information Age Publishing, Inc.
Charlotte, North Carolina • www.infoagepub.com

Library of Congress Cataloging-in-Publication Data

CIP data for this book can be found on the Library of Congress website:
http://www.loc.gov/index.html

Paperback: 978-1-64802-045-2
Hardcover: 978-1-64802-046-9
E-Book: 978-1-64802-047-6

Printed in the United States of America.

CONTENTS

Acknowledgments ix

1. Setting the Stage 1
Organization of Text 1
   Why Curricular? 2
   Why Cocurricular? 2
   Why Technology Enhanced? 2
   Why Followership Focused? 2
   Why Assessment? 3
How to Use This Text 3
   Beginning With the End in Mind: Developing Learning Outcomes for Your Leadership Program 3
   Types of Leadership Learning Outcomes 3
The Leadership Learning Framework 5
The Leadership Learning Framework as a Vehicle for Learning Outcomes 5
Why the Leadership Learning Framework Works: Leader and Follower Experiences
   as a Source of Transformational Learning 6
Table of Activities 7

2. Discussion 13
Discussion in Leadership Education 13
Braving the Fishbowl: Using Concentric Circles to Facilitate Dialogue
   (Darren Pierre, Shelby Hearn, and Cristian Noriega) 14
Talking Popsicle Sticks (Trisha Teig) 15
Live Twitter Chats (Kathy L. Guthrie and Josie Ahlquist) 17
Exploring Preconceived Understandings of Followership Through Group Discussion (Cameron C. Beatty) . . . 18
Let's Discuss Learning: Assessing Learning of Discussion Activities (Trisha Teig) 19
Untangling the Destructive Leadership Web: The Case of Team Foxcatcher (Jasmine D. Collins) 22

3. Case Study Methods 25
Case Study Methods in Leadership Education 25
Making a Case for Leading Critically (Daniel M. Jenkins and Amanda Cutchens) 26
Protests and Student Activism on Your Campus: Are You Ready?
   (Brian T. Magee and Anne-Marie Algier) 27
Cracking the Case: Learning Through Student-Written Teaching Case Studies (Eric Kaufman) 29
Peer Consultation (Justin Greenleaf, Thomas Stanley, and Kerry L. Priest) 30
Practice Case Study: Preparing Students to Become Leadership Consultants (Lindsay J. Hastings) 31
"Living Leadership" Case Studies (Melissa L. Rocco) 33

4. Reflection 37
Reflection-Based Pedagogy in Leadership Education 37
Reflection Through Mind Mapping Leadership and Change Concepts (Cameron C. Beatty) 38
Mirror Your Experience: Peer-Teaching Through Reflection (Aaron D. Clevenger) 39
Photographing Leadership: Making Meaning of Our World (Jackie Bruce and Daniel Collins) 40

Follow the Leader or Leading the Follower? Asking Critical Questions
About Followers and Followership (Julie E. Owen) 41
Beyond "Dear Diary": Feedback Driven Journaling (Jillian M. Volpe White) 43
You Think What?: Utilizing Reflection to Enhance Understanding of Self and Comfort
With Differing Perspectives (Eric Grospitch and Michael Gleason) 45

5. Team-Based Learning **47**
Team-Based Learning in Leadership Education 47
Organizational Change Case Study Project (Corey Seemiller) 48
Post-It Note Introductions (Brittany Brewster) 50
Globally Networked Learning: An International Lens on Leadership (Lisa Endersby) 51
Escape Games as a Learning Assessment (John Banter and John Egan) 53
Examining Identity and Expanding One's Self-Awareness as a Leader (Sara E. Thompson) 54
Ready—Set—Action: Multimedia Teach-Back Group Activity (Bobby Kunstman) 56

6. Service-Learning **59**
Service-Learning in Leadership Education 59
Are You Sure We Can Do This? Tackling Concerns Around Service-Learning (Marianne Lorensen) 60
Iterative Concept Mapping in Service-Learning (Rian Satterwhite) 61
Reflecting 1 Second Each Day (Kathy L. Guthrie) 63
Appreciative Service-Learning (Tamara Bauer and Kerry L. Priest) 64
The Service and Leadership Integration (Eric Buschlen) 65
Root Causes, Connections, and Systems (Julie LeBlanc) 67

7. Self- and Peer-Assessments **69**
Self- and Peer-Assessments in Leadership Education 69
Strengths-Spotting (Rachel Pridgen and Abigaile VanHorn) 70
Leadership You Admire (Jennifer Batchelder) 71
Virtual Values Sort (Vivechkanand S. Chunoo) 72
Humility Exercise: Self- and Peer-Assessment (Matthew Sowcik and Austin Council) 74
Luck of the Draw Discussion Groups: Using Self-Assessment
to Promote Lifelong Leadership Learning (Beth Hoag) 78
In My Feelings: Individual and Collective Capacities for Emotional Intelligence (Erica Wiborg) 81

8. Role-Play **83**
Role-Play in Leadership Education 83
Leadership Behaviors and Fast Food (Daniel M. Jenkins and Amanda Cutchens) 84
A "Starring Role" in Processing Diversity and Inclusion (Jason Headrick) 86
Uncovering Challenges Working through Technology (Kirstin C. Phelps) 87
Architects, Inventors, Creators: Exploring Follower Behavior in Groups (Maritza Torres) 89
Conscious Selection and Review of Role-Playing Activities (Michaela Shenberger) 90
Empathic Listening Triads (Gayle Spencer) 93

9. Simulation **97**
Simulation in Leadership Education 97
What if There Is No "Right" Answer? Preparing for the "Grey Areas"
of Ethical Decision Making (Sonja Ardoin) 98
Diversifying the Vision of Leadership (Jesse Ford) 100
Gamified Test (Elizabeth Goryunova) 101
Finding the Path: Leadership and Followership as a Relationship (Jillian M. Volpe White) 102
Game On! Using Barnga to Facilitate Cultural Awareness
in Leadership Education (Amber Manning-Ouellette) 104
On Campus Simulations as Leadership Development (Kathleen Callahan) 105

10. Games **107**
    Games in Leadership Education 107
    Green Apple Group Scramble Game (Natalie Coers) 108
    The Power of Thoughtful Directions (Brittany Devies) 109
    Using a Video Game for Learning Ethical Decision Making (Virginia L. Byrne) 110
    Five Types of Followers and You (Ali Raza) 112
    Perfect Storm (Cara Lucia) 113
    Game Change Management (Michael Miller) 114

11. Arts-Based Learning **117**
    Arts-Based Learning in Leadership Education 117
    The Mirror Exercise: "Follow The Follower" (Christopher Ruiz de Esparza) 118
    Theater of Bad Leadership (Sally R. Watkins) 120
    Leadership: Changing the Narrative (Natasha H. Chapman and Naliyah Kaya) 121
    Encouraging Creative Reflection Through Journaling (Jessica Chung) 122
    Oozing Leadership Slime (Sally R. Watkins) 124
    The Eyes Have It: Using Images as a Leadership Assessment Tool
        (J. Preston Yarborough and S. Todd Deal) 125

Editor and Contributor Bios **127**

Acknowledgments

When we decided to answer the call to create a companion manual to *The Role of Leadership Educators: Transforming Learning*, we knew we needed to call on the diverse leadership educators we know and love. We are fortunate to work in a field with such intelligent, passionate, and engaged practitioners and scholars who answered our plea. A total of 68 leadership educators agreed share their brilliance and experience in creating dynamic and influential leadership learning opportunities. We are especially grateful to Brittany Devies whose commitment, organization, and determination kept this text moving forward. Honestly, without her, this book would not exist. Brittany Devies, remember her name, she is a new leadership educator to watch out for.

CHAPTER 1

Setting the Stage

Facilitating Leadership Learning Opportunities

This text was developed to fill a significant resource gap in leadership education. Very few instructor's and facilitator's guides are available to leadership educators. Of those existing, the vast majority are associated with specific textbooks (e.g., Dugan, Turman, Barnes, & Associates, 2017), tied to particular leadership theories or models (e.g., Kouzes, Posner, High, & Morgan, 2013), or only accessible through subscription services (i.e., electronic guides tied to the purchase of an adopted textbook). We sought out not only to offer an addition to the sparse number of leadership education instructor's and facilitator's guides, but more importantly to create a resource grounded in educational, pedagogical, and instructional design. In their roundtable discussions with leadership educators at professional conferences, Jenkins and Priest (2013; and later, Priest, Seemiller, & Jenkins, 2013), found that the chief area leadership educators were seeking professional development in was teaching and learning—the knowledge of the theory and practice of teaching, knowledge about theory and practice of student learning and student development, and the implementation of student-centered strategies.

In response to leadership educators' call for professional development related to teaching and learning, this text is grounded foremost in the college teaching and leadership education literature. Respectively, each learning activity in this book includes learning outcomes, facilitation and debriefing notes, and additional resources offered by the authors. We not only want educators to use the learning activities provided in this text, but also develop their capacity to be leadership educators. That is, we want leadership educators to be better facilitators, to debrief learning activities with more intentionality, to understand the importance of beginning with learning outcomes and objectives in mind, and ultimately foster their acumen to make informed educational, instructional, and programmatic decisions; perhaps inspiring them to create their own learning activities as well.

ORGANIZATION OF TEXT

We organized this text very differently than other instructor's or facilitator's guides out there. Specifically, instead of organizing this text topically by leadership theories, models, or their components, it is organized by the pedagogical methods covered in f *The Role of Leadership Educators: Transforming Learning* (Guthrie & Jenkins, 2018): (a) discussion; (B) case studies; (c) reflection; (d) team-based learning; (e) service-learning; (f) self- and peer-assessments; (g) role-play; (h) simulation; (i) games; and (j) art. Intentionally, each chapter in this text contains six learning activities for each pedagogical method, at least one in each of the following categories:

1. **Curricular:** These learning activities were designed with academic credit-bearing leadership education courses in mind.
2. **Cocurricular:** These learning activities were designed with nonacademic leadership education programs—often situated in higher education within student affairs and/or academic affairs—in mind.
3. **Technology Enhanced:** These learning activities were designed with asynchronous and synchronous online learning in mind.
4. **Followership Focused:** These learning activities were designed with the role of the leader *and* follower in mind and provide opportunities to explore both leadership and followership dynamics and experiences.
5. **Learning Assessment—Curricular:** These learning activities were designed with a focus on the assessment of learning in academic credit-bearing leadership education courses.

Transforming Learning: Instructional and Assessment Strategies for Leadership Education, pp. 1–12

6. **Learning Assessment—Cocurricular:** These learning activities were designed with a focus on the assessment of learning in nonacademic leadership education programs.

While each learning activity was designed with a particular contextual category in mind, many are interchangeable. That is, just because a specific learning activity is categorized as "curricular" does not mean it could not slightly be altered to fit a student affairs-based leadership program (and vice versa). Likewise, simply because a learning activity is categorized as "technology enhanced" does not mean that it is only for a fully online courses, rather it is focused on how various forms technology can improve leadership learning. In any case, we also want to provide some context around these categories (see Table on pages 9–11).

WHY CURRICULAR?

Since the 1980s, institutions of higher education have been offering academic credit-bearing leadership studies courses (Guthrie & Jenkins, 2018). Guthrie, Teig, and Hu (2018) report there are 1,558 curricular-based programs in the United States, ranging from associates, certificates, bachelors, master's, and doctoral degree types. Accordingly, many of the learning activities in this text build upon leadership knowledge derived from popular leadership textbooks often utilized in leadership studies coursework such as *Leadership: Theory and Practice* (Northouse, 2019) and *Exploring Leadership: For College Students Who Want to Make a Difference* (Komives, Lucas, & McMahon, 2013), as well as scholarship from peer-reviewed journals such as the *Journal of Leadership Education,* the *Journal of Leadership Studies,* and the *Journal of College Student Development.* Equally, some learning activities, such as "Leadership You Admire" in Chapter 7, refer to self-assessments, case studies, or other resources in the abovementioned texts.

WHY COCURRICULAR?

Beginning in the 1970s, cocurricular leadership programs started to emerge in higher education (Guthrie & Jenkins, 2018). These include standalone programs in dedicated centers of leadership, civic engagement, service-learning, and social justice, as well as within offices and units of student activities and organizations, residence and Greek life, and living/learning communities, to name but a few. And while these programs are also grounded in leadership knowledge, the academic component is oftentimes more implicit (i.e., little or no expectations related to reading textbooks or completing graded assignments), the programs tend to be more focused on leadership training (i.e., skill development)

and leadership development, and no academic credit is earned. Nonetheless, cocurricular leadership programs have traditionally included a significant service-learning component (Guthrie, 2016; Guthrie & McCracken, 2010) and provide leadership learning touchpoints for students in higher education who may not have flexibility in their academic programs to engage in for-credit leadership coursework. Correspondingly, several learning activities in this text build upon commonly used theoretical frameworks in student leadership development such as the social change model of leadership development (Higher Education Research Institute, 1996; Komives, Wagner, & Associates, 2016) or provide opportunities for students to build or practice skills in group work (see Chapter 5), facilitation (see Chapter 2), or critical thinking and communication in cross-cultural interactions (see Chapter 9).

WHY TECHNOLOGY ENHANCED?

There is vast growth in technology-enhanced leadership education (Phelps, 2012). Although there is growing scholarship related to the use of technology in leadership education (e.g., Guthrie & McCracken, 2010; Jenkins, 2016; Jenkins, Endersby, & Guthrie, 2015; Phelps, 2012), there is little in the way of specific resources for leadership educators to use as a quick reference. And, as stated above, technology-enhanced learning activities need not be limited to online courses—leadership educators can integrate technology into multiple facets of their instruction and facilitation. For example, the learning activity "Cracking the Case: Learning Through Student-Written Teaching Case Studies," in Chapter 3, develops students' capacity to utilize collaborative technology in order to explore leadership theories and apply shared leadership in a small group setting. Similarly, in Chapter 6, the learning activity "Reflecting 1 Second Each Day" utilizes students' smart devices as a vehicle for critical reflection on service-learning engagement.

WHY FOLLOWERSHIP FOCUSED?

Only recently has the theoretical construct followership emerged as an accepted critical and foundational component of leadership knowledge taught in leadership programs (Raffo, 2013). Case in point, until now, in its eight edition, the most widely utilized leadership textbook, *Leadership: Theory and Practice* (Northouse, 2019), finally has a full chapter dedicated to followership. Although substantial literature such as *Followership: How Followers Are Creating Change and Changing Leaders* (Kellerman, 2008) and *The Courageous Follower: Standing Up to and for Our Leaders* (Chaleff, 2009) exist, there is a void of resources related to followership education. As Rost (1991) and Murji (2015) point out, if leadership is really a relationship between the leader and follower, why are leadership educators so focused on one half of the equation: the leader? Thus, this text seeks to build upon the publications of Hoptin (2014), Raffo (2013), and Hurwitz (2017), and provide learning activities focused on the understanding and application of followership. For example, the learning activity "The Mirror Exercise: 'Follow the Follower'" in Chapter 11 utilizes play to broaden participants' understanding of the leader-follower relationship as fluid, interactional, and shared. Likewise, the learning activity "Architects, Inventors, Creators: Exploring Follower Behavior in Groups" in Chapter 8 utilizes role-play as a vehicle for exploring Kellerman's (2008) follower typology and provides opportunities for participants to observe each behavior in the typology influences group outcomes.

WHY ASSESSMENT?

Assessment is inextricably linked to learning and development; in this way, assessment is intrinsic to education (Ewell, 1988). And, while assessing the unseen and social construction of leadership is not easy (Guthrie & Jenkins, 2018), there is increased pressure on leadership educators in both curricular and cocurricular roles to demonstrate that student learning is occurring at individual, program, and institutional levels (Dugan, 2012; Goertzen, 2012; Roberts & Bailey, 2016). In response to this demand, we included learning activities designed to assess leadership learning in curricular as well as cocurricular contexts. It is important to note that while not all learning activities have an assessment component, doing so intentionally through design provides a more comprehensive learning experience for participants (Fink, 2013). For example, in the learning activity for curricular learning assessment, "Let's Discuss Learning: Assessing Learning of Discussion Activities," in Chapter 2, participants not only engage in a learning activity focused on group communication, but also have opportunities to assess their learning, discern their clarity of understanding for course content, and reflect on the communication dynamics observed during the discussion. Similarly, "'Living Leadership' Case Studies," the learning activity for cocurricular assessment in Chapter 3, offers participants opportunities to collaborate and apply personal leadership knowledge as well as assess their own critical thinking skills.

HOW TO USE THIS TEXT

The following sections describe the intentionality and process we aim to illustrate throughout this text and in each learning activity in the subsequent chapters. First, we outline the importance of developing leadership learning outcomes first and foremost prior to considering the instructional and assessment strategies to employ in your course or program. Additionally, this section includes an overview of commonly used leadership learning outcomes and related examples. Next, we introduce the leadership learning framework from our text, *The Role of Leadership Educators: Transforming Learning* (Guthrie & Jenkins, 2018), and explain how each aspect of learning depicted in the framework can be applied to intentional program design. Finally, we present our model of leader and follower experiences as a source of transformational learning (Guthrie & Jenkins, 2018) and illustrate how intentional educational design, such as the learning activities in this text, offer opportunities for participants to make sense of their leadership and followership experiences as a conduit to leadership discovery, development, and metacognition. Applicably, in each section, we include examples from the learning activities in this text. We encourage you to flip through the learning activities as a reference tool to enhance your own learning as you read through the following sections.

BEGINNING WITH THE END IN MIND: DEVELOPING LEARNING OUTCOMES FOR YOUR LEADERSHIP PROGRAM

Effective leadership program design starts by developing a set of learning outcomes, that is, beginning with the end in mind (Covey, 1989; Guthrie & Jenkins, 2018). This method, referred to as "backwards design" (Wiggins & McTighe, 2005), is critical to the effectiveness of any leadership learning experience (Guthrie & Jenkins, 2018). Accordingly, as with program design, we suggest a scaffolding approach to designing learning activities where educators plan and execute the creation of curriculum and learning experiences to meet defined learning outcomes and objectives (Wiggins & McTighe, 2005). Conversely, beginning with a list of readings, such as the 15 chapters of a textbook that align with the 15 weeks of a typical curricular course is misguided. Instead, focus first on what Fink (2013) describes as deciding "your big dream" for your students as an instructor or facilitator—what do you want your students to be able to know, be, or do as a result of participating in your leadership program?

TYPES OF LEADERSHIP LEARNING OUTCOMES

High-quality learning outcomes are critical in curricular planning and intentionally designing a leadership program (Guthrie & Jenkins, 2018). In leadership education, learning outcomes generally fall into two broad categories: (a) technical knowledge of the expertise and skills deemed requisite to leadership either generally or in particular areas; and (b) humanistic knowledge about people, both as individuals and as members of groups (Harvey & Jenkins, 2014). In both categories, the learning outcomes are reinforced through essential leadership content knowledge such as theories, models, and concepts. To demonstrate this, Northouse (2009) adapted Fink's (2003) taxonomy of significant learning and organized leadership learning outcomes into six categories:

1. **Foundational Knowledge:** Understand and remember key assumptions and components of various leadership models;
2. **Application:** Know how to apply leadership models to real-life situations;
3. **Integration:** Be able to relate leadership theory to other academic subjects and current events;
4. **Human Dimension:** Understand the personal and social implications of knowing about leadership;
5. **Caring:** Care about leadership and learning more about it; and
6. **Learning How to Learn:** Know how to keep on learning about leadership.

Correspondingly, most leadership learning outcomes should fall within one or more of the categories described above. For example, learning objectives from a "Teams & Leadership" program/workshop might look like these (Seemiller, Jenkins, & Associates, 2017):

Foundational Knowledge:

- remember some of the terminology associated with teams and teamwork (for example, groupthink, roles);
- be able to identify the key elements of team and group processes (for example, forming, storming, norming, and performing);

Application

- be able to do a formal analysis of team roles in order to meet specific goals;
- be able to observe a team in the real world and identify specific group dynamics;

Integration

- identify some of the differences between effective and ineffective team leaders and how context affects each;
- relate ideas about teamwork to group processes, for example, communication, shared decision making;

Human Dimension

- come to see themselves as people more educated about teams and teamwork than the average person;

- be able to inform and educate other organizational members about the roles and responsibilities of team members in group work;

Caring

- value the importance of assigned roles in group work as a part of effective team leadership;
- be anxious to critically evaluate group dynamics that they encounter regularly in the public media.

Learning How to Learn

- be able to identify important resources for their own subsequent team-based work;
- continue to be proactive with team-based work and shared decision making, for example, what group roles to take on and how to delegate responsibilities

The example learning objectives above utilize Fink's (2013) interactive taxonomy of significant learning, leadership educators may just as well use Bloom's (1956; see also Anderson, Krathwohl, & Bloom, 2001) hierarchical taxonomy of learning which begins with surface knowledge, that is, what can a learner recall or remember information covered within a lesson (remembering) and increases stepwise through five additional domains: (a) Understanding—can a learner explain ideas or concepts? (b) Applying—can a learner use information, or connect it to other ideas or concepts? (c) Analyzing—can a learner distinguish between different parts of an idea or concept? (d) Evaluating—can a learner justify the significance of an idea of concept? and (e) Creating—can a student create something original founded upon prior knowledge? The point of the matter is not which learning taxonomy you choose to utilize, but rather we are learner-centered leadership educators who begin with the end in mind and structure and design our leadership programs intentionally.

For resources related to developing learning outcomes visit the homepages of most faculty development centers at U.S. colleges and universities such as the Center for Innovative Teaching and Learning (2019) at the Indiana University Bloomington, the Iowa State University Center for Excellence in Learning and Teaching (2019), and the Teaching Commons at DePaul (DePaul Teaching Commons, 2019). The next step in intentionally designing a leadership program is to connect the learning outcomes with appropriate learning activities and procedures for assessing student learning. Hence, the learning and assessment activities offered in this text provide exemplars and put the leadership learning framework introduced in the next section in motion.

THE LEADERSHIP LEARNING FRAMEWORK

The leadership learning framework is a student-centered approach leadership educators can use theoretically, conceptually, and in practice to create programs that intentionally connect pedagogy (i.e., instructional and assessment strategies) with learning outcomes. Accordingly, the leadership learning framework includes six aspects of leadership learning as depicted by Guthrie and Jenkins (2018, pp. 58–70):

- **Leadership Knowledge**: the content knowledge of leadership theories, concepts, and skills is foundational for all leadership learning and encompasses the entire wheel;
- **Leadership Development**: the human and interpersonal aspects of leadership learning, focuses on learners' values and needs, personal motivation and readiness to lead, identity, and dimensions of self;
- **Leadership Training**: the skills- and competency-based behavioral aspects of leadership, focuses on what learners are able to do when they leave our leadership programs;
- **Leadership Observation**: the social, cultural, and observational aspects of leadership learning, focuses on learners' construction of knowledge through making meaning about how effective and ineffective leaders and followers act in relation to others in sociocultural contexts (it is passive in nature);
- **Leadership Engagement**: the experiential, relational, interactional, and interpersonal aspects of leadership learning, focuses on learners' construction of knowledge through direct engagement and participation with the activities of leadership (it is active in nature); and
- **Metacognition**: the conduit among critical thought, meaning making, and reflection of the leadership learning experience, is centered within the framework, because without it, learners are unable to adapt and apply what they learn.

THE LEADERSHIP LEARNING FRAMEWORK AS A VEHICLE FOR LEARNING OUTCOMES

The leadership learning framework is a mechanism for instructors to better understand how students learn and develop leadership. When used as a channel for delivering learning outcomes, the leadership learning framework offers clarity related to the different types of learning students should experience in an intentional leadership program. As demonstrated in the framework:

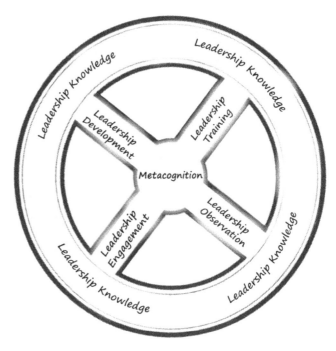

Source: Guthrie and Jenkins, (2018, p. 58).

Figure 1.1.   Leadership learning framework.

Knowledge of leadership theories, concepts, and skills is foundational for all leadership learning and needs to be adjoined to all of its aspects. We believe leadership knowledge acquisition occurs in all programs, even if only by using language about leadership that may not have been used previously. Working in from the leadership knowledge rim of the framework, the four aspects of development, training, observation, and engagement all contribute to metacognition. Metacognition sits at the heart of leadership learning because, without critical thought and reflection of the learning experience, we cannot make meaning or begin to apply and adapt what we learn. (Guthrie & Jenkins, 2018, p. 57)

Accordingly, leadership educators have myriad instructional and assessment strategies to choose from when designing learning activities (Guthrie & Jenkins, 2018). That being stated, we proposed that each component of the leadership learning framework may be underscored by intentionally pairing appropriate instructional and assessment strategies (see for example Guthrie & Jenkins, 2018, pp. 75–77). To illustrate this phenomenon, in Table 1.1. Table of Activities, we have identified the aspects of learning from the leadership learning framework present for each learning activity in this text. For example, the learning activity "Leadership Behaviors and Fast Food" in Chapter 8, includes all six aspects of learning from the leadership learning framework. Specifically, the learning aspects of leadership knowledge and development are present through the activity of having participants complete and self-assess their results on the Leadership Behaviors Questionnaire (Northouse, 2019). Further, participants also have opportunities to experience the learning aspects of leadership engagement, training, and observation through participation in and observing the performed role-play and assessing the student actors propensity to be more task- or relationship-focused in their assigned roles. Through structured debriefing including questions that require students to critically reflect on their feelings related to the role-play scenario, what leadership behaviors were present in the activity, what they learned from the experience, and how this scenario relates to a real world, the learning aspects of leadership metacognition, observation, knowledge, and development are explored and reinforced. While not every learning activity should include all six learning aspects from the leadership learning framework, most learning activities should include at least two aspects. We hope the learning activities in the current text will inspire you to create your own innovative instructional and learning strategies to construct leadership learning opportunities of all students.

WHY THE LEADERSHIP LEARNING FRAMEWORK WORKS: LEADER AND FOLLOWER EXPERIENCES AS A SOURCE OF TRANSFORMATIONAL LEARNING

Leadership is a process of learning in which individuals make sense of their experiences, uncover leadership within themselves, and work in communities of leadership practice with others (Antonacopoulou & Bento, 2004). To illustrate this phenomenon through building upon learners' existing knowledge about leadership, followership, and experiential bases (Kolb, 1984; Wisniewski, 2010), in Figure 1.2 we offer a model of leader and follower experiences as a source of transformational learning (Guthrie & Jenkins, 2018, pp. 150–151). Like Kolb's (1984) model of experiential learning, the learning process is activated by a learner's experience—in a leader *or* follower role in a particular context. The second stage—critical reflection—involves learners in an iterative process of reflecting on experience and synthesizing lessons, conclusions, uncertainties, and questions (Harvey & Jenkins, 2014; Owen, 2016). In the third stage, learners make meaning of their leader or follower experiences from the critical reflection in the prior stage through experiential abstraction (Baxter Magolda, 2008; Kegan, 1994). In the fourth and final stage, learners experience metacognitive discovery and exploration through experimentation of new behaviors and skills, while self-monitoring in the present.

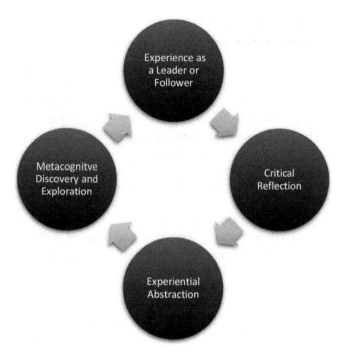

Source: Guthrie and Jenkins (2018, p. 151).

Figure 1.2.   Model of leader and follower experiences as a source of transformational learning.

Each learning activity in this text was intentionally designed with transformative learning in mind. That is, each learning activity invites participants to actively engage, construct personal meaning of the content presented, and build upon their existing experiences and understanding of leadership and followership. For example, the learning activity "Photographing Leadership: Making Meaning of Our World," in Chapter 4, provides opportunities for participants to engage with leadership or followership content, while also using their individual worldview—literally through the use of photography to "photograph leadership"—to make meaning of that content. This learning activity also includes a significant, critical reflection component that ties participants' experiences from the activity to sociocultural aspects, peers' worldviews, and future-focused prompts such as "What struck you about the photo or the explanation that you can take with you in your own journey?" Thus, through the process of "photographing leadership," participants are experiencing leadership or followership in their own worlds and are asked to consider how the photograph demonstrates the enactment or application of course content (Stage 1 of the model). Subsequently, through guided reflection questions, students are asked how their photograph is representative of their world and what leadership challenges and/or opportunities illustrated in the photo and (Stage 2), to respond to the leadership and sociocultural aspects depicted in both their own and their peers' photographs (Stage 3), and finally, to consider how they might enact or apply the theory under study as a result of the influence of the aforementioned process (Stage 4). The cycle begins again when students reflect on their experiences from these experiments, that is new "enactions" or applications.

TABLE OF ACTIVITIES

We acknowledge that whether you are a new or seasoned leadership educator, sometimes creating leadership learning activities can be a challenge. One learning activity can be complex in that it holds several instructional strategies, as well as have multiple leadership learning aspects. As mentioned before, we developed Table 1.1, a Table of Activities, to help guide your selection of learning activities for the specific context in which you seek. We recognize this is not all inclusive, or a slight change in context can shift both what instructional strategy and leadership learning aspect it contains. However, we hope Table 1.1 will give you a start to better understanding the offerings of each learning activity provided. The learning activities and assessment strategies in the following chapters are truly brilliant and we hope you are as inspired as we were to not only use those provided, but continue to create our own.

References:

Anderson, L. W., Krathwohl, D. R., & Bloom, B. S. (2001). *A taxonomy for learning, teaching, and assessing: A revision of Bloom's taxonomy of educational objectives.* Boston, MA: Allyn & Bacon.

Antonacopoulou, E. P., & Bento, R. F. (2004). Methods of "learning leadership": Taught and experiential. *Leadership in organizations: Current issues and key trends* (pp. 81–102). New York, NY: Routledge.

Baxter Magolda, M. B. (2008). Three elements of self-authorship. *Journal of College Student Development, 49*(4), 269–284.

Bloom, B. S. (1956) *Taxonomy of educational objectives, the classification of educational goals—Handbook I: Cognitive domain.* New York, NY: McKay.

Chaleff, I. (2009) *The courageous follower: Standing up to and for our leaders.* San Francisco, CA: Berrett-Koehler.

Covey, S. (1989). *7 habits of highly effective people.* New York, NY: Free Press.

DePaul Teaching Commons. (2019). *Course objective & learning outcomes.* Retrieved from https://resources.depaul.edu/teaching-commons/teaching-guides/course-design/Pages/course-objectives-learning-outcomes.aspx

Dugan, J. P. (2012). Exploring local to global leadership education assessment. In K. L. Guthrie & L. Osteen (Eds.), New *directions for student services, No. 140: Developing students' leadership capacity* (pp. 89–101). San Francisco, CA: Jossey-Bass.

Dugan, J., Turman, N., Barnes, A., & Associates. (2017). *Leadership theory: Facilitator's guide for cultivating critical perspectives.* San Francisco, CA: Jossey-Bass.

Ewell, P. (2002). *Applying learning outcomes concepts to higher education: An overview.* National Center for Higher Education Management Systems.

Fink, L. D. (2003). *Creating significant learning experiences.* San Francisco, CA: John Wiley & Sons.

Fink, L. D. (2013). *Creating significant learning experiences* (2nd ed.). San Francisco, CA: John Wiley & Sons.

Goertzen, B. J. (2012). Assessment adrift: Review of the current state of assessment of academically based leadership education programs. *Journal of Leadership Studies, 6,* 55–60.

Guthrie, K. L. (2016). Expanding leadership education: Teaching service-learning online. *ILA Member Connector, 6,* 15–17.

Guthrie, K. L., & Jenkins, D. M. (2018). *The role of leadership educators: Transforming learning.* Charlotte, NC: Information Age.

Guthrie, K. L., & McCracken, H. (2010). Making a difference online: Facilitating service-learning through distance education. *The Internet and Higher Education, 13,* 153–157.

Guthrie, K. L., Teig, T. S. & Hu, P. (2018). *Academic leadership programs in the United States.* Tallahassee, FL: Leadership Learning Research Center, Florida State University.

Hoptin, C. (2014). Learning and developing followership. *Journal of Leadership Education, 13*(1), 129–137.

Harvey, M., & Jenkins, D. M. (2014). Knowledge, praxis, and reflection: The three critical elements of effective leadership studies programs. *Journal of Leadership Studies, 7*(4), 76–85.

Higher Education Research Institute. (1996). *A social change model of leadership development (Version III).* Los Angeles, CA: University of California Higher Education Research Institute.

Hurwitz, M. (2017), Followership: A classroom exercise to introduce the concept. *Management Teaching Review, 2*(4), 218–288.

Indiana University Bloomington Center for Innovative Teaching and Learning. (2019). *Developing learning outcomes.* Retrieved from https://citl.indiana.edu/teaching-resources/course-design/developing-learning-outcomes

Iowa State University Center for Excellence in Learning and Teaching. (2019). *Tips on writing course goals/learning outcomes and measurable learning objectives.* Retrieved from http://www.celt.iastate.edu/teaching/preparing-to-teach/tips-on-writing-course-goalslearning-outcomes-and-measureable-learning-objectives/

Jenkins, D. M. (2016). Teaching leadership online: An exploratory study of instructional and assessment strategy use. *Journal of Leadership Education, 15*(2), 129–149.

Jenkins, D. M., Endersby, L., & Guthrie, K. L. (2015). Leadership education 2050: Changing the spaces and faces of experience. In M. Sowcik, A. C. Andenoro, M. McNutt, & S. E. Murphy (Eds.), *Leadership 2050: Critical challenges, key contexts, and emerging trends* (pp. 127–139). Bingley, England: Emerald.

Jenkins, D. M., & Priest, K. L. (2013, July). *Creating teacher resiliency: A dialogue on professional development for leadership educators.* Roundtable discussion facilitated at the 2013 Association of Leadership Educators Conference. New Orleans, LA.

Kegan, R. (1994). *In over our heads: The mental demands of modern life.* Cambridge, MA: Harvard University Press.

Kellerman, B. (2008). *Followership: How followers are creating change and changing leaders.* Boston, MA: Harvard Business Press.

Kolb, D. A. (1984). *Experiential learning: Experience as the source of learning and development.* Upper Saddle River, NJ: Prentice-Hall.

Komives, S. R., Lucas, N., & McMahon, T. R. (2013). *Exploring leadership: For college students who want to make a difference* (3rd ed.). San Francisco, CA: Jossey-Bass

Komives, S. R., Wagner, W., & Associates. (2016). *Leadership for a better world: Understanding the social change model of leadership development* (2nd ed.). San Francisco, CA: Jossey-Bass.

Kouzes, J. M., Posner, B. Z., High, B., & Morgan, G. M. (2013). *The student leadership challenge: Facilitation and activity guide.* San Francisco, CA: Jossey-Bass.

Murji, S. (2015). Taking followership education to the next level. *Journal of Leadership Education, 14*(3), 168–177.

Northouse, P. G. (2009). *Introduction to leadership concepts and practice* (5th ed.). Thousand Oaks, CA: SAGE.

Northouse, P. G. (2019). *Leadership: Theory and practice* (8th ed.). Thousand Oaks, CA: SAGE.

Owen, J. E. (2016). Fostering critical reflection: Moving from a service to a social justice paradigm. In W. Wagner & J. M. Pigza (Eds.), *New directions for student leadership, No. 150: Leadership development through service-learning* (pp. 37–48). San Francisco, CA: Jossey-Bass.

Phelps, K. (2012). Leadership online: Expanding the horizon. In K. L. Guthrie & L. Osteen (Eds.), New *directions for student services, No. 140: Developing students' leadership capacity* (pp. 65-75). San Francisco, CA: Jossey-Bass.

Priest, K. L., Seemiller, C. R., & Jenkins, D. M., (2013, October-November). *Creating teacher resiliency: A dialogue on professional development for leadership educators.* Roundtable discussion facilitated at the 15th Annual International Leadership Association Global Conference, Montreal, Canada.

Raffo, D. M. (2013). Teaching followership in leadership education. *Journal of Leadership Education, 12*(1), 262–273.

Roberts, D. M., & Bailey, K. J. (2016). Setting the stage: The intersection of leadership and assessment. In D. M. Roberts & K. J. Bailey (Eds.)., *New directions for student leadership, No. 151: Assessing student leadership* (pp. 7–18). San Francisco, CA: Jossey-Bass.

Rost, J. (1991). *Leadership for the twenty-first century.* New York, NY: Praeger.

Seemiller, C., & Jenkins, D., & Associates. (Eds.). (2017). *Leadership education academy facilitator's guide* (Unpublished manuscript). Denver, CO.

Wiggins, G., & McTighe, J. (2005). *Understanding by design* (2nd ed.). Alexandria, VA: Association for Supervision and Curriculum Development.

Wisniewski, M. A. (2010). Leadership and the millennials: Transforming today's technological teens in tomorrow's leaders. *Journal of Leadership Education, 9*(1), 53–68.

TABLE OF ACTIVITIES

Chapter	Activity	Context	Page	Other Pedagogy	Knowledge	Development	Training	Observation	Engagement	Metacognition
Discussion	Braving the Fishbowl: Using Concentric Circles to Facilitate Dialogue	Curricular instructional	14			X		X		
	Talking Popsicle Sticks	Cocurricular instructional	15	Reflection				X		X
	Live Twitter Chats	Technology enhanced	17	Reflection		X			X	X
	Exploring Preconceived Understandings of Followership Through Group Discussion	Followership focused	18	Reflection						X
	Let's Discuss Learning: Assessing Learning of Discussion Activities	Curricular learning assessment	19	Reflection Self-assessment			X			X
	Untangling the Destructive Leadership Web: The Case of Team Foxcatcher	Cocurricular learning assessment	22	Art	X	X				
Case Study	Making a Case for Leading Critically	Curricular instructional	26	Discussion	X	X	X			
	Protests & Student Activism on Your Campus: Are You Ready?	Cocurricular instructional	27				X			
	Cracking the Case: Learning Through Student-Written Teaching Case Studies	Technology enhanced	29	Peer Assessment	X		X			
	Peer Consultation	Followership focused	30	Peer Assessment		X	X			X
	Practice Case Study: Preparing Students to Become Leadership Consultants	Curricular learning assessment	31	Team-based learning Peer assessment	X		X		X	X
	"Living Leadership" Case Studies	Cocurricular learning assessment	33	Team-based learning	X		X		X	
Reflection	Reflection Through Mind Mapping Leadership and Change Concepts	Curricular instructional	38	Art Discussion	X					X
	Mirror Your Experience: Peer-Teaching through Reflection	Cocurricular instructional	39		X		X			X
	Photographing Leadership: Making Meaning of Our World	Technology enhanced	40	Art	X			X		X
	Follow the Leader or Leading the Follower?: Asking Critical Questions About Followers and Followership	Followership focused	41	Discussion	X	X				X
	Beyond 'Dear Diary': Feedback Driven Journaling	Curricular learning assessment	43			X	X			X
	You Think What?: Utilizing Reflection to Enhance Understanding of Self and Comfort with Differing Perspectives	Cocurricular learning assessment	45	Self-assessment	X	X				X

Leadership Learning Framework

TABLE OF ACTIVITIES (CONTINUED)

Chapter	Activity	Context	Page	Other Pedagogy	Knowledge	Development	Training	Observation	Engagement	Metacognition
									Leadership Learning Framework	
Team-Based Learning	Organizational Change Case Study Project	Curricular instructional	48	Case Study	X					
	Post-It Note Introductions	Cocurricular instructional	50	Reflection		X			X	X
	Globally Networked Learning: An International Lens on Leadership	Technology enhanced	51			X			X	
	Escape Games as a Learning Assessment	Followership focused	53	Simulation		X			X	X
	Examining Identity and Expanding One's Self-Awareness as a Leader	Curricular learning assessment	54	Art Reflection	X	X				X
	Ready—Set—Action: Multimedia Teach-Back Group Activity	Cocurricular learning assessment	56	Art	X	X			X	
Service-Learning	Are You Sure We Can Do This? Tackling Concerns Around Service-Learning	Curricular instructional	60	Discussion			X			X
	Iterative Concept Mapping in Service-Learning	Cocurricular instructional	61	Art Reflection			X			X
	Reflecting 1 Second Each Day	Technology enhanced	63	Art Reflection		X				X
	Appreciative Service-Learning	Followership focused	64	Art Reflection		X				X
	The Service and Leadership Integration	Curricular learning assessment	65	Reflection Self-Assessment		X				X
	Root Causes, Connections, and Systems	Cocurricular learning assessment	67	Reflection	X	X			X	X
Self- and Peer-Assessments	Strengths-Spotting	Curricular instructional	70	Discussion Reflection	X	X				X
	Leadership You Admire	Cocurricular instructional	71	Discussion Reflection		X		X		X
	Virtual Values Sort	Technology enhanced	72	Discussion Reflection		X			X	X
	Humility Exercise: Self- and Peer-Assessment	Followership focused	74	Reflection		X			X	X
	Luck of the Draw Discussion Groups: Using Self-Assessment to Promote Lifelong Leadership Learning	Curricular learning assessment	78	Discussion Reflection		X			X	X
	In My Feelings: Individual and Collective Capacities for Emotional Intelligence	Cocurricular learning assessment	81	Reflection		X				X

TABLE OF ACTIVITIES (CONTINUED)

Chapter	Activity	Context	Page	Other Pedagogy	Knowledge	Development	Training	Observation	Engagement	Metacognition
Role-Play	Leadership Behaviors and Fast Food	Curricular instructional	84	Reflection / Self-Assessment	X	X	X	X	X	X
	A "Starring Role" in Processing Diversity & Inclusion	Cocurricular instructional	86	Art / Reflection	X					X
	Uncovering Challenges Working through Technology	Technology enhanced	87	Team-based learning		X			X	
	Architects, Inventors, Creators: Exploring Follower Behavior in Groups	Followership focused	89	Reflection / Team-based learning		X	X		X	X
	Conscious Selection and Review of Role-Playing Activities	Curricular learning assessment	90	Reflection			X		X	X
	Empathic Listening Triads	Cocurricular learning assessment	93	Reflection		X	X	X	X	X
Simulation	What if There is No "Right" Answer?: Preparing for the "Grey Areas" of Ethical Decision-Making	Curricular instructional	98	Reflection / Team-based learning	X	X	X		X	X
	Diversifying the Vision of Leadership	Cocurricular instructional	100	Art	X	X			X	
	Gamified Test	Technology enhanced	101	Reflection	X	X	X			X
	Finding the Path: Leadership & Followership as A Relationship	Followership focused	102	Team-based learning			X	X	X	
	Game on! Using Barnga to Facilitate Cultural Awareness in Leadership Education	Curricular Learning assessment	104	Games / Reflection		X	X	X	X	X
	On Campus Simulations as Leadership Development	Cocurricular learning assessment	105	Art / Role-Play		X	X		X	X
Games	Green Apple Group Scramble Game	Curricular instructional	108	Reflection / Self-Assessment	X	X	X		X	X
	The Power of Thoughtful Directions	Cocurricular instructional	109	Reflection			X		X	X
	Using a Video Game for Learning Ethical Decision-Making	Technology enhanced	110		X	X	X		X	X
	Five Types of Followers and You	Followership focused	112	Reflection / Team-based learning	X					X
	Perfect Storm	Curricular learning assessment	113	Reflection / Team-based learning		X	X		X	X
	Game Change Management	Cocurricular learning assessment	114				X		X	

TABLE OF ACTIVITIES (CONTINUED)

Chapter	Activity	Context	Page	Other Pedagogy	Leadership Learning Framework					
					Knowledge	Development	Training	Observation	Engagement	Metacognition
Arts-Based Learning	The Mirror Exercise: "Follow the Follower"	Curricular instructional	118	Reflection	X				X	X
	Theater of Bad Leadership	Cocurricular instructional	120	Reflection Team-based learning						X
	Leadership: Changing the Narrative	Technology enhanced	121	Discussion	X	X		X		
	Encouraging Creative Reflection through Journaling	Followership focused	122	Reflection		X				X
	Oozing Leadership Slime	Curricular learning assessment	124	Reflection	X					X
	The Eyes Have It: Using Images as a Leadership Assessment Tool	Cocurricular learning assessment	125	Games	X	X	X		X	X

CHAPTER 2

Discussion

Spoken language is the central medium by which instructors teach, as well as the primary means by which students learn. Communication helps individuals reflect and connect new knowledge and content to what they already know (Cazden, 2001; Dudley-Marling, 2013). Correspondingly, discussion is the pedagogical method through which an instructor facilitates discussion to lead students through the process of analyzing a piece of material (Guthrie & Jenkins, 2018). Material might range from a poem to a statistical table or a new theoretical approach. In any case, the discussion method puts students in active learning mode and gives them first-hand appreciation of, and experience with, the application of that material—that is, the knowledge—to practice (Christensen, 1987). In the same way, discussion transforms students into "cocreators of knowledge" (Brookfield & Preskill, 2005, p. 22) providing them opportunities to construct and disclose deeper meaning of the material by drawing on the knowledge and experience they bring to their courses, thereby enriching understanding for all participants (Eeds & Wells, 1991; Hardman & Mroz, 1999). It is primarily through this process of sharing one's experience that makes discussion the signature pedagogy (see Shulman, 2005) of leadership education (Jenkins, 2012, 2013).

DISCUSSION IN LEADERSHIP EDUCATION

Discussion-based pedagogy is the most widely used instructional strategy in leadership education, regardless of academic level or modality (Jenkins, 2012). Whether it is through instructor-facilitated class discussion, interactive lecture/discussion, small-group discussion, or instructor-led, student-led, or shared instructor- and student-led online discussion boards, discussion pedagogy transcends undergraduate and graduate leadership education (Jenkins, 2016, 2018). Namely, leadership education is and should be chiefly dialogical (Dugan, 2017). High-quality leadership programs should incorporate student-centered experiential learning (e.g., meaningful discussion), and to be effective, leadership must be taught through learner-centered pedagogies (Eich, 2008, 2012), meaning the pedagogy lends itself to the learner being responsible for contributing to his or her own learning by engaging in discussions (Guthrie & Jenkins, 2018). In this way, the primary goal of the leadership educator is to empower students in the task of making meaning from content and their experiences; this requires communication and contemplation of what we know and what we are exposed to (Guthrie & Jenkins, 2018). Put another way—show, don't tell. "The role of the leadership educator is not to deliver or transmit information," Wisniewski (2010) states, "but ... to actively engage the learners in constructing personal theories and philosophies of leadership by creating a learning environment that builds upon learners' existing knowledge and experiential base" (p. 65).

For more, check out the "tips for facilitating discussion-based pedagogy in your leadership course" in *The Role of Leadership Educators: Transforming Learning* (Guthrie & Jenkins, 2018, pp. 178–179).

References:

Brookfield, S. D., & Preskill, S. (2005). *Discussion as a way of teaching: Tools for democratic classrooms* (2nd ed.). San Francisco, CA: Jossey-Bass.

Cazden, C. B. (2001). *Classroom discourse: The language of teaching and learning* (2nd ed.). Portsmouth, NH: Heinemann.

Christensen, C. R. (1987). *Teaching and the case method*. Boston, MA: Harvard Business School.

Dudley-Marling, C. (2013). Discussion in postsecondary classrooms: A review of the literature. *SAGE Open*, pp. 1–13.

Dugan, J. P. (2017). *Leadership theory: Cultivating critical perspectives*. San Francisco, CA: Jossey-Bass.

Eeds, M., & Wells, D. (1991). Talking, thinking, and cooperative learning: Lessons learned from listening to children talk about books. *Social Education*, *55*, 134–137.

Eich, D. (2008). A grounded theory of high-quality leadership programs: Perspectives from student leadership programs in higher education. *Journal of Leadership & Organizational Studies*, *15*(2), 176–187.

Eich, D. (2012). *Root down and branch out: Best practices for leadership development programs*. Madison, WI: Darin Eich.

Guthrie, K. L., & Jenkins, D. M. (2018). *The role of leadership educators: Transforming learning*. Charlotte, NC: Information Age.

Hardman, F., & Mroz, M. (1999). Post-16 English teaching: From recitation to discussion. *Educational Review, 51*, 283–293.

Jenkins, D. M. (2012). Exploring signature pedagogies in undergraduate leadership education. *Journal of Leadership Education, 11*(1), 1–27.

Shulman, L. S. (2005). Signature pedagogies in the professions. *Daedalus, 134*(3), 52–59.

Wisniewski, M. A. (2010). Leadership and the Millennials: Transforming today's technological teens in tomorrow's leaders. *Journal of Leadership Education, 9*(1), 53–68.

BRAVING THE FISHBOWL: USING CONCENTRIC CIRCLES TO FACILITATE DIALOGUE

Darren Pierre, Shelby Hearn, and Cristian Noriega

Discussion, Curricular Instructional

The term "brave space" refers to Arao and Clemens' (2013) framework and is defined as a learning space that will push participants to "the edge of their comfort zones to maximize learning" (p. 143). This learning activity encourages risk taking and a brave space implies that risk will always be taken when discussing diversity and social justice (Guthrie & Chunoo, 2018). This is a facilitated dialogue, one of many methods to consider in developing participants' facilitation skills. Participants are split into two discussion groups, encouraging active listening and participation while participants are able to facilitate within both smaller and large group discussions.

Learning Outcomes:

Participants will have opportunities to:

- communicate benefits of using discussion as an effective pedagogical method.
- articulate the importance of "brave spaces" when engaging in discussion.

- identify how their various identities and experiences impact their meaning making structures.

Setting Up the Activity:

- Group size: 10–30 participants
- Time: 45–60 minutes

- Materials: Various resources to aid in discussion, technology (if participants request), chairs

Instructions:

1. In a class setting, as part of the assignments outlined on the syllabus, participants will be asked to facilitate an in-class dialogue.

   - Each week, 2–3 participants sign-up to facilitate class discussion.
   - Discussion would be based on the readings assigned for that particular session of the course.

2. One week prior to class, participants assigned to facilitate discussion will meet with the instructor (outside of class) to clarify the key points of the readings, share the discussion questions developed for class, and ask any remaining questions of the instructor.

   - For the instructor, this is a great opportunity to share with participant facilitators any helpful tips (e.g. class dynamics, insights from previous groups, general suggestions).

3. The activity begins with the class being randomly split into two groups. The 2–3 participant facilitators will split up, each with a group.

   - Group #1 will sit in a circle in the middle of the room.
   - Group #2 will sit in a larger circle around group #1 (the outer circle group serves in an observatory fashion of the inner circle group)

4. The timer starts and the facilitator assigned to Group #1 facilitating a discussion on the readings. (15–20 minutes)

5. The facilitators should engage in a discussion that elicits from participants an understanding of their personal impressions of the readings, challenges to the texts, and connections to lived experiences. Suggested debriefing questions may be:

   - How do your identities impact how you engage with the questions and topics being discussed?
   - How do your lived experiences impact how you engage with the questions and topics being discussed?

6. While Group #1 is participating in the discussion, Group #2 will observe the interactions within Group #1. Group #2 will be asked to pay attention to body language and major themes that emerged

from the conversation had by Group #1. (15–20 minutes)

7. The same process will occur with the inner circle now becoming the outer circle, and the facilitator assigned to Group #2 will lead the discussion. This time, the discussion should focus on the second half of readings assigned for that session, which were not covered in the first circle. Group #1 will then engage in the same observatory tasks as Group #2 did the first round. (15–20 minutes)

8. Group #2 participant facilitator will close the discussion and the two circles will then organize into a large group. The facilitators will engage their peers in a discussion on how the readings covered in both rounds speak to one another (15–20 minutes).

Facilitator Notes:

- It is highly encouraged to do this activity in a longitudinal form (over the entirety of the semester/quarter) as participants will become more familiar with each other overtime, which as a byproduct may elicit growth in their comfort with and ability to improve facilitate group dialogues.
- Using the discussion pedagogy, educators need to diversify the types of questions asked. In other words, have a mix of questions that elicit both high and low-level responses.
- Educators should be active participants in the discussion, focused on listening and fostering the sharing of diverse viewpoints/perspectives.
- This activity should be done with a class of 10–30. If you have more than 30 participants, consider doing this activity in four circles with four facilitators.
- As you are engaging participants in the activity debrief, be sure to acknowledge the differences in brave vs. safe spaces. Note, "safety" is not necessarily simultaneously conferred based on identities (e.g., race, class, ability, status, etc.) (Bacchetta, Tayeb, & Haritaworn, 2015). Therefore, the use of the term, "brave spaces" serves as a more accurate depiction of what is intended for environments of various communities to share openly with others (Ali, 2017).
- For the observations taken during the Fish Bowl Activity, the point is not to make assumptions. Rather, the goal is to bring the interactions observed to the space for the group to discuss.

References

Ali, D. (2017). *Safe spaces and brave spaces: Historically context and recommendations for student affairs Vol. 2.* NASPA

Arao, B., & Clemens, K. (2013). From safe space to brave space: A new way to frame dialogue around diversity and social justice. In L. Landreman (Ed.), *The art of effective facilitation: Reflections from social justice educators* (pp. 135–150). Terre Haute, IN: Stylus.

Bachetta, P., El-Tayeb, F., & Haritaworn, J. (2015). Queer of colour formations and translocal spaces in Europe. *Environment and Planning D: Society and Space, 33*(5), 769–778.

Guthrie, K. L., & Chunoo, V. S. (Eds.). (2018). *Changing the narrative: Socially just leadership education.* Charlotte, NC: Information Age.

TALKING POPSICLE STICKS
Trisha Teig

Discussion, Cocurricular Instructional

By engaging in a structured process to progress discussion, participants can consider their own and others' contributions to the conversation in a reflective manner. This can lead to important conversation about how a learning environment is shaped by who speaks, how frequently some participants speak, and/or some participants remain silent, and the power of experiential observation and reflection on how and why these normative practices unfold (Adams, 2007; Beatty & Tillapaugh, 2017; Mahoney, 2016). This learning activity provides an opportunity for participants to consider personal and others' contributions.

Learning Outcomes:

Participants will have opportunities to:

- reflective on observations about the process of a discussion activity.
- identify who is contributing most and least in the conversation and why.

Setting Up the Activity:

- Group size: 10–30 participants
- Time: 60 minutes–1 hour 15 minutes
- Materials: Popsicle sticks, three per participant.

Instructions:

1. Set up (5–10 min)

   - Separate large group into groups of 4-6 participants.
   - Hand out three Popsicle sticks to each participant.

- Give each group discussion questions on a sheet of paper or projected on a screen.
- Facilitator should share the following to explain the Popsicle sticks and the structure of the discussion:
  - You and your group should discuss the following questions from our reading.
    * Before you begin the discussion, please place your three Popsicle sticks in front of you.
    * Each time you speak (no matter what you say) you should place a Popsicle stick in the center of the table.
    * Once you have used your three Popsicle sticks, you cannot rejoin the conversation until everyone in your group has used all of their Popsicle sticks. Your job is to listen and observe the discussion as it progresses.
    * Once everyone has used all three sticks, everyone in the group regains three sticks again and may start over with the same process.

2. Discussion (30 minutes)

- The group should continue using this structure for 30 minutes while discussing the questions regarding the course content.

3. Debriefing (30–40 minutes)

- Facilitators may debrief this activity in a variety of formats.
- First, to allow for reflection time for all learners, provide participants 3–5 minutes for written reflection on what happened in their group. This can be guided by specific questions or by simply allowing space for open reflection. Next, consider if your participant group would better reflect initially in small or large groups. It may be helpful to maintain the small group environment but change groups for participants to share what they experienced.
- Finally, the facilitator may choose to open the observation and debriefing of the activity to the large group. Please anticipate and notice, again, *who* is speaking and not speaking in this large group space. Debriefing questions could include:
  - What did you observe in the Popsicle activity? Who spoke first/last? Who used their sticks first or last? Did the same people use their Popsicle sticks first/last in each round?
  - How did this activity make you feel? Was it more difficult to speak or not speak? Why?

- What did you observe about the ideas presented in your group? Did you feel like you were able to hear from everyone? Did the Popsicles help or hinder the ability to have an active discussion?
- The Popsicle sticks may also be utilized in large group debrief. In this format, participants again have three sticks in front of them. However, once a participant has spoken one time, they may not use another stick until everyone in the group has also used at least one stick. This constructs the debrief conversation to also be a space for all voices to be heard and to continue the observation process. However, it can also inhibit a more dynamic discussion during debriefing by enforcing a more stringent structure.

Facilitator Notes:

- It is important facilitators are watching each group throughout the activity to bring up your own observations, encouraging participants who usually contribute excessively to consider what this means, and alternatively encouraging reflection and sharing from participants who rarely offer their voice.
- Topics of identity, especially gender identity and race, will likely arise as participants notice who tended to speak first/most or last/least. Be prepared with research to support the conversation in helping participants consider why more men, White people, or other privileged identities tend to dominate discussion.
- The activity may also be implemented in a shorter timeline by shortening the discussion time, using the Popsicle sticks directly in a debriefing, or allowing participants to reflect on their observations of the experience outside of the learning space in written formats such as reflection papers or an online discussion board.

References:

Adams, M. (2007). Pedagogical frameworks for social justice education. In M. Adams, L. A. Bell, & P. Griffin (Eds.), *Teaching for diversity and social justice* (2nd ed., pp. 15-34). New York, NY: Routledge.

Beatty, C., & Tillapaugh, D. (2017). Masculinity, leadership, and liberatory pedagogy: Supporting men through leadership development and education. In D. Tillapaugh & P. Haber Curran (Eds.), *New directions for student leadership: No. 154, Critical perspectives on gender and student leadership* (pp. 47–58). San Francisco, CA: Jossey-Bass.

Mahoney, A. D. (2016). Culturally responsive integrative learning environments: A critical displacement approach. In K. L. Guthrie, T. Bertrand Jones, & L. Osteen (Eds.), *New directions for student leadership: No. 152, Developing culturally relevant leadership learning* (pp. 47–59). San Francisco, CA: Jossey-Bass.

LIVE TWITTER CHATS

Kathy L. Guthrie and Josie Ahlquist

Discussion, Technology Enhanced

Twitter is a social networking platform used globally. It connects users through the use of hashtags, which is a symbol that precedes a word or phrase to identify a specific topic. This learning activity provides an opportunity for leadership learning to occur in a digital space. Dr. Josie Ahlquist created this learning activity as an assignment for LDR 2116: Leadership in a Digital Age, an undergraduate leadership studies course at Florida State University. Although this activity is framed in the context of an academic course, this could be done in a cocurricular context as well.

Learning Outcomes:

Participants will have opportunities to:

- experience relational process in digital environment through use of Twitter.
- become an active learner and content contributor online.
- engage in leadership learning through an online platform.

Setting Up the Activity:

- Group size: 5–25 participants
- Time: 1 hour 15 minutes
- Materials: Twitter account, personal device, internet connection

Instructions:

1. Introduce the concept of a live Twitter chat to participants, which are scheduled gatherings to discuss a topic with a moderator. Explain that this chat will cover at least six questions over a period of one hour that must be responded to within that hour. The time for the live Twitter chat can either be decided collectively or the facilitator can set a predetermined time. (10 minutes)

2. Instruct participants to prepare for the live Twitter chat by understanding the expectations and viewing tutorial videos. (5 minutes)

   - Expectations (can be given to participants)
     - Before the chat, watch the Twitter tutorial video (http://janetfouts.com/how-to-partici-pate-in-a-tweet-chat/#axzz3h7DsXm7I).
     - Stay active online for the full hour.
     - Always use the course hashtag in each tweet.
     - Reply to at least one person per question, in addition to answering each of the six prompts.
     - Ideally you should be on computer or laptop, so viewing the feed & posting tweets are easier.

3. During the determined hour in which the live Twitter chat will take place, the facilitator will want to pose questions every 8 minutes. Potential questions may include:

   - Introductions: What has been a highlight this semester? Share a photo of that experience.
   - Introductions: Name, dream job, and if you could make the perfect app for college students, what would it include?
   - From taking this class, how has your perspective/use of social media changed? Be specific.
   - What do you see as the difference between responsible/professional social media utilization and being silenced/censored?
   - For your personal application, how do you plan to define and act out digital leadership both online and face to face?
   - Who do you hope to be a digital role model to and how do you plan to display leadership on social media?
   - Post one question you want your classmates to answer related to this course. Reply to at least three of your classmates questions
   - How can this class (and your instructor) further support students to discover their digital identity, reputation, and leadership presence online?
   - What would you describe as your life mission/motto?
   - In this course learning about digital leadership, what is one thing you would want to tell your high school self about social media

4. With 5 minutes left in the allotted hour for the live Twitter chat, pose a survey to get feedback from the experience. Figure 2.1 is a visual from feedback Dr. Josie Ahlquist received from a live twitter chat in

LDR 2116 at Florida State University. It provides a visual to what poll results may look like.

Dr. Josie Ahlquist
@josieahlquist

Great chat #LDR2116! Share what you thought

63%	Wow, crazy but cool
13%	Too much for me
6%	Just alright
18%	LOVED

16 votes • 1 hour left

Figure 2.1.   Live Twitter chat poll results.

Facilitators Notes:

- It is critical the facilitator is active the entire hour the live Twitter chat is occurring. Encouraging participation and responding to participant's post will only increase potential learning.
- Although this learning activity was shared as part of a digital leadership course, it could be revised to focus on any leadership topic of online platform.

Resources:
http://janetfouts.com/how-to-participate-in-a-tweet-chat/#axzz3h7DsXm7I
http://www.postplanner.com/how-to-participate-in-twitter-chats/
http://www.business2community.com/twitter/become-an-industry-thought-leader-with-twitter-chats-01231988

EXPLORING PRECONCEIVED UNDERSTANDINGS OF FOLLOWERSHIP THROUGH GROUP DISCUSSION
Cameron C. Beatty

Discussion, Followership Focused

This discussion based classroom engagement activity focuses on discussion of concepts of followership. As Guthrie and Jenkins (2018) noted, a key component of quality classroom discussion in leadership education is questioning that is focused and flexible. Questioning that is focused allows for appropriate and needed learning opportunities for the class as a community. Discussion elicits higher level reflective thinking, problem solving, and retention of information (Ewens, 2000). The activity is intended to provide opportunities for participants to reflect on followership in their own personal context and challenge participants' preconceived understandings of followership in relation to leadership.

Learning Outcomes:

Participants will have opportunities to:

- gain an understanding of their preconceived notions of followership and where those beliefs regarding followership come from.
- articulate their definition of followership in relation to leadership and offer a critical critique of their definition in relation to the reading for class (Kellerman, 2008).
- participate in small pairs and large group discussion.

Setting Up the Activity:

- Group size: 15–25 participants, but smaller groups are fine.
- Time: 30–45 minutes
- Materials: Participants will need a piece of paper and writing utensil or laptop

Instructions:

1. Have the participants write out: (5 minutes)

   - Their definition of followership
   - A time they were a good follower.
   - What made them a good follower? How did others respond to the way they were following?
   - What characteristics or behaviors do "good followers" exhibit? How does this inform your understanding of followership?

2. Have participants share in pairs their definition of followership and a story of a time when they felt they were a good follower. (7–10 minutes)

- Once participants have shared, ask participants to come to a consensus on their definition and create one definition of followership.

3. Large-Class Discussion (10 minutes)

- Was writing a definition of followership difficult? What was difficult about writing the definition? What was easy?
- How often do you think about the ways in which you are engaging in the leadership process as a follower? How self-aware are you of how decisions have impacted the way you lead and follow?
- What did hearing other's stories around followership feel like for you?
- We oftentimes use followership in our leadership practice, but what does that really mean and what does that look like in action for you?

4. Discussion Follow-Up (Large Group) (7–10 minutes)

- Do you have to be a good leader to be a good follower? Why or why not?
  - For participants who are resistant to the concept of followership, call these participants into the conversation by encouraging them to think about followership as a part of the leadership process. Questions for these participants might include:
    * How do/would followers respond to different approaches to leadership?
    * If we consider leadership to be a process, then what role do we all play in the process?
    * What role does followership play in the leadership process besides idea of positional roles?

References:
Ewens, W. (2000). Teaching using discussion. In R. Neff & M. Weimer (Eds.), *Classroom communication: Collected readings for effective discussion and questioning* (pp. 21–26). Madison, WI: Atwood.

Guthrie, K. L., & Jenkins, D. M. (2018). *The role of leadership educators: Transforming learning.* Charlotte, NC: Information Age.

Kellerman, B. (2008) *Followership: How followers are creating change and changing leaders.* Cambridge, MA: Harvard Business Review Press.

LET'S DISCUSS LEARNING: ASSESSING LEARNING OF DISCUSSION ACTIVITIES
Trisha Teig

Discussion, Curricular Learning Assessment

Assessing learning from discussion can also focus upon the learning environment created through a discussion activity. Participants' reflection on whose voices are most represented in the conversation as well as whose voices are not present, can offer leadership educators excellent foundations for assessing the learning for both the content *and* process of discussion.

This activity is to be implemented after a significant discussion led in class. The assessment activity may be employed in class after discussion or be given as an outside of class assignment.

Learning Outcomes:

Participants will have opportunities to:

- assess their learning from the discussion activity.
- discern their clarity of understanding for course content following the discussion activity.
- reflect on the discussion in consideration for who is contributing most and least in the conversation and why.

Setting Up the Activity:

- Group size: 10–30 participants
- Time: 40–60 minutes
- Materials: Discussion feedback and reflection handout

Instructions:

1. Following the discussion, the instructor should pass out the discussion feedback and reflection handout to each participant.
2. Instructor should explain the purpose/directions for the handout:

- "This discussion feedback and reflection handout is intended to review your understanding and learning from the class discussion we just completed. This handout will also allow you to reflect upon how you learned from your peers by giving feedback about the discussion. Please consider not only what you learned today, but also who you learned it from, and how you learned it. Consider also, who spoke in class today, who did not speak, and why. Finally, based on this reflection, consider how that contributed to your learning during the discussion. Do you have any questions about the handout?" (Instructor responds to any questions with further clarity).

3. Participants complete the handout. (10–15 minutes)
4. In the following class, the instructor should discuss the overall information from the handouts to inform the learning from the discussion with the class. (30–45 minutes)
5. Instructors should take time to read through the handouts and aggregate the feedback. Debriefing of the handout should take place in the next class period with the facilitator sharing overall comments on learning, clarifying concepts that were missed or unclear, and sharing how participants are learning from each other in the discussion format. Debriefing should also include discussion on which voices in general were most and least represented, and if that reflects varying identities in the group.

Facilitator Notes:

•   Aggregating the data and facilitating a conversation about learning from peers should be influenced by the feedback participants give. Often, there are a vocal majority of a few voices being represented in a discussion, which limits the amount participants can learn from each other by constricting the amount of diverse perspectives shared. If this is the outcome of the assessment, facilitators can focus on processing the learning environment created.
•   Debriefing can also focus on missed concepts based on the learning assessment data received through the handout. It is possible one or two participants in the group will be identified in the worksheet by many participants. The sharing of any data regarding specific participants, rather than speaking on general feedback given, should be determined by the instructor based on the level of comfort/trust built into the group. It may be more helpful to share broad information about the aggregated data with the large group and then share any specific feedback directly in a one on one capacity with participants.

Discussion Feedback and Reflection Handout

What did you learn from the discussion?	What inhibited you from learning in the discussion? Why?
	What ideas/concepts are unclear?

Who did you learn from in the discussion?	Whose voices were represented in the discussion? Why?
	Whose voices were not represented in the discussion?

UNTANGLING THE DESTRUCTIVE LEADERSHIP WEB: THE CASE OF *TEAM FOXCATCHER*
Jasmine D. Collins

Discussion, Cocurricular Learning Assessment

The following activity uses the 90-minute documentary film *Team Foxcatcher* (Greenhalgh, 2016) as a starting point for a preplanned, facilitator-led discussion focused on the topic of destructive leadership. Increasingly, leadership literature is beginning to recognize that destructive leadership outcomes are not only a function of toxic leaders, but a result of interactions among toxic leaders, followers who are prone to conformity and/or collusion, and environments which contribute to destructive leadership processes (Johnson, 2018; Kellerman, 2005; Thoroughgood, Padilla, Hunter, & Tate, 2012). This activity is designed to assess participant holistic understanding of pertinent leader behaviors, follower characteristics, and contextual pressures that contribute to destructive leadership outcomes.

Learning Outcomes:

Participants will have opportunities to:

- identify and describe how destructive leader behaviors, susceptible follower characteristics, and environmental factors compromise quality of life for the involved parties, and detract from group or organizational goals.
- deepen understanding of toxic leadership beyond a solely leader-centric perspective.
- connect key ethical issues raised in film to their own experiences as leaders.

Setting Up the Activity:

- Group size: Groups no larger than 20 participants, unless additional facilitators can lead small group discussion of 8-10 participants
- Time: 2 hours 15 minutes
- Materials: *Team Foxcatcher* film, screen, projector, list of key terms, note-taking materials, debriefing questions, flip chart paper, chalkboard, whiteboard (optional)

Instructions:

1. Set up (5 minutes)

    - After providing relevant topical instruction related to leader behaviors, follower characteris-

tics, and contextual pressures, transition to the film.
    - Set up the room in such a way that all participants are able to view the screen. It is also recommended that the facilitator turn on the "closed captioning" function to maximize comprehension and accessibility for all participants in the room.
    - Provide each participant with a handout of key terms or concepts covered earlier in the program in addition to note-taking materials.
    - Instruct participants to take notes related to destructive leader, follower, and contextual factors they observe.

2. Watch the film (90 minutes)
3. Break (5 minutes)
4. Set up for discussion (5 minutes)

    - After the completion of the film, move participants into one large circle (if only one group) or into smaller discussion group clusters.
    - You may choose to use a visual aid such as a large flip chart, chalkboard or whiteboard to aid in the facilitation of the discussion.

5. Facilitate discussion (30 minutes)

    - What are your initial reactions to the film? (May opt to use an "around the room" debriefing strategy wherein all participants share a brief thought).
    - Who were the key people and groups involved in this case?
    - What red flags did you notice along the way that indicated that there might be a problem?
    - What connections can you make between John DuPont's behaviors and the destructive leader behaviors we introduced earlier in the day?
    - What kinds of susceptible follower behaviors did you observe throughout the film?
    - Why do you think no one "stepped up" upon witnessing the increasingly dangerous situation?
    - What kinds of contextual pressures contributed to this tragedy?
    - Do you think this could have been prevented? Why or why not?
    - Who do you think is ultimately to blame for what happened to Dave Schultz?
    - How would you have tried to prevent this tragedy if you were living on the Foxcatcher estate? If you were a member of USA Wrestling? If you were a police officer?
    - How does what you witnessed in this film today apply to your own life?

Facilitator Notes:

- This activity is designed to take place as part of a larger discussion of leadership ethics and toxic leadership processes. In a cocurricular context, this activity would be more appropriate for a day-long (or longer) leadership retreat or workshop. For example, the Illinois Leadership Center hosts a day-long i-Program called *Integrity,* which supports participants in developing the skills necessary to navigate ethical challenges they may face (leadership.illinois.edu).
- To best prepare participants for discussion, they will need to be familiar with concepts of "bad" or "destructive" leader behaviors (Johnson, 2018; Kellerman, 2005), characteristics of susceptible followers (Johnson, 2018; Thoroughgood, et al., 2012) and contextual pressures (Kellerman, 2005; Johnson, 2018; Thoroughgood et al., 2012).
- Although the run time for the film is 90 minutes, the film could be cut shorter by offering a verbal or written introduction of the film—thus skipping some of the beginning—and/or ending the film once it begins to focus on the legal aspects of the case. Keep in mind, participants will want to know what happened!
- One additional strategy to help with the length of the film is to break it up into segments, with debrief questions in between.

References:

Greenhalgh, J. (2016). *Team Foxcatcher* [Documentary film]. USA: Netflix.

Johnson, C. E. (2018). *Meeting the ethical challenges of leadership: Casting light or shadow* (6th ed.) Thousand Oaks, CA: SAGE.

Kellerman, B. (2005). How bad leadership happens. *Leader to Leader, 35,* 41–46.

Thoroughgood, C. N., Padilla, A., Hunter, S. T., & Tate, B. W. (2012). The susceptible circle: A taxonomy of followers associated with destructive leadership. *The Leadership Quarterly, 23*(5), 897–917.

Resources:

Illinois Leadership Center (2018). Programs and Services. Retrieved from https://leadership.illinois.edu/programs-services/i-programs

CHAPTER 3

Case Study Methods

Case study refers to a written description of a problem or situation for analysis used to bring experiences that learners may not be able to access, bridging the gap between theory and application (Bonwell & Eison, 1991; Erskine, Leenders, & Mauffette-Leenders, 1998), and stimulating the application of research techniques, decision-making skills, and critical thinking analysis (Herreid, 2011). In most instances, case studies are:

> stories about situations (including characters, issues, and environmental factors), with a set of facts, arranged in chronological order, specifically crafted to promote engaged discussion and focused analysis. The student's role begins by reading and analyzing the case, identifying the objectives and goals of key characters, and putting him or herself in each character's shoes. (Guthrie & Jenkins, 2018, p. 194)

Although a case study is most often explored through facilitated discussion, it can also be the basis for simulations, role-plays, written exercises, and a wide variety of other pedagogical methods. In this way, the classroom experience differs from a traditional question-and-answer session. Instead case studies develop through a progression of thinking, goes beyond the specific story, includes the students and instructor in dialogue, and allows students to generalize to similar situations and experiences (Herreid, 2011). Case study methods range from an individual or direct approach where the instructor assigns a case study for students to read and analyze to utilizing multimedia, interviews, stories or personal narratives, to have students create their own cases.

CASE STUDY METHODS IN LEADERSHIP EDUCATION

There are countless ways to frame case studies in leadership education beyond the typical decision-making process. These include cases focused on leadership processes, a particular leader or follower, a system of leaders and followers within a particular context, as well as the relational dynamics of leadership and followership among individuals. Correspondingly, cases that are framed in accessible ways for students, that is, inclusive of student experiences and contexts (e.g., Marshall & Hornak, 2008) create opportunities for transformational learning (Guthrie & Jenkins, 2018). Likewise, guest speakers, current events, and relevant cases that include characters or situations depicted in popular media such as film, television and streaming video, music, YouTube, TED talks, and literature are also prime for this method (Guthrie & Jenkins, 2018). And in some scenarios, such as the case-in-point method (Heifetz, 1994; Parks, 2005), the in-class dialogue or interaction among a group of students becomes the case itself. In any event, the case study method is both an activity and a pedagogy that can be used to provide learners with complex scenarios to analyze, discuss, and make meaning of when compared to their own experiences.

For a survey and several examples of various case study method approaches in leadership education ranging from a case study competition to interviews, see *The Role of Leadership Educators: Transforming Learning* (Guthrie & Jenkins, 2018, pp. 192–202).

References:

Bonwell, C. C., & Eison, J.A. (1991). *Active learning: Creating excitement in the classroom.* Washington, DC: George Washington University ERIC Clearinghouse on Higher Education.

Erskine, J. A., Leenders, M. R., & Mauffette-Leenders, L. A. (1998). *Teaching with cases.* London, Canada: Ivey.

Heifetz, R. A. (1994). *Leadership without easy answers* (Vol. 465). Boston, MA: Harvard University Press.

Herreid, C. F. (2011). Case study teaching. In W. Buskist & J. E. Groccia (Eds.), *New directions for teaching and learning, no. 128: Evidence-based teaching* (pp. 31–40). San Francisco, CA: Jossey-Bass.

Guthrie, K. L., & Jenkins, D. M. (2018). *The role of leadership educators: Transforming learning.* Charlotte, NC: Information Age.

Marshall, S. M., & Hornak, A. M. (2008). *A day in the life of a college student leader.* Sterling, VA: Stylus.

Parks, D. S. (2005). *Leadership can be taught.* Boston, MA: Harvard Business School Press.

Making a Case for Leading Critically
Daniel M. Jenkins and Amanda Cutchens

Case Study Methods, Curricular Instructional

This learning activity uses case studies to explore curricular concepts related to leadership education. Small group and larger class discussion centers on leadership theories or models highlighted in a brief scenario, similar to the one provided below. In this case study, critical leadership is the focus. After reviewing the theory, groups will analyze the situation and answer supplementary discussion questions, then share those findings with the class as a whole. The activity will end with a class debrief.

Learning Outcomes:

Participants will have opportunities to:

- apply critical thinking skills to leadership situations.
- apply leadership theories or models to real-world situations.
- analyze decision-making skills.

Setting Up the Activity:

- Group size: 5–35 participants
- Time: 35–45 minutes
- Materials: Several handouts of the same case study and flip chart paper or scrap paper

Instructions:

1. The instructor provides groups with a case, preferably one in the participants' context. The case should have a few general, open-ended discussion questions.
2. Each group of 4–5 participants should be given time to discuss and answer the questions related to the case. (10 minutes)
3. The instructor should allow each group time to present the case and answers to discussion questions to the class. During this time, the instructor should allow participants from the larger group to give respectful, constructive feedback to participants in the smaller group. (5 minutes)
4. Debrief.

- Note: Best practice is "Six Phases of Debriefing" (for more information, see Guthrie & Jenkins, 2018, pp. 166–169). Specifically, consider the following debriefing questions using critical leadership theory:

  - Were you frustrated by a particular part of the case study? Were you satisfied with any of the leader's actions in the case study?
  - As the leader, what would you have done differently (if anything) in this situation?
  - What decision did you make?
  - Which of the "12 actions" did your group use in making the decision?
  - What communication strategies did you use in your group as you worked through this case study?
  - What is one thing you learned about leaders or leadership by doing this activity?
- Has anyone experienced something similar to this case study in real life?

Scenario (given to participants):

You are the former president of a newly created organization chapter on campus. Under your leadership, the organizational membership doubled and the institutional leadership took notice. The organization became well respected and members were often called upon to represent the institution in various ways like participating in student government, appearing at formal school functions, and even providing a training session for other new organizations. A mentorship program also emerged. In fact, your mentee, Sam, is the newly elected president of the organization and you moved on to serve on the organization's national chapter.

However, many of your peers, who are still members involved in the chapter, recently expressed concern about Sam's leadership abilities. They told you things like, "We don't understand the direction Sam is moving in" and "It just doesn't feel the same." You tried to address their concerns by suggesting they talk to Sam, but they told you Sam was "never around" and "unresponsive." Therefore, you decided to reach out.

When you call Sam, you get an immediate response. Sam is enthusiastic and tells you networking has paid off because a community partner just agreed to start an even stronger mentoring program with the organization. You are happy for Sam and your former organization, but you are conflicted on whether or not to tell Sam about the current state of the members. Would it be better for Sam to figure it out, or should you coach Sam? If you decide to coach Sam, how should you approach the situation?

Facilitator Notes:

- Small groups of 4–5 participants allow for greater participation by providing a safe environment for reflection and discussion. Afterward, large class discussion regarding the smaller groups' application of the material may further diversify ideas and opinions.

- Case studies that put leaders in positions where decisions are made or where decisions need to be made, are best exercises. It is especially beneficial for larger group discussion if both scenarios are used. A great companion textbook to your course material or a book you may keep as a resource for case studies may be Marshall and Hornak's (2008) *A Day in the Life of a College Student Leader*.

References:

Guthrie, K. L., & Jenkins, D. M. (2018). *Role of leadership educators: Transforming learning*. Charlotte, NC: Information Age.

Jenkins, D. M., & Cutchens, A. B. (2011). Leading critically: A grounded theory of applied critical thinking in leadership studies. *Journal of Leadership Education, 10*(2) 1–21.

Marshall, S. M., & Hornak, A. M. (2008). *A day in the life of a college student leader*. Sterling, VA: Stylus.

Handout: 12 Actions a Leader Can Take to Lead Critically (Jenkins & Cutchens, 2011)

1. Be aware of the context of your situation and evaluate the implications of your decisions.
2. Ask questions and listen appropriately.
3. Take the time to understand the diversity of others' decisions, values, and opinions.
4. Be flexible and open-minded in your decision-making.
5. Accept, internalize, and apply constructive criticism.
6. Evaluate assumptions before you try to challenge them.
7. Understand processes before you try to change them.
8. Know the strengths and weaknesses of your followers and direct or empower accordingly.
9. Be purposeful and take into account your organization's mission and values when making decisions.
10. Engage others where they are, not where you want them to be.
11. Encourage critical followership.
12. Take informed action.

PROTESTS AND STUDENT ACTIVISM ON YOUR CAMPUS: ARE YOU READY?

Brian T. Magee and Anne-Marie Algier

Case Study Methods, Courricular Instructional

Protests and student activism are happening on college and university campuses at an increasing rate. Being familiar with your campus policies and guiding principles on these topics will help make your team ready for when an incident occurs. This activity focuses on campus activism and connecting it to leadership development.

Learning Outcomes:

Participants will have opportunities to:

- understand the importance of having protocols and safety guidelines on campus.
- establish clear expectations on campus about how to handle protests and student activism.
- learn what informs your campus policies and how that impacts the campus response.

Setting Up the Activity:

- Groups Involve: Various institutional context, but campus partners that need to be included: student affairs/dean of students office, student activities office, public safety/campus police, communications, and risk management/legal counsel.
- Time: Two meetings. First meeting—review/develop policies around campus activism/protests. Second meeting—includes case study scenario and application of campus policy to the scenario.
- Materials: Documents for the first meeting include: Current/existing campus policies/guidelines on protests/activism, student code of conduct, faculty handbook, et cetera

Instructions:

First Meeting (60 minutes):

1. All constituents above meet for one hour to review current policies/guidelines. If no policies/guidelines exist, conversations should be had to begin to develop policies/guidelines. (30 minutes)
2. Please consider: Who is covered by the policy? Who is administrating and enforcing the policy? What are the guiding principles? Are there restrictions on when a protest or student activism can happen on campus? (30 minutes)

Second Meeting (2 hours):

1. Constituents meet for two hours and review the campus policies/guidelines that exist or were developed. (30 minutes)
2. Read and discuss the case study. Discuss in detail the universal response by drafting a step by step process of how each constituent is involved. (1 hour 30 minutes)

Case Study (given to participants):

The College Republicans are bringing a famous far-right conservative speaker that is against Deferred Action for Childhood Arrivals and immigration reform. The event is approved by the student organization's primary advisor and is scheduled to be held in the largest auditorium on campus on a weeknight. The event is open to all members of the university community and the public. A week prior to the event, another student organization decides to protest the event because of the beliefs/values of the individual who is speaking. The student organization decides to create a Facebook event noting that they will be protesting the speaker the night of the event. This protest encourages all students to come share their voice in opposition of the speaker by using signs and forming a wall around the venue. The College Republicans' primary advisor is notified that this protest will be happening during the event.

Facilitator Notes:

- While working with participants in the scenario described, it is important to talk through the importance of free speech and the ability to have civil dialogue. This connects to the Social Change Model of Leadership Development (Higher Education Research Institute, 1996; Komives & Wagner, 2017). Specifically, the value of Controversy with Civility highlights that different viewpoints are inevitable and they can help move the group toward change if viewpoints are discussed in a positive and respectful way (Barnhardt, Sheets, & Pasquesi, 2015; Komives & Wagner, 2017). When individuals commit to understanding the source of a disagreement, it helps the group remember their common purpose.
- Important questions to address with campus partners include:
  - What meetings should take place prior to the scheduled event?
    * Meetings with the student organizations hosting event. Inform participants of the campus policies, student code of conduct, available resources, and potential safety issues that may arise during the event.

- Coordination with all service providers and host a logistics meeting with detailed documentation about location/venue and event details. Having a point of contact for the event in case there is an emergency.
  - What resources would your university provide the students in response to a protest?
    * *Student Activities:* Provide a megaphone (property of student government). Remind them of protest/student activism policies and student code of conduct.
    * *Facilities:* Monitor exits and make sure all are clear prior to protest. Make sure bathrooms and trash are emptied prior to event. Be ready to assist if need to shut power off or other facilities requests.
    * *Communications Office:* Response to media (TV, social media, etc.).
    * *Public Safety:* Help to provide adequate staffing of event should a problem arise. Establish the perimeter of the protest to make sure event is secure and safe.
  - How would you handle a protest that includes a large increase of general public? Vandalism?
    * Notify public safety/campus police to discuss the increase in attendance. This could lead to an event shut-down or increase of local law enforcement agencies
    * In recent protests, "Black Bloc" protesters have caused issues and vandalism on campuses (Tate, 2017). Is your campus aware of these individuals and how they protest?
    * Large amounts of public usually bring an increased media attention.
    * What happens if the increased public start violating policies that the original student protesters had no intention of violating?
  - Who should be notified that a protest is happening on campus? Who initiates your protest/student activism policy?
  - Should outside law enforcement officers be notified prior to the event?
  - Who makes the decision to shut down or end an event effected by a protest? Is it only public safety/campus police? Or can an advisor or student make those decisions?

References:

Barnhardt, C. L., Sheets, J. E., & Pasquesi, K. (2015). You expect "what"? Students' perceptions as resources in acquiring commitments and capacities for civic engagement. *Research in Higher Education, 56*(6), 622–644.

Higher Education Research Institute. (1996). *A social change model of leadership development: Guidebook version III*. College Park, MD: National Clearinghouse for Leadership Programs.

Komives, S. R., & Wagner, W. (2017). *Leadership for a better world: Understanding the social change model of leadership development* (2nd ed.). San Francisco, CA: Jossey-Bass.

Tate, E. (2017, February 13). Bracing for Black Bloc. *Inside Higher Ed.* Retrieved from https://www.insidehighered.com/news/2017/02/13/wake-violent-protests-colleges-prepare-chaos

CRACKING THE CASE: LEARNING THROUGH STUDENT-WRITTEN TEACHING CASE STUDIES
Eric Kaufman

Case Study Methods, Technology Enhanced

The purpose of the case study development assignment is to produce verification of participants' ability to analyze and synthesize multiple concepts of leadership in real world contexts. In addition, the assignment offers participants experience in applying shared leadership in a small group setting. This assignment is a culminating course experience that has the potential to align with a variety of the learning objectives. Beyond satisfaction, research on student case writing reveals relationships with improved final exam and course grades (Escartín, Saldaña, Martín-Peña, Varela-Rey, Jiménez, Vidal, & Rodríguez-Carballeira, 2015).

Learning Outcomes:

Participants will have opportunities to:

- define and describe leadership in the contexts of interest to them.
- apply shared leadership in a small group setting.
- identify, discuss, and apply prominent leadership theories.

Setting Up the Activity:

- Group size: 5–7 participants per group
- Time: Varies depending on desired complexity and quality. Academic term or at least 6 weeks is appropriate
- Materials: Internet access and collaborate work software (e.g., wikis, Google Docs).

Instructions:

1. Begin by facilitating exploration and discussion of a short case study, such as one available through Stanford's "Leadership in Focus" website: http://leadershipinfocus.net/. Experience with a variety of different case studies will enhance participants' creativity in developing their own cases.

2. Assign participants to groups that will be conducive for collaborative development of a teaching case during the time frame available and encourage them to brainstorm topics and options for a case that would easily feature concepts that are the focus for the course (e.g., specific leadership theories). As participants consider problems that would make for a great case study, encourage them to draw upon their own experience and recent events in the news.

3. Direct participants to prepare a case narrative and teaching notes following guidance from *Writing Case Studies: A Manual*, available at https://www.slideshare.net/hudda2020/writing-case-studies-a-manual.

4. Arrange time for student groups to facilitate a case study discussion using the teaching case study they have developed. Although the participants should consider plausible solutions to the case, encourage them to be open to alternate views and explanations. (60 minutes)

5. Facilitate reflection on the experience, including appropriate peer evaluation (e.g., participants provide both qualitative and quantitative feedback to those with whom they collaborated to develop and deliver the teaching case).

- How did the case study reveal perspective and insight on the leadership concepts?
- In what ways did teaching about leadership help you learn about leadership?

Facilitator Notes:

- There are a variety of resources available to help guide case writing, including faculty reflections on implementing student-written, instructor-facilitated (SWIF) case projects (Boulocher-Passet, 2016; Careaga, Rubaii, & Leyva, 2017; Corrigan, & Craciun, 2012; McDonald, 2013; Tarter & Beal, 2013).
- When guiding and evaluating student cases, pay particular attention to what Herreid (1997) has identified as the characteristics of a good case: (1) tells a story, (2) focuses on an interest-arousing issue, (3) is set in the past 5 years, (4) creates empathy with central characters, (5) includes quotations, (6) is relevant to the reader, (7) serves pedagogic utility, (8) is conflict provoking, (9) is decision forcing, (10) has generality, and (11) is short.

References:
Boulocher-Passet, V. (2016, June). *Developing a teaching case study: The difficulties faced by students, as viewed by faculty.*

Paper presented at the 23rd International Education Innovation in Economics and Business Conference, EDHEC Business School, Nice.

Careaga, M., Rubaii, N., & Leyva, S. (2017). Beyond the case method in public affairs education: Unexpected benefits of student-written cases. *Journal of Public Affairs Education*, 23(1), 571–590.

Corrigan, H., & Craciun, G. (2012). Wearing more than one hat: Improving student-authored case longevity while encouraging additional student roles. *Marketing Education Review*, 22(1), 33–38.

Escartín, J., Saldaña, O., Martín-Peña, J., Varela-Rey, A., Jiménez, Y., Vidal, T., & Rodríguez-Carballeira, Á. (2015). The impact of writing case studies: Benefits for students' success and well-being. *Procedia—Social and Behavioral Sciences*, 196, 47–51.

Herreid, C. F. (1997). What makes a good case. *Journal of College Science Teaching*, 27(3), 163–165.

McDonald, L. M. (2013). Using student-constructed cases to investigate crises. *Journal of Management Education*, 37(1), 115–134.

Tarter, J., & Beal, B. D. (2013). Implementing a "SWIF" program in an undergraduate strategy course: Processes, results and recommendations. *Journal of Learning in Higher Education*, 9(1), 151–160.

PEER CONSULTATION

Justin Greenleaf, Thomas Stanley, and Kerry L. Priest

Case Study Methods, Followership Focused

The peer consultation process is a case study method in which participants' own challenges are the "case" (Green & Fabris McBride, 2015). Central to the process is the adaptive leadership practice of "getting on the balcony"—being able to metaphorically step back (or up) from the field of action (also known as "dance floor") in order to see and reflect on patterns of interaction, context, or system dynamics (Heifetz, Grashow, & Linsky, 2009). This activity helps build leaders' capacity to diagnose problems, gain insights and generate new ideas to make progress on tough challenges.

Learning Outcomes:

Participants will have opportunities to:

- explain a challenging issue or problem to peers.
- reframe thinking about their own issue or problem.
- formulate a plan for working toward a solution.
- practice diagnosing situations from an adaptive lens.

Setting Up the Activity:

- Group size: Intended for small groups of 5–6 participants
- Time: 50 minutes per consultation
- Materials: Peer consultation guide (copy of directions/instructions for each participant)

Instructions:

1. Identify roles in advance: facilitator, case presenter, timekeeper, and notetaker. The case presenter should come prepared to share details specific leadership challenge they are facing. Some guiding questions may include: *What is the background of the problem? Who are major players? Why is it important to you? What actions have you taken so far?* The facilitator will guide the group discussion through six steps of the consultation process:

   - Case Presentation: verbally present to the peer group by case presenter. (5 minutes)
   - Data Gathering: Peer group members ask powerful questions and gather additional data regarding the challenge. (10 minutes)
   - Diagnostic Brainstorming: Case presenter "gets on the balcony" (turns back to peer group to just listen) as group engages in diagnostic brainstorming (making observations and interpretations), notetaker begins capturing notes. (15 minutes)
   - Action Step Brainstorming: Case presenter remains "on the balcony" while the peer group brainstorms action steps. (10 minutes)
   - Presenter Reflections: The case presenter returns to the "dance floor" by rejoining the group and reflecting on what they heard. (5 minutes)
   - Group Debrief: The group debriefs the consultation process. (5 minutes)

2. Upon completion of the peer consultation process, there are several questions that may be useful in determining what went well and what could be done better for next time. These questions include, but are not limited to, the following:

   - What parts of the process were done well and which ones were a struggle?
   - Were the interpretations offered in the diagnostic brainstorming stage helpful useful in making progress or were they largely protective of the presenter?
   - How might future consultations with this group be improved?

Facilitator Notes:

- In the first phase of the process, only the case presenter can talk and the timekeeper ensures that the full five minutes are used even if the case presenter is not able to speak for the whole time.
- In the second phase, the facilitators will work with participants to help them keep their questions and responses short and to the point to make good use of time and allow a deeper understanding of the challenge.
- The third phase is often the most difficult for participants. When the presenter "gets on the balcony," the facilitators must work to help the group stay away from offering solutions and *only offering interpretations*. It may seem strange to have the presenter turn their back; however, it emphasizes that the presenter is to simply listen and reflect on what is being said. Only after the group has spent the full 15 minutes in diagnosis are they be allowed to move onto the fourth phase where they will be able to offer solutions or ideas the presenter might consider implementing to make progress on their challenge.
- When the presenter "comes back to the dance floor" in phase five to reflect on what they have heard, they should not try to confirm or disconfirm statements that were made, but rather share initial thoughts and ideas that they may be willing to try out.
- Finally, the last 5 minutes is no longer focused on the case presenter and their challenge, but on the group's engagement in the peer consultation process. What did they do well? What was difficult for them? How can they improve the process for next time?

References:

Green, C., & Fabris McBride, J. (2015). *Teaching leadership: Case-in-point, case studies, and coaching.* Wichita, KS: Kansas Leadership Center.

Heifetz, R., Grashow, J., & Linsky, M. (2009). *The practice of adaptive leadership: Tools and tactics for changing your organization and the world.* Boston, MA: Cambridge Leadership Associates.

PRACTICE CASE STUDY: PREPARING STUDENTS TO BECOME LEADERSHIP CONSULTANTS
Lindsay J. Hastings

Case Study Methods, Curricular Learning Assessment

In this practice case study model, participants are given a case and a theory that elucidates the issues within the case. Participants will be asked to analyze a human system using leadership theory and propose training and development solutions to help that human system operate more effectively.

Learning Outcomes:

Participants will have opportunities to:

- critically evaluate information about leadership from both academic and popular sources.
- create novel ways of using abstract theoretical approaches to leadership in real world situations.
- assess a situation and make decisions about what theoretically based leadership skills and behaviors are likely to be most effective.
- resolve a complex leadership challenge by evaluating the intersection between leader, follower, and context.

Setting Up the Activity:

- Group size: 6–8 participants with one teaching assistant
- Time: 2 hours 30 minutes
- Materials: Case study (Northouse's 2019 *Leadership: Theory and Practice* is a good resource), information on a leadership model or theory that elucidates the issues within the case

Instructions:

The practice case study model allows for the highest amount of scaffolding by providing both the case and the theory that elucidates the issues within the case. The goal for the participants is to analyze the case using the provided leadership theory and propose a leadership training and development solution. The ultimate intention is to prepare participants to be able to serve as in-house leadership consultants for any organization in which they are engaged.

1. Individually participants read the case and answer the following questions in small groups: (30 minutes)

- How does [theory] elucidate the issues presented in the case?
- How did we see the model components of the theory demonstrated in the case?

2. Small groups are to act as if they have been hired by the case study organization as leadership consultants. The objective for each small group is to critically evaluate the case using the assigned leadership theory that applies and formulate a theoretically based training and development solution. Each group needs to be prepared to orally present as a group using the following questions as a guide: (1 hours 30 minutes)

- Based on the applicable theory, what assessments will your group use to collect data?
- How will that data be used in devising a training and development solution?
- What training and development activities will be involved?
- What will be the intended outcomes from this training and development program?
- How will the program be evaluated for effectiveness?

3. Each group will be allowed 5 minutes to present their analysis. (30 minutes)
4. Facilitators should offer overall oral evaluative feedback to the small groups or written individual feedback to each group. The key in debriefing the learning outcomes associated with the practice case study is to ensure that the chosen theory is threaded throughout the training and development solution. The assessments, training and development activities, and evaluation plan should all reflect the theory that elucidates the issues within the case. Consider these questions:

- Based on the applicable theory, what assessments will your group use to collect data? For example, if authentic leadership elucidates the issues within the case, participants should recommend using the Authentic Leadership Questionnaire (Avolio, Gardner, & Walumbwa, 2007).
- How will that data be used in devising a training and development solution? Participants will need to predict the outcomes of the assessment since they are not able to administer it. For example, if authentic leadership is chosen due to

a violation of relational transparency (a component of the model of authentic leadership; Gardner, Avolio, Luthans, May, & Walumbwa, 2005) demonstrated in the case, then participants might predict low scores in Transparency on the Authentic Leadership Questionnaire and build training and development activities around relational transparency.

- What training and development activities will be involved? Some participants have teaching and/or facilitation experience, but most do not. Offering participants a sample lesson plan or program planning template (see https://www.mindtools.com/pages/article/planning-training-session.htm) might be highly useful. Participants should be able to articulate a formal plan for training and development activities.
- What will be the intended outcomes from this training and development program? Participants should articulate how the training and development activities target growth in areas of need from the assessment results and develop leadership capacity within the theoretical framework chosen. Participants should be challenged to consider research relative to its effect on followers and/or organizational outcomes.
- How will the program be evaluated for effectiveness? A basic program evaluation plan with metrics around meaningful gains expected as a result of the training and development should be articulated, such as a 10% gain in total score, or an average total score among the executive team moving from moderate to high range.

References:

Avolio, B. J., Gardner, W. L., & Walumbwa, F. O. (2007). Authentic leadership questionnaire. Retrieved from https://www.mindgarden.com/69-authentic-leadership-questionnaire.

Gardner, W. L., Avolio, B. J., Luthans, F., May, D. R., & Walumbwa, F. (2005). "Can you see the real me?" A self-based model of authentic leader and follower development. *The Leadership Quarterly, 16*(3), 343–372.

Northouse, P. G. (2019). *Leadership: Theory and practice* (8th ed.). Thousand Oaks, CA: SAGE.

Resources:

Mind Tools Content Team. (n.d.). Planning a training session: Organizing key concepts for learning. Retrieved from https://www.mindtools.com/pages/article/planning-training-session.htm

"LIVING LEADERSHIP" CASE STUDIES

Melissa L. Rocco

Case Study Methods,
Cocurricular Learning Assessment

Though, observation and reflection on leadership happening in real time can be a transformational learning experience for participants, as well as a helpful indicator of learning and development for leadership educators (Rocco, 2017; Shankman, Allen, & Haber-Curran, 2015). In this live case study project, participants serve as peer consultants by working in small teams to observe and analyze the leadership and organizational culture of select organizations. Consulting teams use their findings to tell the current leadership story of their selected organization and apply their knowledge of leadership theory and practice to recommend action steps for the organization moving forward. Findings and recommendations are presented to the other consulting teams and, if desired, to the organization.

Learning Outcomes:

Participants will have opportunities to:

- collaborate with others to observe and analyze leadership in practice in an unfamiliar context.
- apply personal leadership knowledge and experience to assist others in developing leadership capacity.
- demonstrate cognitive complexity and critical thinking skills associated with advanced leadership understanding and practice.

Setting Up the Activity:

- Group size: 8–20 participants divided into small consulting teams of 2–4 participants
- Time: 3–4 weeks minimum (2 large group meetings, plus time for teams to work on own)
- Materials: Computer, audio/visual connection, presentation software, projector, screen

Instructions:

Initial Meeting (approximately 60 minutes):

1. *Activity Introduction:* Share with participants that they will be working together in small groups as organization consultants with the goal of helping a fellow organization improve their leadership capacity and practice. Each team will choose an organization to which none of them belong to observe and interact with over the course of a few weeks. Using the insight and information gained (data), they will determine the organizations' current leadership patterns, successes, and challenges (analysis) and then come up with recommendations for the organization moving forward. They will present their findings and recommendations to one another and, if desired, to their organization at the end of the project. Participants will also have the opportunity to provide feedback to those on their team as well as to other consulting teams. (5 minutes)

2. *Determine Consulting Teams and Organizations:* Divide participants into teams of 2–4 people each, taking care to promote diversity of background, identity, and thought within each team. Team members should take time to get to get familiar with one another and decide on an organization they would like to consult; it should be an organization to which none of the team members belong. (30 minutes)

3. Organizational Analysis Instructions: Share advice for engaging in organizational observation and analysis, including but not limited to the below suggestions. (5 minutes)

   - Contacting their chosen organization in advance to ensure their willingness to engage in this activity and gather information about meetings and events.
   - Determining the best ways to gather information about their organization to conduct a thorough analysis. This may include but is not limited to; attending organization meetings, interviewing organization members and advisors, observing at organization events, and volunteering to help with one of the organization's projects.
   - Gathering information about the organization's leadership philosophy and approach (both stated and enacted), organizational structure and culture, individuals' leadership styles, and other aspects of leadership theories and models of interest to the consulting team.
   - Noticing aspects of leadership as both positional and as a process.
   - Asking members and positional leaders about their approach to leadership and their view of how leadership happens in the organization overall.
   - Determining the organization's strengths and challenges and making connections to their leadership practice.

4. *Recommendations Instructions*: Share that the consulting team should use their analysis to determine

what the organization could do to improve and/or develop their leadership capacity and organizational culture. Recommendations may include, but are not limited to: (a) potential leadership learning and development goals; (b) suggestions for educational interventions such as workshops and trainings; (c) adjustments in organizational structure or process that may lend to a more effective or appropriate approach to leadership; (d) membership selection and retention considerations; (e) actions related to diversity in identity, background, and thought; and (f) connections to organizational purpose and mission. (5 minutes)

5. *Questions and Team Planning:* Solicit and respond to any questions from the participants regarding the project instructions. Provide time for the consulting teams to plan their work together. Explain how many days/weeks they will have to work as consulting teams to observe and interact with their chosen organization. Share the date and time of the final meeting at which each consulting team will present their findings and recommendations. Teams should utilize presentation software and should have 10–15 minutes each to present. (15 minutes)

6. *Consulting Team Work:* During this time, consulting teams should work on their own to observe and interact with their organization as they deem appropriate. In addition to the suggestions in #3 "Organizational Analysis Instructions", consulting teams should be looking to learn more about: the ways in which positional leaders and members engage in leadership; how the organization's work gets done, including organizational structure and processes; challenges and successes of the organization; the spoken and unspoken aspects of the organization's culture as well as consistencies and discrepancies in that culture; what member and organization actions say about their values, mission, and purpose; and examples of particular leadership models or theories in practice. (3–4 weeks minimum)

7. *Final Meeting and Debriefing:* Provide time for each consulting team to present their analysis and recommendations to the other consulting teams. Participants' presentations should indicate clear connections to leadership knowledge, as well as demonstrate complexity in leadership understanding. Following each consulting team presentation, the large group should have the opportunity engage in dialogue. Facilitators should ask questions to help participants dig deeper into their analysis and recommendations. Participants should be encouraged to ask other consulting teams questions or share insights/connections. This is also an appropriate time for facilitators and par-

ticipants to share verbal and/or written feedback to the presenting team. Feedback should be shared both on content of the analysis/recommendations as well as on presentation skills and effectiveness. After all consulting teams have presented, the facilitator should facilitate a large group dialogue by asking questions to gauge participants' critical thinking related to a broadening understanding of leadership theory and practice. (10–15 minutes per team, plus 15–20 minutes for large group debrief) For example:

- What leadership patterns or themes exist between the various organizations represented in this project? What differences?
- What contextual or environmental factors contribute to the way leadership happens in our organizations?
- What did you learn about the practice of analyzing/recommending/consulting related to leadership and culture? What was most interesting? Challenging?
- What did this project teach you about the nature of leadership in organizations? What did it teach you about your peers and their leadership practice?

8. *Peer Feedback and Team Self-Assessment:* Following final presentations and debrief (can be done at a separate time, if necessary), ask consulting teams to group together to provide one another with feedback on the group's process throughout the experience. They should discuss successes and challenges in how they worked together as a group, roles individuals played in the group process, and suggestions for further personal development. This can be done in verbal and/or written format, and can be specific to each person or kept as a more general team assessment. Facilitators may wish to provide guidelines and prompts for this conversation. (20–30 minutes, or in writing on own time)

Facilitator Notes:

- This project can be adapted for as many people as time and space allow.
- If done as a part of an academic course, instructors can consider the following adaptations; peer assessment check-ins throughout the project for credit; written analysis and recommendations paper for credit; requirement to demonstrate knowledge of particular leadership theories or models in final presentations and any written assignments; dividing up the project into parts due throughout the academic term.

- Facilitators may wish to provide time and space in a large group setting for consulting team planning and debrief meetings at various times throughout the duration of the project. In an academic course, instructors can provide time during class for these meetings.
- Having participants prepare and provide peer feedback for one another during and after final presentations can aid with learning assessment and also reinforce important lessons shared in presentations. In an academic course, written feedback can be used as both information for participants as well as a check for the instructor that other participants were engaged during their peers' presentations. Providing quality peer feedback can be a portion of participants' grades.

References:

Rocco, M. L. (2017). *Moving beyond common paradigms of leadership: Understanding the development of advanced leadership identity* (Doctoral dissertation). Retrieved from Proquest Dissertations and Theses. (10285840)

Shankman, M. L., Allen, S. J., & Haber-Curran, P. (2015). *Emotionally intelligent leadership: A guide for students* (2nd ed.). San Francisco, CA: Jossey-Bass.

CHAPTER 4

Reflection

Reflection is the process whereby learners construct and make meaning of their experiences (Ash & Clayton, 2009). Reflection goes beyond just thinking about something that occurred. It is more complex with mental and emotional components that require you to look at past experiences, draw conclusions, make meaning, and then think about how to use this new knowledge in the future (Volpe White, Guthrie, & Torres, 2019). As an instructional method, reflection comes in many forms such as journaling, stream-of-conscious writing, and debriefing. In any case, the reflection method is experiential in nature, providing learners the opportunity to make sense of a specific experience or set of experiences (Fink, 2013; Kolb, 1984). Likewise, intentionally designed reflection-based pedagogy emphasizes the link between thought and action, the metacognitive process of continuous intertwining of thinking and doing and the relationship between them (Ash & Clayton, 2009; Schon, 1983).

REFLECTION-BASED PEDAGOGY IN LEADERSHIP EDUCATION

Reflection is essential for leadership learning (Volpe White et al., 2019). Effective leadership educators need to actively engage learners in critical reflection within learning environments, using processes that build on learners' existing knowledge and experiential background (Guthrie & Jenkins, 2018). Namely, through an individual's reflection on an experience or set of experiences they might have in a leader or follower role in a particular context, they are empowered to consider, for example, what they thought, did, and felt, construct meaning (e.g., knowledge, skill, value) from that experience, and then experiment with the behaviors or skills gained from the process (Guthrie & Jenkins, 2018). Accordingly, we know that reflective opportunities that guide the meaning-making process, assist in the growth of students' identity, awareness, and individual, cognitive, and moral development (Densten & Gray, 2001; Jones & Abes, 2013; Strain, 2005; Wang & Rodgers, 2006). Moreover, reflection-based activities provide a meaningful way for leaders to gain a genuine understanding of themselves; their perceptions of experiences and events; their relationships; their feelings, needs, expectations, and values; and self-care and balance in their leadership roles (Densten & Gray, 2001; Eich, 2008; Hughes, Ginnett, & Curphy, 2015; White, 2012). Within leadership education programs, forms of reflection include written activities in the form of journals, essays about readings, verbal reflection in reaction to class discussions, questions posed, and current events to programs that formally engage students in completing vision- and goal-setting activities and other projects to personalize the concepts to the individual (Eich, 2008). Providing such intentional reflection-based instructional strategies in leadership learning opportunities is essential for learners to make meaning of leadership experiences.

For an in-depth illustration depicting the process of reflection as a vehicle for leadership learning, review the "Model of Leader and Follower Experiences as a Source of Transformational Learning" in *The Role of Leadership Educators: Transforming Learning* (Guthrie & Jenkins, 2018, pp. 150–151).

References:

Ash, S. L., & Clayton, P. H. (2009). Generating, deepening, and documenting learning: The power of critical reflection in applied learning. *Journal of Applied Learning in Higher Education, 1*(1), 25–48.

Densten, I. L., & Gray, J. H. (2001). Leadership development and reflection: What is the connection. *The International Journal of Educational Management, 15*(3), 119–124.

Eich, D. (2008). A grounded theory of high-quality leadership programs: Perspectives from student leadership programs in higher education. *Journal of Leadership & Organizational Studies, 15*(2), 176–187.

Fink, L. D. (2013). *Creating significant learning experiences*. San Francisco, CA: John Wiley & Sons.

Guthrie, K. L., & Jenkins, D. M. (2018). *The role of leadership educators: Transforming learning*. Charlotte, NC: Information Age.

Hughes, R., Ginnett, R., & Curphy, G. (2015). *Leadership: Enhancing the lessons of experience* (8th ed.). New York, NY: McGraw-Hill.

Jones, S. R., & Abes, E. S. (2013). *Identity development of college students: Advancing frameworks for multiple dimensions of identity*. San Francisco, CA: John Wiley & Sons.

Transforming Learning: Instructional and Assessment Strategies for Leadership Education, pp. 37–46

Kolb, D. A. (1984). *Experiential learning: Experience as the source of learning and development.* Upper Saddle River, NJ: Prentice-Hall.

Schon, D. (1983). *The reflective practitioner: How professionals think in action.* New York, N Y: Basic Books.

Strain, C. R. (2005). Pedagogy and practice: Service-learning and students' moral development. In N. S. Laff (Ed.), *New directions for teaching and learning: No. 103. Identity, learning, and liberal arts* (pp. 61–72). San Francisco, CA: Jossey-Bass.

Volpe White, J. M., Guthrie, K. L., & Torres, M. (2019). *Thinking to transform: Reflection in leadership learning.* Charlotte, NC: Information Age.

Wang, Y., & Rodgers, R. (2006). Impact of service-learning and social justice education on college students' cognitive development. *NASPA Journal, 43*(2), 316-337.

White, J. V. (2012). Students' perception of the role of reflection in leadership learning. *Journal of Leadership Education, 11*(2), 140–157.

REFLECTION THROUGH MIND MAPPING LEADERSHIP AND CHANGE CONCEPTS

Cameron C. Beatty

Reflection, Curricular Instructional

This reflection-based classroom activity focuses on cumulative learning and understanding of leadership curriculum. Many individuals struggle with structured reflection so it is important to start with the learning outcome you are aiming to achieve and then select reflection-based pedagogies that center those outcomes (Guthrie & Jenkins, 2018). The following activity offers a mind mapping reflection activity centered on cumulative learning from a leadership course on the topic of change. This activity example draws from concepts of Robert Quinn's (1996) book, *Deep Change: Discovering the Leader Within.*

Learning Outcomes:

Participants will have opportunities to:

- reflect on the key concepts of deep change in leadership.
- apply the key concepts deep change to their personal lives and society around them.
- participate in small group work related to their own cumulative learning on the topic of deep change, including discussion and reflection.

Setting Up the Activity:

- Group size: 15-25 participants
- Time: 30-45 minutes
- Materials: Paper, colorful writing utensils, laptop if notes will be recorded electronically

Instructions:

Mind mapping begins with a main concept or idea that the rest of the map revolves around, so choosing that idea or topic is the first step (Hopper, 2015). Begin by creating an image or writing a word that represents that first main idea. For the purpose of this example for a course titled Leadership and Change of the cumulative content, begin with writing the concept "deep change" on the board. Give participants the following instructions:

1. From the main idea, deep change, create branches (as many as needed), that each represent a single word that relates to the main topic. It is helpful to use different colors and images to differentiate the branches and subtopics (feel free to use different color writing utensils).

2. Then, create subbranches that stem from the main branches to further expand on ideas and concepts around deep change. These subbranches will also contain words that elaborate on the topic of the branch it stems from. This helps develop and elaborate on the overall theme of and concepts of the *Deep Change* book (Quinn, 1996). Including images and sketches can also be helpful in brainstorming and creating the subbranch topics. (10–12 minutes to develop mind map).

3. Next, include examples of where you have seen examples of the concepts included on your mind map. These could be personal examples or examples from society. (3–5 minutes to add on to mind map).

4. Next, pair up and share your mind maps and reflect on the concepts from *Deep Change* (Quinn, 1996) and make connections to your own lives. (10 minutes for pairs to share).

5. Finally, we will come back to together as a community to process.

6. By listening to their peers' reflection, this might spark further personal reflection. Discussion questions could include:

   - What was difficult about coming up with key concepts for your mind map?
   - What key applications from *Deep Change* do you see in your own life?
   - What concepts did you feel were missing from *Deep Change*?

Facilitator Notes:

- This activity can be adapted to cocurricular programming and activities. With cocurricular programs, consider doing the mind mapping with cut out shapes and having participants write their one word on shape and taping the shape to a board. Next start to create the mind map with the shapes on the board. Then continue with discussion questions as previous outlined.

References:

Guthrie, K. L., & Jenkins, D. M. (2018). *The role of leadership educators: Transforming learning*. Charlotte, NC: Information Age.

Hopper, C. H. (2015). Practicing college learning strategies (7th ed). Boston, MA: Cengage Learning.

Quinn, R. E. (1996). *Deep change: Discovering the leader within*. San Francisco, CA: Jossey-Bass.

MIRROR YOUR EXPERIENCE: PEER-TEACHING THROUGH REFLECTION
Aaron D. Clevenger

Reflection, Cocurricular Instructional

Grossman (2009) provides structure and suggestions that can lead to the critical reflection necessary for reflective pedagogy. Grossman's (2009) four types of reflections include: *content-based*, *metacognitive*, *self-author*, and *transformative* reflections. The following activity utilizes an individual's past leadership experiences and Grossman's (2009) reflection model to assist in teaching a chosen leadership topic.

Learning Outcomes:

Participants will have opportunities to:

- design an activity to teach a predetermined leadership topic (utilizing content-based and metacognitive reflection).
- analyze their experience teaching peers a predetermined leadership topic (utilizing self-author and transformative reflection).

Setting Up the Activity:

- Group size: 18 participants (2–3 participants per presentation and 5–6 participants for small group discussion)

- Time: 2 hours (60 minutes for preparation and 10 minutes per presentation)
- Materials: flip charts and colorful writing utensils and technology for presentations

Instructions:

1. Begin by explaining the activity and prompting reflection by providing a list of leadership topics, for example conflict management, active listening, empowering others, or leadership styles such as transformational leadership, servant leadership, or transactional leadership.

2. Set aside time for participants to choose one of the leadership topics and to write a short reflection of their experience with the chosen topic. (15 minutes)

3. Participants will design a lesson answering the following questions: (45 minutes)

   - Learning outcome: What do you expect your peers to know or be able to do?
   - Teaching strategies: What will you do to teach your lesson? Will you present, show a short film and hold a discussion, design an activity that will be used in your presentation?
   - Material or resources needed: What supplies are needed to teach your lesson?

4. At the 15-minute point of the lesson planning time, have participants meet in small groups of five to six people to reflect for 15 minutes on how they are thinking about the activity and the leadership topic. Reflecting on their thought process and explaining their thought process to other participants can lead to a better outcome. At the conclusion of this reflection time have the participants return to their presentation group for the last 15 minutes of their lesson planning.

5. Set aside 10 minutes per presentation to allow the participants to provide their peer lesson, which will include the specific leadership topic and learning outcome along with any personal experience and reflection that the participants have on the topic.

6. Debrief: Utilize the following reflective questions for a debrief: (15 minutes)

   - What did you learn about your leadership topic from this activity? (Content-based reflection)
   - What strategies did you use to create and complete your lesson? What other strategies might you have used to think through the activity? (Metacognitive reflection)

- Describe your behavior, thoughts, and attitudes as you went through this activity. (Self-author reflection)
- Reflect on your previous assumptions and how, through this experience, they have changed. (Transformative reflection)

Facilitator Notes:

- Be sure to encourage creativity in presentations to eliminate numerous PowerPoint presentation style delivery.

References:

Grossman, R. (2009). Structures for facilitating student reflection. *College Teaching, 57,* 15–22.

PHOTOGRAPHING LEADERSHIP: MAKING MEANING OF OUR WORLD
Jackie Bruce and Daniel Collins

Reflection, Technology-Enhanced

This asynchronously delivered activity provides an opportunity for participants to engage with leadership content under study, while also using their own world-view, literally, to make meaning of that content. Participants have the entirety of their world, however they define those boundaries, to use to photograph leadership, in whatever ways they see it. Then, using the guided questions provided as a catalyst, will share their reflections and reactions with classmates to extend their learning.

Learning Outcomes:

Participants will have opportunities to:

- analyze and evaluate major leadership theories and models.
- explore the relationship between leadership theories and models in daily life.
- construct plans to apply or enact the theories under study based on evaluation of the success or failure of their observations.

Setting Up the Activity:

- Group size: 5–35 participants (smaller reflection groups of 4–5 participants)

- Time: Offered asynchronously, 7 days (4 days to create and post original thoughts, and 3 days to reflect and respond to classmates' original posts)
- Materials: access to a learning management system to host asynchronous discussions, photo capturing device, such as camera or phone, textbook/supplementary material to frame the leadership theory(ies) under study

Instructions:

Provide to participants:

1. Read the textbook chapter to review the theory(ies) under study and attend the lecture or review the PowerPoint/lecture notes. (2–4 hours)
2. Go out into your worlds and take a picture/s you believe demonstrates the enactment or application of the theory under study. (1–3 hours)

   - Your pictures must come from PUBLIC settings (anywhere that is not restricted, for example, club meetings and political rallies). Someone's private home/apartment/condo is not a public setting. A classroom sits somewhere in the middle, so error on the side of caution and ask permission of your facilitator and classmates if photographing a class. If you choose to take photos of people, they must be of public figures doing their jobs as public figures.
   - If you take pictures of private citizens, you will need to fuzz out their faces, or take the photos from far enough distance that the faces are not easily identifiable *unless you have their consent/permission.* Talk with your facilitator about using photo release forms for the purposes of this course. All institutional guidelines related to photographing members of the campus community should be followed. All photographs of private citizens outside the university should have a photo permission/release. If you are unsure about whether someone is a private or public figure, error on the side of caution and use a photo release and get their permission to be photographed for purposes of the course.

3. Post the photo to the learning manage system. Once the photo is posted, reflect on and respond to the guided reflection questions provided. (1–2 hours).
4. After your original post is completed, take a few days to review, read and reflect on the posts of your classmates. Take the time to respond to two of your classmates' original posts; paying special attention to the guided reflection response ques-

tions, while also allowing for your own organic responses to arise as they will. (1–2 hours)

Debrief with participants:

5. The guided reflection questions for the original posts are:

- What is happening in your photograph and how does it demonstrate the enactment or application of the course content under study this week?
- Why did you take a photo of this and how is it representative of "your world"?
- Describe the leadership challenges and/or opportunities illustrated in your photo?
- How will your own enactment or application of the theory under study be influenced both now and in the future?

The guided reflection questions for the response posts are:

- Describe your initial, gut reaction to your classmate's photograph. What were your first thoughts when you saw the photo?
- Respond to the social and cultural pieces of the photograph. What is resonating with you in terms of the sociocultural aspects depicted? Why?
- What kinds of leadership did you see depicted in the photograph beyond or in addition to what the original poster shared? How does it resonate with you?

Facilitator Notes:

- Encourage participants to think broadly about the photos they take including locations and objects to help illustrate their leadership stories. Participants often use Photovoice to search for examples of positive enactment of theories. We also encourage them to find examples where the enactment is unsuccessful with the reminder that they (and their fellow participants and facilitators) can learn as much from those attempts that are unsuccessful as from those that are. In order to adapt Photovoice to the virtual classroom, some considerations to reflect on as you embark on the planning and implementation of the method:

  ○ Planning includes making decisions on the aim and scope of the learning activity, how much direction facilitators provide for the reflections prompts (if at all), and directions for photographs should be considered.

○ Understanding the technology skills of your participants is important, and the intensity of the reflection that will be required. In some cases, more than one response might be needed, while in others, replying to one other participant might be sufficient.

○ Rubrics should be implemented for both the photos and the posts in order to encourage participant success. In the case of these facilitators, Photovoice reflection prompts have been used in a variety of leadership courses with success.

Resources:

Chio, V. C., & Fandt, P. M (2007). Photovoice in the diversity classroom: Engagement, voice, and the 'eye/I' of the camera. *Journal of Management Education, 31*(4), 484–504.

Farley, L. A., Brooks, K., & Pope, K. (2017). Engaging students in praxis using Photovoice research. *Multicultural Education, 24*(2), 49–52.

FOLLOW THE LEADER OR LEADING THE FOLLOWER? ASKING CRITICAL QUESTIONS ABOUT FOLLOWERS AND FOLLOWERSHIP
Julie E. Owen

Reflection, Followership Focused

There is ample debate in the field of leadership studies about the notion of "followership." Rost (1991) tried to untangle the differences between follower and followership, referring to followers as "those who follow," and followership as "the process of following." This activity invites participants to reflect on diverse conceptions of followership, to think critically about interdependence in the leadership process, and to consider examples from their own experiences.

Learning Outcomes:

Participants will have opportunities to:

- learn diverse conceptions of the terms follower and followership, and their relationship to leaders and leadership.
- explore possible differences of leaders and followers in characteristics (e.g., motivation, agency), behaviors (e.g., initiation, communication) and outcomes.
- trouble the idea of followership and who benefits from such connotations.
- consider the interdependence of people in shared leadership processes.

Setting Up the Activity:

- Group size: Any size which allows for ample group discussion and interaction; 3–18 recommended range
- Time: 30–45 minutes
- Materials: Diverse definitions of followers and followership, reflection prompts

Instructions:

Each of the prompts below can be conducted as a large group conversation. It may be helpful to have participants first reflect individually on the questions and make a few notes for themselves, or pair and share with a partner, before entering the large group discussion.

1. Introduce the concept of followership and ask participants to brainstorm ways followers might be different from leaders using reflection Prompt #1 (Parts a–c) below. Encourage them to draw on their own past experiences with leadership. (10 minutes)
2. Present three different taxonomies of followers presented in Prompt #2 (parts a–c) below (and expounded upon in Northouse, 2019, Chapter 12: Followership) and ask corresponding reflection questions. (15 minutes)
3. Invite participants to interrogate the underlying concepts of followership using the prompts presented in Prompt #3 below. Explore how a focus on followership might detract from the creation of leader-full environments. (15 minutes)

Reflection Prompts:

1. Uhl-Bien, Riggio, Lowe, and Carsten (2014) define followership as involving "characteristics (a), behaviors (b), and processes (c) of individuals acting in relation to leaders" (p. 96). Have participants brainstorm responses to the following:

   - What are prototypical characteristics of followers? How does their role shape their motivations, abilities, and affect?
     - (a) Followership characteristics: characteristics that impact how one defines and enacts followership. Examples may include role orientations, motivations, intellectual and analytical abilities, affect, and social constructions of followers and/or individuals as engaging in following behaviors.
   - What actions or behaviors are involved in followership?
     - (b) Followership behaviors: behaviors enacted from the standpoint of a follower role

or in the act of following. Examples include the multiple expressions of overt followership including obeying, deferring, voicing, resisting, advising, et cetera.
   - What outcomes are associated with being a follower at the individual, organizational, and systemic levels?
     - (c) Followership outcomes: outcomes of followership characteristics and behaviors that may occur at the individual, relationship and work-unit levels. Examples include leader reactions to followers, such as burnout or contempt, follower advancement or dismissal, whether leaders trust and seek advice from followers, and how followership contributes to the leadership process, that is, leadership and organizational outcomes.

2. There are many taxonomies where scholars try to name diverse approaches to followership. Three are summarized below (see Northouse, 2019, Chapter 12, for more detailed descriptions).

   - (a) Kelley (2008) labels followers as passive, conformist, alienated, pragmatist, or exemplary based on their levels of dependence, critical thinking, and activity.
   - (b) Chaleff (2008) labels followers as resources, individualists, implementers, partners, or diehards based on the level of support they received and the level of challenge.
   - (c) Kellerman (2008) labels followers as isolated, bystanders, participants, and activists based on their level of engagement with the leader and group's goals.
   - How might being labeled as any of the above affect your motivation, participation, and commitment to a group or organization? What is the function/purpose of such labels? Who has the power to label?
   - Uhl-Bien et al. (2014) suggest that rather than focusing on how followers are affected by leaders, we focus on how followers affect leaders and organizational outcomes. What is the impact of followers on the followership process? On leaders? On the achievement of shared goals?

3. Now that we have established commonly held views of followers and followership, let's apply a critical lens:

   - Who or what larger purpose is served by separating leaders and followers into distinct categories? Can you think of a time when you have acted as both follower and leader within the same role, group, or organization?

- In her foreword to Guthrie and Jenkins (2018), Komives exhorts readers to move from an entity (focus on "the leader") approach to a leadership (focus on the group process) approach which involves the creation of "leader-full environments, not just leader-led environments" (p. xx). How might a focus on followership detract from the creation of leader-full environments?

Facilitator Notes:

- Facilitators should be prepared for a wide variety of reactions to interrogating and relanguaging the idea of followers and followership. The dominant leader/follower discourse is pervasive and it may even create anxiety in participants to critically question this dualism.

References:

Chaleff, I. (2008). Creating new ways of following. In R. E. Riggio, I. Chaleff, & J. Lipman-Blumen (Eds.), *The art of followership: How great followers create great leaders and Organizations* (pp. 67–88). San Francisco, CA: Jossey-Bass.

Guthrie, K. L., & Jenkins, D. M. (2018). *The role of leadership educators: Transforming learning*. Charlotte, NC: Information Age.

Kellerman, B. (2008). *Followership: How followers are creating change and changing leaders.* Boston, MA: Harvard Business Press.

Kelley, R. E. (2008). Rethinking followership. In R. E. Riggio, I. Chaleff, & J. Lipman-Blumen (Eds.), *The art of followership: How great followers create great leaders and organizations* (pp. 5–16). San Francisco, CA: Jossey-Bass.

Northouse, P. (2019). *Leadership: Theory and practice* (8th ed.). Thousand Oaks, CA: SAGE.

Rost, J. C. (1991). *Leadership for the twenty-first century.* New York, NY: Praeger.

Uhl-Bien, M., Riggio, R. E., Lowe, K. B., & Carsten, M. K. (2014). Followership theory: A review and research agenda. *The Leadership Quarterly, 25*(1), 83–104.

BEYOND "DEAR DIARY": FEEDBACK DRIVEN JOURNALING
Jillian M. Volpe White

Reflection, Curricular Learning Assessment

Journals are a common tool for reflection in curricular and cocurricular settings (Stevens & Cooper, 2009). However, many instructors fail to capitalize on the power of journaling by not providing timely, written feedback to participants (Hubbs & Brand, 2010). Additionally, participants benefit from journal prompts to guide their writing (Correia & Bleicher, 2008). This sequenced journaling activity challenges participants to reflect consistently and with increasing cognitive complexity as well as respond to feedback from peers or instructors.

Learning Outcomes:

Participants will have opportunities to:

- document reflections with increasing cognitive complexity.
- evaluate experiences using feedback from others.

Setting Up the Activity:

While journaling can be a one-time occurrence, this activity is intended to recur consistently over a period of time. It works for most any size group, though the instructor should consider how much time they have to provide consistent, written feedback to participants.

- Group size: 8–25 participants
- Time: ongoing over the course of a semester or set period of time; the amount of time required in any one setting could vary from 10–20 minutes
- Materials: a notebook or journal, participants could also use a phone, tablet, or laptop to document reflections electronically

Instructions:

Beginning of the semester/experience:

1. Explain the goal of this reflective learning assessment is for participants to process experiences and obtain feedback. Introduce participants to reflective journaling (Stevens & Cooper, 2009). This provides participants with shared language and context for what is expected during the semester.
2. Introduce the "What? So what? Now what?" reflection format (adapted from Kolb, 1984, by Campus

Opportunity Outreach League in 1995; Ash & Clayton, 2009).

- What? Observations and occurrences; objective reporting without judgment or interpretation
- So what? Consequences of actions; shifts from descriptive to interpretive
- Now what? Applying insights to the future; big picture, goal setting, and planning

3.   Set expectations. You might include a minimum length (250–500 words), depending upon where journaling fits in the context of other assignments. Journal writing should go beyond a log of tasks to include thoughtful reflections on experience.
4.   Provide a handout which includes dates for reflective journals and prompts.

Following each journal entry:

5.   Set aside time to provide feedback. If you are using paper journals, use a page to ask questions or share reactions. If you are using an online format, such as discussion boards or a blog, write comments for participants asking questions or sharing feedback.
6.   Allow time in class for participants to exchange materials and share thoughts. Invite participants to react to the content of what they are writing and/or the process of journaling.

End of semester/experience:

7.   During the final few weeks of the semester/experience, ask participants to read back through their journal entries and the feedback they were provided throughout the semester.
8.   Ask them to write a meta-analysis of their journals including insights they gleaned from reading back over the content of the semester.

These prompts are designed for an experiential learning opportunity such as service-learning, community engagement, internship, et cetera. They could also work for reflecting on course material or leadership learning broadly. The following list of questions is a guide, and can be adapted to fit specific experiences. The questions build in cognitive complexity as they progress.

1.   What are you most excited or nervous about as you begin this experience?
2.   What do you hope to learn as a result of this experience?
3.   What assumptions or expectations do you bring to this experience?

4.   Describe your experience. What does it look like, sound like, and feel like?
5.   What is the culture of the organization, including the underlying values and assumptions? What has been the most challenging aspect of adapting to a new place or learning a new organizational culture?
6.   Describe something specific you have done or seen that has revealed something new to you personally or intellectually.
7.   How do you think you are perceived with the people with whom you are working? How are interactions with people causing you to reevaluate stereotypes?
8.   What differences in communication have you faced in a new place (language, customs, gender roles, etc.)? How have you adapted to these differences and been an effective member of your organization?
9.   How can you use your knowledge, skills, and abilities to create positive change?
10. Addressing complex issues is rarely simple, and there is not a magic bullet for creating change. How do you identify multiple perspectives on and facets of complex issues?
11. What are your values? How do you know these are your values?

Facilitator Notes:

When providing feedback, ask questions, help participants connect to course content, affirm complex thinking, and challenge stereotypes. Over the course of the semester, the journals may become asynchronous conversations as participants address questions in subsequent entries. Throughout the course of the semester, prompts should build in cognitive complexity. You can use Bloom's Taxonomy (1956) to ensure prompts are aligned with developing complex thinking. The final prompt should push participants toward metacognitive thinking where they evaluate their own growth and development via a look back through their journals. This could also include a reflection on how they responded to feedback provided by the instructor or peers.

References:

Ash, S. L., & Clayton, P. H. (2009). Generating, deepening, and documenting learning: The power of critical reflection in applied learning. *Journal of Applied Learning in Higher Education, 1*, 25–48.

Bloom, B. S. (1956). *Taxonomy of educational objectives: The classification of educational goals, by a committee of college and university examiners.* New York, NY: Longman.

Correia, M. G., & Bleicher, R. E. (2008). Making connections to teach reflection. *Michigan Journal of Community Service Learning*, 41–49.

Hubbs, D., & Brand, C. F. (2010). Learning from the inside out: Methods for analyzing reflective journals in the college classroom. *Journal of Experiential Education, 33*(1), 56–71.

Kolb, D. A. (1984). *Experiential learning: Experience as the source of learning and development.* Upper Saddle River, NJ: Prentice-Hall.

Stevens, D. D., & Cooper, J. E. (2009) *Journal keeping: How to use reflective writing for learning, teaching, professional insight, and positive change.* Sterling, VA: Sterling.

You Think *What*?: Utilizing Reflection to Enhance Understanding of Self and Comfort With Differing Perspectives
Eric Grospitch and Michael Gleason

Reflection, Cocurricular Learning Assessment

This five step activity provides participants multiple opportunities for self and group reflection, all centered on the participant's initial results on a leadership inventory of the facilitator's choosing (examples listed below). This activity is intended to enhance participants' competence in several areas of the social change model of leadership development (Higher Education Research Institute, 1996). More specifically participants should progress in consciousness of self, congruence, collaboration and controversy with civility.

Learning Outcomes:

Participants will have opportunities to:

* constructively reflect on their individual experience in a group event/activity.
* evaluate feedback from other group members and contrast with one's own perspective.
* translate feedback into their future experiences.
* explore the value of multiple perspectives in gaining a better understanding of self.

Setting Up the Activity:

* Group size: 4–6 participants per small group following the use of an individual leadership self-assessment tool
* Time: 50 minutes
* Materials: paper and writing utensil

Instructions:

1. Encourage participants to complete a self-assessment tool such as the Student Leadership Practices Inventory (Kouzes & Posner, 2003). Facilitators might also consider Northouse (2019) inventories as initial assessment tools as well. (10 minutes)
2. After completing and evaluating the self-assessment, ask participants to individually reflect on their results by writing responses to the following questions: (5 minutes)

   * Based upon what I learned, what is an area that I want to emphasize (perceived strength)?
   * Based upon what I learned, what is an area of opportunity to grow and develop (perceived weakness)?
   * How do I perceive my role in a group project/ experience (vocal leader/worker bee/taskmaster, etc.)?

3. Participants are asked to share their responses to the above questions with other members of the group. Members of the group are encouraged to share candid feedback with one another and present *tough interpretations* about the participant's current self-assessment. O'Malley and Cebulla (2015) describe tough interpretations as "uncomfortable explanations" (p. 33). Considering tough interpretations can allow leaders to better understand situations (and in this case, themselves), and thus consider more useful solutions to make progress (O'Malley & Cebulla, 2015). (15 minutes)
4. Participants are then asked to complete the following verbal reflection with their group members. (10 minutes)

   * Why was it difficult to share differing perspectives about a participant's own interpretation of his or her results?
   * Why was it difficult to receive information that presented a different perspective about your own results?
   * What are the behaviors of the group that promoted a climate that was productive and reduced the amount of interpersonal conflict?
   * How can we apply these behaviors to other group settings?

5. As a final step in the process, participants individually write responses based on Ash and Clayton's (2009) articulated learning guiding questions: (10 minutes)

   * What did I learn?
   * How, specifically, did I learn it?

- Why did this learning matter, or why is it significant?
- In what ways will I use this learning; or what goals shall I set in accordance with what I have learned in order to improve myself, the quality of my learning, or the quality of my future experience or service (p. 143).

Facilitators Notes:

- Learning how to give critical feedback in a way that can be received is a learned skill. The verbal feedback itself is less important than the delivery and how it is received. Pay particular attention to the nonverbal communication during the shared response time. This will give you the guidance for future engagement.

References:

Ash, S. L., & Clayton, P. H. (2004). The articulated learning: An approach to reflection and assessment. *Innovative Higher Education, 29*(2), 137–154.

Higher Education Research Institute. (1996). *A social change model of leadership development: Guidebook version III.* College Park, MD: National Clearinghouse for Leadership Programs.

Kouzes, J. M., & Posner, B. Z. (2003). *The student leadership challenge practices inventory.* San Francisco, CA: Jossey-Bass.

Northouse, P. G. (2019). *Leadership: Theory and practice* (8th ed.). Thousand Oaks, CA: SAGE.

O'Malley, E. & Cebulla, A. (2015). *Your leadership edge: Lead anytime, anywhere.* Wichita, KS: KLC Press.

CHAPTER 5

Team-Based Learning

Team-based learning (TBL) is a structured and systematic instructional strategy in which small groups work together to produce a common product in preparation for the teamwork they are likely to encounter in the workplace (Humphreys, Greenan, & McIlveen, 1997; Michaelsen, Knight, & Fink, 2004; Thomas & Busby, 2003). TBL is also a cooperative learning approach where students endure challenges while striving toward a common goal, learn how to work interactively, and share responsibility and accountability for each other's' learning. When used effectively, TBL moves beyond content delivery and provides students opportunities to apply course concepts to resolve issues, develop critical thinking skills, and give and receive feedback through peer evaluation (Michaelsen & Sweet, 2011). Moreover, effective TBL provides an environment ripe for promoting team development or "teambuilding" processes and encouraging communication and delegation skills (Moorehead & Griffin, 2010). Nonetheless, it is critical that instructors who use TBL structure both the duration of student teams' work together and the final group product, provide opportunities for group development in the form of learning activities early and often, and offer feedback and support to student teams (Allen & Hartman, 2008; Barbour, 2006; Chriac & Granstrom, 2012).

TEAM-BASED LEARNING IN LEADERSHIP EDUCATION

Used primarily to foster team building and reinforce learning outcomes in leadership programs, TBL is a significant component of leadership education (Guthrie & Jenkins, 2018; Jenkins, 2018). As leadership educators, "we have an opportunity and responsibility to ensure that our student working teams are more efficient, relational, process-oriented, and prepared" (Guthrie & Jenkins, 2018, p. 224) and that our students understand the difference between working *in* a group and working *as* a group (Chriac & Granstrom, 2012). Accordingly, focusing on the process components and learning objectives of TBL through integrating reflective activi-

ties, opportunities for group dialogue, and feedback and debriefing versus the final group product is critical (Guthrie & Jenkins, 2018). Specifically, TBL in leadership education programs should promote not only the stages of group development (Tuckman, 1965) but also model effective group development activities such as icebreakers, exploring individual differences through dialogue, setting expectations, assigning roles, and giving and receiving feedback (Baker, 2009; Holmer, 2001; Kayes, Kayes, & Kolb, 2005; McKendall, 2000). At its best, TBL in leadership education is a practice field for team-based work outside of the classroom where students have opportunities to make meaning of their experiences as a team collectively and give one another appropriate feedback.

It is all about process. For a step-by-step guide from creating to facilitating to debriefing TBL in your leadership program, see *The Role of Leadership Educators: Transforming Learning* (Guthrie & Jenkins, 2018, pp. 221–230).

References:

Allen, S. J., & Hartman, N. S. (2008). Leadership development: An exploration of sources of learning. *SAM Advanced Management Journal, 73*(1), 10–15.

Baker, A. C. (2009). *Catalytic conversations: Organizational communication and innovation.* Armonk, NY: M. E. Sharpe.

Barbour, J. (2006). Team building and problem-based learning in the leadership classroom: Findings from a two-year study. *Journal of Leadership Education, 5*(2), 28–40.

Chiriac, E. H., & Granstrom, K. (2012). Teachers' leadership and students' experience of group work. *Teachers and Teaching, 18*(3), 345–363.

Guthrie, K. L., & Jenkins, D. M. (2018). *The role of leadership educators: Transforming learning.* Charlotte, NC: Information Age.

Holmer, L. L. (2001). Will we teach leadership or skilled incompetence? The challenge of student project teams. *Journal of Management Education, 25*(5), 590–605.

Humphreys, P., Greenan, K., & McIlveen, H. (1997). Developing work-based transferable skills in a university environment. *Journal of European Industrial Training, 21*(2), 63–69.

Kayes, A. B., Kayes, D. C., & Kolb, D. A. (2005). Experiential learning in teams. *Simulation and Gaming, 36,* 330–354.

McKendall, M. (2000, May/June). Teaching groups to become teams. *Journal of Education for Business, 75*(5), 277–282.

Guthrie, K. L., & Jenkins, D. M. (2018). *The role of leadership educators: Transforming learning*. Charlotte, NC: Information Age.

Michaelsen, L. K., & Sweet, M. (2011). Team-based learning. In W. Buskist & J. E. Groccia (Eds.), *New directions for teaching and learning, no. 128: Evidence-based teaching* (pp. 41–51). San Francisco, CA: Jossey-Bass.

Michaelsen, L. K., Knight, A. B., & Fink, D. L. (2004). *Team-based learning: A transformative use of small groups in college teaching*. Sterling, VA: Stylus.

Thomas, S., & Busby, S. (2003). Do industry collaborative projects enhance students' learning? *Education + Training*, 45(4/5), 226–235.

Moorehead, G., & Griffin, R. W. (2010). *Organizational behavior: Managing people and organizations*. South-Western/Cengage Learning.

Tuckman, B. W. (1965). Developmental sequence in small groups. *Psychological Bulletin*, 63(6), 384–400.

ORGANIZATIONAL CHANGE CASE STUDY PROJECT
Corey Seemiller

Team-Based Learning, Curricular Instructional

The organizational change case study project provides an opportunity for participants to employ group development principles to a team-based organizational consulting scenario.

Learning Outcomes:

Participants will have opportunities to:

- synthesize and apply their learning to an organizational situation.
- employ strategies for effective group functioning.
- summarize their ideas into a coherent and professional written paper.

Setting Up the Activity:

- Group size: Each group of 3 participants, as many groups as needed
- Time: 6 weeks
- Materials: Copies of a 1–2 page case study of a fictional organization focusing on several organizational issues such as culture, morale, and change. The case study will be designed by the instructor so as to ensure that (a) it is fictional and does not lead to participants spending time researching a real

organization, and (b) includes the types of issues related to the course.

- Outline with prompts that help the groups structure their papers. Outlines should be designed to match the assignment expectations and grading rubric.
- Video-based collaboration space or learning management system with option for recording.
- Writing checklist that includes content, grammatical, and formatting expectations for the paper. These may include formatting, references/citations, organizational/logical structure, writing, and sources.
- Team Evaluation for participants to evaluate both their individual contribution and the contribution of others.

Instructions:

1. Week 1: Setting expectations/forming groups

- The project is designed to simulate a consulting team tasked with diagnosing organizational issues and developing strategies for addressing those issues. Instructions for the project are as follows:
  - Your group will evaluate and make recommendations for an organizational scenario that will be provided to you. In an 8–10 page paper, your group will need to incorporate five concepts/research findings from the class content and/or readings to analyze the scenario and provide recommendations. All participants in the group will receive the same grade regardless of effort or contribution, with two exceptions. Participants who do not contribute in any manner to the Consulting Meeting or Outline will be removed from the group and required to complete the assignment on their own. And, participants who do not contribute at all to the final paper will receive a zero.
    - Give participants a deadline to form their own groups; place remaining participants into groups of three (you may have one group of four depending on class size).

2. Week 2: Provide opportunities for group development early and often

- The project begins with a 1-hour virtual consulting meeting, which is recorded, where the group engages in a discussion about group expectations, formulates an approach to the case study using an outline worksheet designed specifically for this assignment, and then strategizes the division of labor for the project. Instructions for the consulting meeting are as follows:

- You will need to meet for a minimum of one hour with your assigned group for the Organizational Change Case Study Project to discuss the scenario, brainstorm how you believe you should address the issue, and discuss the concepts that best apply to this situation. You will need to audio record the meeting. Your grade will be determined by your participation and active engagement in the meeting. Participation and engagement will be determined by the quantity and quality of your verbal contributions during this meeting. While there is no minimum amount of time or number of instances in which you will be required to contribute, participants who contribute very little or not at all will not receive credit for this meeting.

3. Week 3: Team building

- By the end of Week 3, groups need to finalize the outline and submit it to the instructor. The outline is divided into the sections required for the paper and must include the name of the person writing each section along with a brief overview of the content that will be included in the final paper. Much of the content for the outline will be discussed, negotiated, and even completed during the consulting meeting.

4. Week 4: Offer feedback and support

- After the consulting meeting and outline have been completed, the instructor provides feedback to the group on both the process and content of their project thus far.

5. Weeks 5 and 6: Course experience/ending

- After receiving instructor feedback, groups work for 2 weeks (Weeks 5 and 6) to complete the paper. Upon submitting the paper, each participant also turns in a writing checklist, where they must "sign off" on a number of items that they assert have been accounted for in the paper. Instructions for the writing checklist are:
  - As you write and proofread your Organizational Change Paper, use the Organizational Change Paper Checklist to double check that you have completed all the required writing and formatting elements of this assignment. On the checklist, please put an X in the blank space to the left of each checklist item (con-

firming that you have completed the item). Each individual member of the group will need to complete and submit a copy of the Organizational Change Paper Checklist. This ensures all group members have adhered to the expectations on the checklist and have had the opportunity to proof a near-final version of the assignment.

- Participants also submit their Team Evaluations. Instructions are as follows:
  - Please indicate the responsibilities that each team member, including yourself, fulfilled in order to complete this assignment. Also, give each team member a score from 0–10 in regard to their successful completion of their assigned work on the assignment. These scores will be averaged and then awarded to each participant for a grade. Zero is contributed nothing and 10 is did everything assigned on time and in an effective manner. Numbers in between are on a scale.

Facilitator Notes:

- It is really important to give thorough feedback throughout the project to ensure groups are set up for success.
- Consulting meeting: It is critical to listen to the consulting meeting recordings. These sessions are very telling in discerning group dynamics and work distribution. Any participants who are not present at the consulting meeting because they failed to show up after agreeing to a meeting time will be required to do the project on their own.
- Outline: If any group is moving in the wrong direction or appears to not understand the project based on their outline submissions, it is ideal to catch that before the groups start writing the final paper. For example, any groups that appear to have selected concepts that are not well-suited should be given feedback immediately, asking them to rethink their direction.
- Final Paper: For the final paper, it is best to use a grading rubric that includes a set number of points that groups can earn based on accuracy, quality, and depth related to the content. Once the content points have been totaled, it is recommended to use a reverse point scale for writing errors where instead of accumulating points for writing, the group loses points for errors. Deductions based on writing should be reflective of the same categories on the writing checklist: Formatting, references/citations, organizational/logical structure, writing, and sources.

References:
Seemiller, C. (2016). *Organizational change case study project.* Dayton, OH: Wright State University.

POST-IT NOTE INTRODUCTIONS
Brittany Brewster

Team-Based Learning, Cocurricular Instructional

Introductions to groups often scratch the surface of understanding the complex nature of individual members. Creating shared group identity is essential to the development of a community (Bordas, 2007). This large shared group identity reflects the complex experiences brought by each member that are often lost in everyday introductions. To assist in better understanding people as dynamic individuals, we must create space for members to articulate their experiences and needs when introducing themselves.

Learning Outcomes:

Participants will have opportunities to:

- articulate individual values, assumptions, and needs within a group.
- explore the similarities and differences of members within a group.
- identify areas for support of group members.

Setting Up the Activity:

- Group size: 20 participants
- Time: 60 minutes (5 minutes for introduction, 10 minutes for individual work, 25 minutes for group work, 20 minutes for debriefing)
- Materials: Flip chart sticky paper (one per participant), Post-it Notes or sheets of paper, colorful writing utensils

Instructions:

1. Provide each participant with a sheet of flip chart paper and give the group a minute to create the layout found under the facilitator notes section. (2 minutes)
2. Guide participants through filling each box with the following prompts/questions. The subsequent information can be utilized to frame statements: (3 minutes)

- My name is/I answer to …
  - To appropriately welcome you to conversations.
- My Preferred Gender Pronouns (PGP's) are…
  - To ensure your appropriate gender pronouns are utilized without assumption.
- I consider home to be …
  - To give voice to the many ways you can view home outside of your birth location.
- I value …
  - To spotlight what is important to you.
- People assume I am …
  - To debunk common assumptions made about you.
- I need from you …
  - To share ways our community can support your success in this shared space.

3. Ask participants to answer the prompts/questions provided above on their flip chart paper. (10 minutes)
4. Ask participants to place their flip chart paper on the walls when finished and grab a stack of Post-It notes and a pen/pencil.
5. Participants should read responses posted around the room in silence. During this time, participants should use the post it notes to write questions and comments and place them directly on the flip chart papers. (15–20 minutes)
6. Request participants to spend five minutes reading and reflecting on their responses using the following prompt: (5 minutes)

- At this time, please find a comfortable place to sit with your large Post-It Note. Please spend 5 minutes reading and reflecting on the responses left for you.

7. Gather participant's attention for a large group reflection on the activity. (20 minutes)

- What did it feel like to introduce yourself like this?
- What was the most challenging prompt/question to answer? Why?
- What did you learn about others? What did you learn about yourself?
- What do we think we know about the group? What do we not know?
- How does what we know/don't know about others impact our group?
- What do you take away from this experience?

Facilitator Notes:

- If you play a consistent role in the community as a member, consider completing the activity alongside participants.
- Create a sample of the flip chart paper layout to show participants prior to the activity. An example is displayed below:

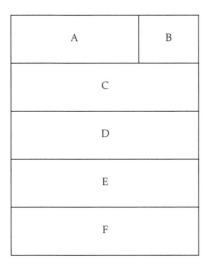

Reference:

Bordas, J. (2007). *Salsa, soul, and spirit: Leadership for a multicultural age*. San Francisco, CA: Berrett-Koehler.

Resources:

Bertrand Jones, T., Guthrie, K. L., & Osteen, L. (2016). Critical domains of culturally relevant leadership learning: A call to transform leadership programs. *New Directions for Student Leadership*, *152*, 9–21.

Jones, S. R., & McEwen, M. K. (2000). A conceptual model of multiple dimensions of identity. *Journal of College Student Development*, *41*(4), 405–414.

GLOBALLY NETWORKED LEARNING: AN INTERNATIONAL LENS ON LEADERSHIP
Lisa Endersby

Team-Based Learning, Technology-Enhanced

The goal of integrating globally networked learning (GNL) into leadership pedagogy is to offer participants the opportunity to explore the definition of and actions inherent in leadership from an intercultural, international lens. GNL connects participants and facilitators across geographic boundaries, leveraging technology as a means to analyze, create, and disseminate knowledge across cultures. While the work of GNL can expand to an entire course, it can also serve as a single activity that can be implemented as part of a lecture or classroom activity.

Learning Outcomes:

Participants will have opportunities to:

- identify similarities and differences in approaches to leadership across cultures.
- discuss the integration of a global awareness or focus in their leadership style/approach.
- employ an awareness of the cultural impact of and on leadership to their work in groups.

Setting Up the Activity:

- Group size: 5–30 participants
- Time: It is recommended to consider learning outcomes when determining how much time to spend on this activity. For example, if the goal is to gather information to inform a larger project, less time may be required than if the goal is to build and practice particular leadership skills
- Materials: None

Instructions:

A challenging, but also exciting opportunity in facilitating GNL in your classroom is the ability to modify the instructions below to suit your desired timeline. Incorporating GNL into your teaching can follow a similar approach that you take in designing a course or in class activity—an up-front investment in your participants' success, even if it does take some extra time, will go a long way in creating an organized, meaningful learning opportunity.

1. Determining an assignment or lesson that would benefit from the real-time integration and exploration of cultural differences.
2. Finding a partner facilitator in another country who teaches a topic either similar or complimentary to what you are teaching. This step can take the most time if you have not yet or often engaged with colleagues in this way.
3. With your partner facilitator, determine how both groups of participants may benefit from interacting with each other.

   • What knowledge, skills, and/or perspectives may be helpful in completing the assignment? If your participants are completing an assignment related to leadership for social change, how might insight from another culture influence their thinking about this topic? How might they understand how leadership for social change could look in a country and culture other than their own?
   • A helpful way to begin this process is to determine, together, your desired learning outcomes for the activity. Agreeing on a common goal or endpoint can help you to explore and finalize which path may make the most sense to travel. This process could take anywhere from a single meeting to a few weeks or months of dialogue.

4. Consider the technology you will need to connect participants. You may also wish to consider asynchronous technologies (e.g., discussion forums) alongside or in place of synchronous tools as a means to mitigate challenges related to time zones, access to technology, and other potential issues.
5. Prepare participants to engage with their partner class. This is often where an initial lesson on intercultural/global competencies is helpful, alongside a discussion of what skills may be developed in and/or most useful for completing this activity.
6. Facilitate an opportunity for engagement with the partner class. At the first attempt, it is often helpful for facilitators to be on hand to guide participants through the initial encounter. Typically, this initial engagement happens within a single class (synchronously) or over a finite period of time (e.g., a week prior to the first portion of the activity or assignment). Synchronous and asynchronous opportunities are both sound pedagogically, but it

will be up to you to determine what will work best for your participants. Factors to consider include time differences/time zones, participant readiness/willingness to engage, and your intended learning outcomes (e.g., if the development of interpersonal communication skills are an intended learning outcome, synchronous communication may be one valuable way to practice and demonstrate these skills).

Facilitator Notes:

• Finding a partner facilitator and/or organization can be challenging. Consider your ongoing or past research partnerships as a place to start.
• Working effectively and collaboratively in groups is a skill in itself. It is helpful to consider having the two groups meet at least once before the project work begins as a way to break the ice and to establish group norms for working together. As the project continues, consider meetings that focus on doing the work itself; sharing updates and information is typically quicker over email or a similar online collaborative platform.
• Remember that assessing this work is more than assigning participants a grade. Consider how you might assess both product and process. For example, providing participants with the opportunity to reflect on this experience (both as a larger group and individually) can offer powerful insights into their own personal growth and the unique nature of working in a cross cultural, interdisciplinary environment.

Resources:

Jenkins, D. M. (2012). Global critical leadership: Educating global leadership with critical leadership competencies. *Journal of Leadership Studies, 6*(2), 95–101.

Soria, K. M., & Troisi, J. (2014). Internationalization at home alternatives to study abroad: Implications for students' development of global, international, and intercultural competencies. *Journal of Studies in International Education, 18*(3), 261–280.

Starke-Meyerring, D., & Wilson, M. (2008). *Designing globally networked learning environments: Visionary partnerships, policies, and pedagogies.* Rotterdam, Netherlands: Sense. Retrieved from https://www.sensepublishers.com/media/243-designing-globally-networked-learning-environments.pdf

ESCAPE GAMES AS A LEARNING ASSESSMENT
John Banter and John Egan

Team-Based Learning, Followership Focused

Escape games are uniquely positioned to serve as a team-based learning activity because the final outcome is secondary to the group process. The LEADescape framework is designed to assist leadership educators in developing their own escape games that meet their specific contextual needs (Banter & Egan, 2018). The debrief provided is constructed as a learning assessment with the expectation that learners have already been exposed to the specific followership content through other instructional strategies.

Learning Objectives:

Participants will have opportunities to:

- distinguish between leadership and followership.
- articulate leadership as a cocreated process (Uhl-Bien, Riggo, Lowe, & Carsten, 2014).
- interpret their level of engagement in this team-based problem solving scenario in connection to the Kellerman follower typology (Kellerman, 2008).

Setting Up the Activity:

- Group Size: 5–10 participants
- Time: 45 minutes–1 hour 15 minutes (30–60 minutes for game, 15 minutes for debrief)
- Materials: See Facilitator's Notes

Instructions:

1. Provide basic rules for the escape game before participants begin that may include: (a) no breaking or tearing items within the game; (b) how much time they have to accomplish their task; (c) when and if any hints will be given (i.e., with 10 minutes and with five minutes left in the game); and (d) players can discard clues/puzzles once they have been used.
2. For this specific learning assessment surrounding followership, it is important to assign one person in each game as the positional leader of the group. This will lead to a richer debrief.
3. Provide the teams with the team goal that has been designed into the game, start a visual timer, and announce you have __ (time) ____ minutes to _____ (goal) _____.
4. Once game has been complete, engage in a debrief of the process. Possible debriefing questions include:

- What interactions or exchanges did you observe between people during the game? Were they positive or negative?
- How did those interactions and individuals influence the group in the escape game?
- How did your experience in the escape game clarify differences between leadership and followership?
- How did you observe the interaction of individuals' influencing or accepting of others' influence in the overall outcome of the game?
- How would you describe these interactions in the context of leadership as a cocreated process?
- How engaged were you in the game trying to escape [on a scale of 1 (*lowest*) to 5 (*highest*)]? Describe how your level of engagement in the game connects to Kellerman's (2008) follower typology. Did you see similarities or differences?

Facilitator Notes:

- The simplest and most expensive approach is to bring learners to an established escape room facility in your area and follow the experience with a debrief. Adventurous or cost-sensitive leadership educators can build escape games to meet the educational needs of their learners. Because locking learners in a room is logistically and fiscally challenging, it may be best to design a game with an alternative goal. As illustrated in Table 5.1, the LEADescape framework guides educators through the method of developing an escape game that can be used as an instructional strategy or as a learning assessment (Banter & Egan, 2018).

The framework begins with the creation of learning objectives while giving careful consideration for appropriate taxonomy levels, and this is followed by selecting a theme that connects with learners. Once an engaging theme has been identified, utilize a web search of images related to the theme to create a written list of items that belong in the escape game world being created. Next, develop a creative storyline connected to the theme that can be revealed during gameplay or introduced at the start of the game. The game can now be designed using a flowchart that should include two to three entry points or threads of the game that later connect to achieving the final goal. This allows players to initially enter into more than one bag, box, or other locked item as well as allowing for asynchronous play. The list of items previously created can now be integrated into the puzzles, clues, and other items in the game. Table 5.2 includes an incomplete list of possible puzzles to consider for an escape game.

Table 5.1. LEADesape Framework

Learning objectives	Taxonomy considerations; leadership behaviors or leadership knowledge?
Theme	What connects with participants? What items belong?
Storyline	Connect to theme; convincing and logical within theme
Game	Determine puzzles and connect to theme; learning objective considerations; build game map or flowchart
Debrief	Connect game to learning objectives; develop debrief questions for deeper learning through reflection
Pilot	Observe and take notes during pilot; enlist informal feedback; modify based on feedback
Evaluation	Include formal feedback process for participants; modify existing game; build new escape games

Table 5.2. Escape Game Puzzles and Game Elements

Number of items	Have physical items in the game that belong in your theme. For instance, glasses, forks, knives, and plates in an Italian restaurant theme. The amount of each item (3 forks, 7 glasses, etc.) corresponds to a correct number in a combination lock. Now you need to find a clever way to reveal the correct order for the numbers in another location. This could be a card or photograph that displays the objects in the proper order.
Puzzle pieces	Hide puzzle pieces tied to your theme inside boxes/bags or just within your game space. The puzzles construction could reveal a final answer (combination lock) or a substitution cipher.
Substitution cipher	A cipher simply makes a previously unreadable message mean something useful. The original message may include strange symbols or emojis. The cipher is a table that allows players to convert the symbols into letters or numbers that provide a combination or clear message.
Overlay	Overlaying paper over another document tied to your theme reveals a hidden message or combination.
Online clues	Make a free website to house puzzles or clues. Hide clues within a Youtube video you've created. Find creative ways to drive players to the hyperlink (QR code, substitution cipher).
Hidden stuff	Hide objects, clues, puzzles or needed keys throughout your game space. For difficult hiding spots, consider leave hints or riddles that tell players where to look.
Team challenge game	Insert instructions to complete a group task that must be accomplished. Drive remote control car blind folded into a specific square on the floor as teammates who have sight provide directions. Get creative!

References:

Banter, J., & Egan, J. (2018). Escape rooms: A student-centered approach to animating leadership learning. Paper presented at the Association of Leadership Educators 28th annual conference: Leadership Innovation and Inclusion in the City of Big Shoulders, Chicago, IL

Kellerman, B. (2008). *Followership: How followers are creating change and changing leaders*. Boston, MA: Harvard Business Press.

Uhl-Bien, M., Riggio, R., Lowe, K., & Carsten, M. (2014). Followership theory: A review and research agenda. *The Leadership Quarterly*, 25(1), 83–104.

Resources:

Clarke, S., Peel, D. J., Arnab, S., Morini, L., Keegan, H., & Wood, O. (2017). escapED: A framework for creating educational escape rooms and interactive games for higher/further education. *International Journal of Serious Games*, 4(3), 73–86.

Humphrey, K. (2017). The application of a serious, non-digital escape game learning experience in higher education. *Sport & Exercise Psychology Review*, 13(2), 48–54.

Nicholson, S. (2015). *Peeking behind the locked door: A survey of escape room facilities*. Retrieved from http://scottnicholson.com/pubs/erfacwhite.pdf

EXAMINING IDENTITY AND EXPANDING ONE'S SELF-AWARENESS AS A LEADER
Sara E. Thompson

Team-Based Learning, Curricular Learning Assessment

Using implicit leadership theories, participants engage in an active learning experience exploring one's leader identity and developmental readiness. This activity provides participants with an opportunity to examine leadership development concepts and uncover limiting beliefs that may be preventing them from activity participating in leadership experiences or self-selecting into training and development opportunities. This activity is adapted from Schyns, Kiefer, Kerschreiter, and Tymon (2011).

Learning Outcomes:

Participants will have opportunities to:

- expand one's self-awareness by uncovering limiting or unconscious beliefs that may be in the way of a participant developing as a leader.

- expand one's social awareness to consider contextual factors that may be limiting communication in a leadership setting.
- identify implicit bias and stereotypes regarding one's leader identity.

Setting Up the Activity:

- Group size: 10–50 participants
- Time: 45 minutes
- Materials: paper, writing utensils

Instructions:

1. Facilitator may share a story about how the term "leader" is overused in society and for many people their definition (prior to taking a leadership course or engaging in a leadership program) is built from our life experiences. (5 minutes)
2. Ask participants to engage in an individual reflection exercise thinking about what they have seen and been taught about leading and leadership throughout their lives. (10 minutes)
3. Sort participants into small groups ranging from 3–5 participants. Then, ask participants to draw a leader. Encourage participants to be creative, share their individual reflections with one another. Consider the qualities and attributes that are necessary to be an effective leader. Questions participants may discuss in their groups are: "What are the qualities, attributes, experiences that are important to you in a leader? Who would you want to follow?" "What matters to you when leading or being led by others?" (15 minutes)
4. Report out. Ask each group to show and describe their drawing. (20 minutes depending on group size)
5. Facilitate discussion about the activity. (10–15 minutes)

    - What are the similarities you notice in each of the drawings? What are the differences you notice? Why do you think those qualities or attributes are important? What is missing from the drawings? Where did these opinions come from? The response is often some form of individual or cultural context. Engage participants in a conversation about context; discuss the ways our context/culture shapes our perspective as leaders.

    - Engage participants in a conversation about followers. Consider asking: What do you notice about followers in these drawings? What percentage of their small group conversation included a discussion of followers? Often it is a small percentage and there is opportunity to engage participants in a discussion about why considering your followers makes you a better leader.
6. After debrief, share the definition of implicit leadership theories:

    - "Implicit leadership theories are images that everyone holds about the traits and behaviors of leaders in general" (Schyns, Kiefer, Kerschreiter, & Tymon, 2011, p. 398). "Similar to stereotypes, implicit leadership theories serve to explain the other person's behavior and also the observer's reaction toward that person" (Schyns, Kiefer, Kerschreiter, & Tymon, 2011, pp. 398–399).
    - The difference between the definition of leader development and leadership development (Day, 2001) including: (a) Leader development focuses on individual skills—what I do, my strengths and weaknesses, what I know, my personality, my life experiences; (b) Leadership development focuses on the broader relational and social context where interaction and exchange takes place, including qualities such as empathy, service, and team dynamics.

Facilitator's Notes:

- Understanding implicit leadership theories may assist you in deepening your social awareness and understanding how others view leadership. Ask: How might your unexamined, implicit leader identity be influencing your perception of others and/or the situational and environmental context where you are leading? Consider ending the class with an in-class journal entry: Where am I comfortable leading and where do I need to expand my self-view as a leader?

References:

Day D. V. (2001). Leadership development: A review in context. *Leadership Quarterly, 11,* 581–613.

Schyns, B., Kiefer, T., Kerschreiter, R., & Tymon, A. (2011). Teaching implicit leadership theories to develop leaders and leadership: How and why it can make a difference. *Academy of Management Learning & Education, 10*(3), 397–408.

READY—SET—ACTION: MULTIMEDIA TEACH-BACK GROUP ACTIVITY
Bobby Kunstman

Team-Based Learning, Cocurricular Learning Assessment

Leadership teach-backs serve as a simple mechanism by which participant understanding of concepts can be shared and assessed. This activity serves as a capstone to a culmination of lessons learned. Rather than simply sharing an instructional teach-back for the group, participants will be divided into teams and asked to create an advanced method of teach-back using various forms of multimedia. Uniquely, participants will be asked to incorporate people, places, and things into their presentation as part of this process while imparting the lessons learned from the material.

Learning Outcomes:

Participants will have opportunities to:

- recall concepts of leadership learning imparted to them through previous group lessons and activities.
- demonstrate an understanding of small group dynamics in a team-based setting learning and teaching from each other in a collaborative environment
- develop and reflect on creative expression and its connection to leadership activities.

Setting Up the Activity:

- Group size: 15+ participants (divided equally into smaller groups for the teach-back)
- Time: 3 hours (10 minutes set-up, 90 minutes team-based learning activity, 60 minutes team-based teach-back, 20 minutes processing learning)
- Materials: Lessons from activity for teach-back, at least one hand-held visual recording device, props for teach-back, computer, and projector

Instructions:

1. This activity is designed to provide opportunities for participants to relearn material, work as a team, present learning with tangible examples related to the community, and reflect on their learning process.
2. Identify lesson (or learning material) to be used for teach-back that can be divided amongst a larger group into equal smaller groups (e.g., Bordas, 2012, developed eight principles that inform leadership

from a multicultural lens. Those eight principles could be divided equally amongst a group for a teach-back activity).
3. Prior to start of the activity, encourage the use of handheld mobile devices to include videos of places, people, and things (Free video editing applications can be downloaded from smartphone application stores).
4. Explain the following to participants:

- Participants will have time to create a 5-minute multimedia teach-back of their assigned lesson. (90 minutes)
  - Participants should ideate and conceptualize approach for teach-back. (15 minutes)
  - The teach-back should contextualize the lesson based on examples seen in the surrounding environment (e.g., Students, staff, faculty, interacting with other people, visiting other places and sites on campus, visiting other places and sites in the community). (approximately 1 hour 10 minutes)
  - Remaining time should be used to enhance presentation (e.g., video editing, practice run-through, etc.). (approximately 5 minutes)

5. After 90 minutes, participants should be prepared to teach-back their lesson. Each group will have approximately time for their teach-back. (5 minutes per group)
6. After all teach-back presentations, engage in a debrief about the lessons and its connection to the environment. (20 minutes)

Facilitator Notes:

- When asking participants to create their teach-backs, let them know that learning, creativity, and fun should be the primary goal of their 90-minute time allotment.
- Encourage them to have fun and get to know their small group partners in this activity.
- Be prepared to offer fun and innovative ideas of what a teach-back can include (e.g., create a news story about a topic, explore an area like a tourist by site-seeing, role-playing scenarios with group members).
- If possible, preselect teams to create new group dynamics amongst individuals who may have little interaction during normal sessions.
- Participants will have high energy from this activity. During the debrief, use this time to ask questions that engage them back to the purpose of this activity about learning, teaching, interacting with each other, and having fun.

References:

Bordas, J. (2012). *Salsa, soul, and spirit: Leadership for a multi-cultural age.* San Francisco, CA: Berrett-Koehler.

CHAPTER 6

Service-Learning

Jacoby (1996) defines service-learning as "a form of experiential education in which students engage in activities that address human and community needs together with structured opportunities intentionally designed to promote student learning and development" (p. 5). This definition allows for both inclusion of curricular and cocurricular contexts. Considered a high-impact educational practice in higher education (Kuh, 2008), educators are faced with challenges in developing service-learning opportunities. One of the major challenges is the miscalculation of time and resources when designing and implementing a service-learning opportunity (Speck, 2001) Another potential challenge for educators implementing service-learning is student resistance for various reasons (Speck, 2001).

SERVICE-LEARNING IN LEADERSHIP EDUCATION

Service-learning pedagogy not only connects participants with the community (Hoover & Webster, 2004) where leadership learning through observation can occur, but also demonstrates learning outcomes in social activism and personal growth (Guthrie & Jenkins, 2018). Service-learning and leadership theories and practices have elements that align which makes service-learning a suitable instructional strategy for leadership learning opportunities (Wagner & Pigza, 2016). Wagner and Pigza (2016) outlined five intersections of service-learning and leadership. These include intentionality, role of failure, participation, prerequisites of agency, and learning across cultures (pp. 11–12). Each of these intersections also demonstrate congru-

ency and tension for service-learning in leadership learning. However, to create successful service-learning opportunities in leadership education, knowing different types of service-learning projects is essential. Guthrie and Jenkins (2018) discuss three major types of service-learning projects that can enhance leadership learning opportunities. These include group service-learning projects, individual service-learning projects, and online service-learning projects.

For examples on the major types of service-learning projects, check out "Types of Service-Learning Projects" in *The Role of Leadership Educators: Transforming Learning* (Guthrie & Jenkins, 2018, pp. 242–247).

References:

Guthrie, K. L., & Jenkins, D. M. (2018). *The role of leadership educators: Transforming learning*. Charlotte, NC: Information Age.

Hoover, T. S., & Webster, N. (2004). Modeling service learning for future leaders of youth organizations. *Journal of Leadership Education, 3*(3), 58–62.

Jacoby, B. (1996). *Service-learning in higher education: Concepts and practices*. San Francisco, CA: Jossey-Bass.

Kuh, G. D. (2008). *High-impact educational practices: What they are, who has access to them, and why they matter*. Washington, DC: Association of American College and Universities.

Speck, B. W. (2001). Why service-learning? In M. Canada & B. W. Speck (Eds.), *New directions for higher education, No. 114, Developing and implementing service-learning Programs* (pp. 3–13). San Francisco, CA: Jossey-Bass.

Wagner, W., & Pigza, J. M. (Eds.). (2016). Fostering critical reflection: Moving from a service to a social justice paradigm. In *New directions for student leadership, No. 150, Leadership development through service-learning* (pp. 11–22). San Francisco, CA: Jossey-Bass.

ARE YOU SURE WE CAN DO THIS? TACKLING CONCERNS AROUND SERVICE-LEARNING

Marianne Lorensen

Service-Learning, Curricular Instructional

This activity is designed for instructors who have made an intentional decision to incorporate service-learning into their courses and are now working to help their participants commit to that decision as well. It is common, in these situations, for participants to display some resistance and skepticism. Rather than dismissing those reactions, facilitators should help participants examine their concerns. While this activity is not a solution to the challenges of service-learning, it is intended to provide some awareness of those challenges and some guidance for discussing them.

Learning Outcomes:

Participants will have opportunities to:

- articulate challenges inherent in service-learning.
- develop strategies for addressing service-learning challenges.

Setting Up the Activity:

- Group size: 10–25 participants
- Time: 40 Minutes
- Materials: White board or flip chart paper, colorful writing utensils, index cards, personal electronic devices (such as phones, tablets, and laptops)

Instructions:

1. Invite participants, as a large group, to generate a list of the concerns they have and challenges they perceive to be part of service-learning. (Variation: If time is a consideration in this activity, the instructor can start with a prepared list and give participants the option to add to that list.) (10 minutes)

    Some of the most common concerns and challenges may include:

    - Timing (How am I going to fit this into my schedule?)
    - Schedule conflicts (I can't be there at times that are expected.)
    - Transportation (How am I going to get to the service-learning site?)
    - Flexibility (What happens if I am sick or have to study and can't make it?)

    - Comfort/competence (I've never done this before and don't know how.)
    - Personal beliefs (My culture or faith does not permit me to support or advocate for certain social issues.)
    - Physical ability (I have severe allergies that prevent me from working with food/animals.)
    - Safety (I'm not sure if it's safe for me to be at the service site or in that part of town.)
    - Responsibility (Am I going to be in charge of something or someone?)
    - Social justice (I worry that this service will do more harm than good for the people we say we are serving.)

    Feel free to add to this list any concerns or challenges that might be specific to your class, program, or institution. Record the list on a white board or flip chart paper at the front of the room.

2. Poll participants or have them "vote" to determine which challenges and concerns are most prevalent in the group. Record results on the list at the front of the room. (With a show of hands, the instructor can record results. If desired, the instructor can invite participants forward to indicate their votes with markers or stickers.) (5 minutes)

3. Once the list is generated, have participants pair off or create small groups (3–4 people). (TIP: If participants are already organized into groups for class or around service-learning sites, those groups can be used. Mixing them up may have some advantages.) Provide each group with index cards or flip chart paper and markers.

4. Assign each group one of the top five concerns expressed by the class. Allow them ten minutes to discuss the concern and identify ways to address it. (Example: If transportation is a concern, the group addressing it may start looking into options for public transit, ride sharing, carpooling, and service sites that are within walking distance.) (10 minutes)

5. Have each group share their assigned concern and corresponding strategies with the class. Encourage the class to share other strategies that might come to mind about a particular concern. (10–15 minutes)

6. Debrief, either in a group discussion or individual written reflection. (5–10 minutes)

    - Are you feeling more comfortable with the prospect of service-learning than you were when you arrived to class today? Why or why not?
    - What did you learn, or find yourself thinking about differently, as a result of the strategies discussed in this activity?
    - What questions or concerns are lingering for you?

- How do you think this service-learning experience might influence your thinking about leadership?
- What do you hope to do/learn in your service-learning experience that will contribute to your leadership development?

Facilitator Notes:

- Depending upon the particular focus of the class, the instructor should feel free to frame the processing questions and discussion in a way that incorporates that focus. For example, if the class is focused on leadership skill development, ask participants about the skills they think will be most useful in service-learning. If the class is focused on community leadership, have participants consider how the community agencies they will be serving provide leadership in a community context.
- An exploration of participant concerns is also likely to be an opportunity to discuss aspects of privilege, social responsibility, and unconscious bias. It is important that participants feel heard and respected in these conversations. It is also important that the instructor help participants distinguish between being unsafe (I have a severe peanut allergy, so I should not be serving at a food bank.) and being uncomfortable (I have never been around people who are dealing with poverty.).
- Be advised this activity may be the start of conversation around participant concerns. It will not be—and should not be—the end. The concerns will likely be revisited and reexamined throughout the course of the semester. It is an ongoing discussion.

Resources:

Einfeld, A., & Collins, D. (2008). The relationships between service-learning, social justice, multicultural competence, and civic engagement. *Journal of College Student Development, 49*(2), 95–109.

Hoover, T. S., & Webster, N. (2004). Modeling service learning for future leaders of youth organizations. *Journal of Leadership Education, 3*(3), 58–62.

Jones, S. R., & Abes, E. S. (2004). Enduring influences of service-learning on college students' identity development. *Journal of College Student Development, 45*(2), 149–166.

Morton, K. (1995). The irony of service: Charity, project, and social change in service-learning. *Michigan Journal of Community Service Learning, 2*, 19–32.

Myers-Lipton, S. J. (1998). Effect of a comprehensive service-learning program on college students' civic responsibility. *Teaching Sociology, 26*(4), 243–258.

ITERATIVE CONCEPT MAPPING IN SERVICE-LEARNING
Rian Satterwhite

Service-Learning, Cocurricular Instructional

Concept mapping blends qualitative and quantitative components as it is used to achieve "both awareness of the issues at hand and agreement on how to proceed" (Kane & Trochim, 2007, p. 2). This learning activity can assist participants in the reflective, meaning-making process that is essential in service-learning (Jacoby & Associates, 1996) and allows for increasing levels of participant autonomy and critical, creative, and practical thinking through the iterative process. This is best suited to service-learning contexts in which participants sustain a level of engagement with a community partner over time, rather than a singular experience in the community, though it can be adapted and shortened for these settings as well.

Learning Outcomes:

Participants will have opportunities to:

- identify at least three ways in which their service-learning experience intersects with different socio-economic challenges in their local communities.
- explore at least three ways in which the responses to challenges in their local communities (i.e., the services provided by the community partner in the service-learning experience) are well adapted and intelligent responses to the provider's immediate environment.
- see themselves as having their own voice and efficacy in civic issues.

Setting Up the Activity:

- Group size: Various depending on size engaging in service-learning experience
- Time: 3–5 meetings and integrated into other instructional strategies
- Materials: Paper versions: large paper (enough for multiple drafts/versions); assorted colorful writing utensils. Electronic versions: access to numerous resources for mind or concept mapping exist online.

Instructions:

1. Before class/program starts

   - Decide if you will use paper or electronic mapping methods. If electronic, research and choose your platform, create an account, and become familiar with its features and limitations.

2. First class/meeting

   • Introduce concept mapping and the intended use of this exercise. (10–20 minutes)

3. Later class/meeting (prior to the start of service-learning experience)

   • Model the mapping process by briefly producing a concept map of a chosen topic (e.g., a parallel or "adjacent" topic to the primary focus of the course/experience). (5 minutes)
   • Guide participants through their first mapping exercise, drawing primarily from the content that you have assigned. This should be a collaborative process either as a whole group or in smaller groups. (15 minutes)

4. Throughout semester or service-learning time frame

   • Depending on available time and duration of the service experience, revisit the first draft of concept maps and ask participants to revise and expand their maps (usually at least twice) as they gain new experiences and knowledge to integrate into earlier iterations. You may wish to include a short and consistent set of reflective prompts for individuals or groups to complete after each iteration, which can effectively prepare participants for the culminated debrief after the final version is constructed. (20 minutes each iteration)

5. Final class/meeting

   • Debrief the concept mapping process as appropriate. (30 minutes)
     ○ Were you surprised by how your map grew over time? What does this tell you about the complexity of addressing socioeconomic challenges in our communities?
     ○ How does this service-learning experience inform your understanding of our course content? Your understanding of the focus area of your community partner (e.g., housing insecurity, food insecurity, sustainability, educational access and attainment, etc.)?
     ○ What did you learn or experience that gave you hope, in spite of the complexity of the problem(s)?
     ○ What wisdom did you encounter in your service-learning experience? How does this inform how you think about the concept of "expertise" and its role in policy making?

Facilitator Notes:

• As stated earlier, this strategy is useful when there is a high degree of scaffolding provided at the beginning. After time, the scaffolding and direct guidance from the facilitator is gradually removed, as participants are encouraged to take greater responsibility for their creative, critical, and practical thinking on the subject.

References:

Jacoby, B., & Associates. (1996). *Service-learning in higher ed: Concepts and practices.* San Francisco, CA: Jossey-Bass.

Kane, M., & Trochim, W. (2007). *Applied social research methods series: Vol. 50. Concept mapping for planning and evaluation* (L. Bickman & D. J. Rog, Eds.). Thousand Oaks, CA: SAGE.

Resources:

Fink, L. D. (2013). *Creating significant learning experiences: An integrated approach to designing college courses.* San Francisco, CA: Jossey-Bass.

Hmelo-Silver, C., Duncan, R., & Chinn, C. (2007). Scaffolding and achievement in problem-based and inquiry learning: A response to Kirschner, Sweller, and Clark (2006). *Educational Psychologist, 42*(2), 99–107.

Lucidchart. (2018, May 31). *How to make a concept map.* Retrieved from https://www.youtube.com/watch?v=8XGQGhli0I0

Novak, J. D. (2010). Learning, creating, and using knowledge: Concept maps as facilitative tools in schools and corporations. *Journal of e-Learning and Knowledge Society, 6*(3), 21–30.

REFLECTING 1 SECOND EACH DAY
Kathy L. Guthrie

Service-Learning, Technology Enhanced

In this activity, participants identify one word that represents their learning each day they are engaged with a service-learning project. After writing this word on a small, portable white board, they will video tape it and upload it to a video diary app. At the end of their service-learning project they are able to watch the evaluation of their reflections in a short video format.

Learning Outcomes:

Participants will have opportunities to:

- reflect on how service-learning project connects to leadership learning.
- identify one word that represents their learning each time they engage in a service-learning project.
- demonstrate learning through developing a short video.

Setting Up the Activity:

- Group size: Any size group (this is done individually)
- Time: At least 6 minutes a day
- Materials: Small white board, dry erase marker, personal device capable of video (phone, tablet, computer), video diary app (optional)

Instructions:

1. Before the service-learning project begins, discuss the importance of critical reflection (Owen, 2016). Introduce activity. (5 minutes)
2. Participants will dedicate time each day they are engaged in their service project to personally reflect on their learning that day. They are encour-

aged to reflect in a preferred method, such as journaling, discussing with a friend, or just thinking. During this reflection, they need to choose one word that describes their learning and/or experience of that day engaging in service. (at least 5 minutes/day)
3. Next, participants need to write their chosen word for the day on their small white board. (1 minute/day)
4. Using a video diary app or software, participants are to record themselves holding the white board with their word printed on it and saying the word. (30 second/day).
5. Depending on context of the service-learning project, participants can share their video with the facilitator, service site volunteer coordinator, or advisor.
6. If for a curricular based course, participants may be required to make a presentation to their class on their video, including any themes in the words they chose or how their words evolved over the semester.

Facilitator Notes:

- Reflection is critical to leadership learning (White & Guthrie, 2016), especially when service-learning is the primarily pedagogy being utilized. Setting up the importance of making meaning of experiences is essential for participants to make time to critically reflect and choose their one word each day.
- This activity was adapted from Kryder (2018).

References:

Kryder, K (2018). *Five creative reflective tools to enhance critical thinking.* Orlando, FL: Leadership Educators Institute.
Owens, J. E. (2016). Fostering critical reflection: Moving from a service to a social justice paradigm. In W. Wagner & J. M. Pigza (Eds.), *New directions for student leadership: No. 150. Leadership development through service-learning* (pp. 37–48). San Francisco, CA: Jossey-Bass.
White, J. V., & Guthrie, K. L. (2016). Creating a meaningful learning environment: Reflection in leadership education. *Journal of Leadership Education, 15*(1), 60–75.

APPRECIATIVE SERVICE-LEARNING
Tamara Bauer and Kerry L. Priest

Service-Learning, Followership Focused

We apply a modified appreciative inquiry process as a model of service-learning in an undergraduate leadership course (Cooperrider, Whitney, & Stravos, 2008; Priest, Kaufman, Brunton & Seibel, 2013). Appreciative inquiry provides an asset-based approach to learning socially responsible leadership (Komives, Wagner, & Associates, 2016), by creating the conditions to exercise leadership with our community to make progress on an urgent challenge—in our case, local food security.

Learning Outcomes:

Participants will have opportunities to:

- diagnose an issue through asset mapping, research, and storytelling.
- develop goals and strategies for positive change.
- critically reflect on socially responsible leadership.

Setting Up the Activity:

- Group size: Any size group
- Time: 7 weeks (including in- and out-of-class activities)
- Materials: Collaboration with community partner for service-learning experience; developed timeline and strategy for overlay of appreciative inquiry model to time period; out-of-class worksheets, in-class facilitation guides, reflection prompts, and final evaluation assignment.

Instructions:

The *Community Leadership Experience* is a 7-week service-learning experience within a 16-week introduction to leadership course. We highlight learning activities at each stage of our modified appreciative inquiry process applied to the leadership challenge of food in/security. (In our case, Week 1 of the project is Week 7 of the course. Participants work in small groups of 10–12, called learning communities, led by an undergraduate teaching assistant.)

1. Discover (Weeks 1–2): Orientation to the service-learning purpose and process. Discover and appreciate personal, organizational, and societal stories/experiences related to the social issue of food security and hunger through watching a documentary, touring local food pantry (community partner), researching the issue, and group asset mapping.
2. Dream and Design (Weeks 2–3): Cocreate a desired future/vision, and develop action steps and organizational structure to bring dream to life. Emphasis on addressing root causes and collaboration.
3. Deliver (Weeks 4–5): Implementation of action steps, including a communitywide food collection. Emphasis on team project management and team performance.
4. Debrief (Weeks 5–6): This addition to the appreciative inquiry process integrates experiential learning. Participants critically reflect on their experience and make meaning of socially responsible leadership through structured writing prompts and small group discussion.
5. Define (Week 7): In this final stage, participants consider how to apply learning into their different spheres of influence to impact change. Learning is evaluated through a final group presentation titled "Synthesis of Learning."

Facilitator Notes:

- At each stage, we use a set of guiding questions to orient our work, followed by a variety of reflection methods (e.g., writing, discussion) to debrief and make meaning of each step. Some example questions are listed below:

  - Discover—*What do we know? What do we need to know?*
    * What does food insecurity (versus hunger) mean? What are statistics of this issue in the United States, in your hometown, in our community?
    * What are possible causes of food insecurity/hunger? What root causes or systems are connected to this issue?
    * How does food insecurity/hunger affect individuals and our society?
    * How might food insecurity affect you? (Think about this in relationship to your major, your future career, your family, your work, your community, etc.) What implications does food insecurity have for you at the individual, group, or global levels?

  - Dream and Design—*What works? What could be? What should be? What can we do?*
    * Based on what we know is currently being done, what types of programs exist to address issues of food insecurity and what other ideas do you have to help make progress on this issue?

* What are our own strengths, interests and spheres of influence that we could leverage to help make progress?
* What personal, group and societal goals do you have for this experience?
* What will be required of you, as a learner, to engage in service-learning?

o Deliver—*What will be?*
* Participants complete two "Reflection on Action" worksheets after engaging in direct service. These worksheets follow the DEAL model (describe, evaluate, and articulate learning), connecting experience to learning objectives (Ash & Clayton, 2009).

o Debrief—*What happened? What did I learn? How did I learn it?*
* What did we learn about exercising leadership from the Community Leadership Experience? (Highlighting connections to/application of Socially Responsible Leadership)
* How did you learn it? Identifying specific/significant actions by individuals or team, connected to learning and specific course concepts.

o Define—*Why does it matter? What's next?*
* As socially responsible leaders, why does it (the learning) matter? Share how the learning has value as part of your leader development journey.
* What will I do as a result of this experience? Address how this experience has changed your way of thinking, feeling and/or behaving.

References:

Ash, S. L., & Clayton. P. H. (2009). Generating, deepening, and documenting learning: The power of critical reflection in applied learning. *Journal of Applied Learning in Higher Education, 1*, 25–48.

Cooperrrider, D. L., Whitney, D., & Stavros, J.M. (2008). *Appreciative inquiry handbook: For leaders of change* (2nd ed.). San Francisco, CA: Berrett-Koehler.

Komives, S. R., Wagner, W., & Associates. (2016). *Leadership for a better world: Understanding the social change model of leadership development* (2nd ed.). San Francisco, CA: Jossey-Bass.

Priest, K. L., Kaufman, E. K., Brunton, K., & Seibel, M. (2013). Appreciative inquiry: A Tool for organizational, programmatic, and project-focused change. *Journal of Leadership Education, 12*(1), 18–31.

THE SERVICE AND LEADERSHIP INTEGRATION
Eric Buschlen

Service-Learning, Curricular Learning Assessment

The purpose of this activity is to outline a process where participants participate in their community through service learning. While the act of service is the participant focal point, that act is not the focus for the participant's assessment. Instead, participants are graded on their reflective narrative—a commonly used measure in leadership education. Additionally, participants have the option for extra points if the participant can find three other participants to serve the site at the same time.

Learning Outcomes:

Participants will have opportunities to:

* assess his/her own servant leadership skills and potential through a process of site evaluation, self-evaluation, and reflection.
* identify and analyze the importance and complexity of leading others to complete a service learning act.
* evaluate the needs of a local nonprofit agency through service learning.

Setting Up the Activity:

* Group size: 1+ participants depending on how many participants service site can accommodate
* Time: 6 hours (5 hours of completed service and 1 hour of needed to set up with site)
* Materials: Service Critique Form for verification

Instructions:

"Service as a Leader" Reflection Paper

1. Embed this assignment/activity into a course syllabus or leadership development program. (several weeks before semester or program)
2. Outline the requirements to participants. (10–15 minutes)

   * Based on a visit to the university's community engagement center, participants will need find a nonprofit organization related to their academic program of choice and offer five hours of time to that agency.
   * It is required to take the Service Critique Form to the site, get it filled out by a site supervisor, and

staple that form to a two-page (can be longer) reflection paper.

- In the reflection paper, reflect on experiences through the eyes of an academic servant leader: what learning occurred in this real-world setting that could not have been learned in a classroom, what did the participant experience, will the participant serve there again, how will this experience impact a participant's career, how challenging was it to find three friends to serve with the participant, what leadership lessons were learned in this project?

3. Make sure participants follow university policies related to service or service learning (early in semester, invite member from appropriate university volunteer center to address participants and discuss policies related to off-campus service, sites, etc.).

4. Facilitate a group-based debriefing discussion. (10–15 minutes)

- Reflecting on the act of service you provided, did this process make you want to serve more? Why is that? In other words, what did you learn about yourself through this process?
- How many of you took others with you to also serve? Explain how you made the "ask"—how did you frame it? Was it easy to find peers to help? Did you view asking peers to serve with you was also as an act of leadership? For those of you who did not find peers to serve with you, what happened?
- What are 2–3 key leadership lessons that you learned from this service assignment?

Table Leadership Service Critique Form

Student Name: _____ Agency: _____

Number of peers serving with the student above: _____

Number of hours served per student: _____

Please answer the following on scale of 1 to 5 (1 = *strongly agree*, 5 = *strongly disagree*)

1. I feel the student(s) worked hard on the project that was assigned.   _____

2. I feel this experience assisted the student(s) leadership learning.   _____

3. I feel the student(s) should have put in more time toward the project.   _____

4. The student(s) showed up on time.   _____

5. The student(s) led his/her peers.   _____

6. I feel the student(s) did everything possible to complete the project.   _____

7. It appears as if the student(s) took this seriously.   _____

8. I would love the opportunity to work with this student(s) again.   _____

9. The student(s) served the entire five hours.   _____

10. I feel this process was a benefit to the community.   _____

Written Comments:

Site Signature _____ Title _____

Date _____

ROOT CAUSES, CONNECTIONS, AND SYSTEMS
Julie LeBlanc

Service-Learning, Cocurricular Learning Assessment

This activity, which ideally occurs after participants have taken part in a service-learning experience, requires participants to critically analyze the interconnected nature of community needs. Participants will brainstorm community needs' root causes and connections in order to understand the broader systems addressed by their partnering community organization(s). It can be used in curricular or cocurricular environments and works most effectively when participant participants represent a diverse array of identities, perspectives, and academic disciplines (Dugan & Komives, 2010).

Learning Outcomes:

Participants will have opportunities to:

- identify topics and concepts related to the primary social issue addressed by their partnering community organization(s) (foundational knowledge).
- analyze root causes of a social issue in the context of a particular community and environment (integration).
- see themselves as change agents, connecting their academic discipline with an actual community need (human dimension).

Setting Up the Activity:

- Group size: The activity is most appropriate for groups ranging in size from 5 to 25 people
- Time: 35–45 minutes
- Materials: 8.5 x 11 sheets of paper for each participant, flip chart paper, colorful writing utensils

Instructions:

1. The facilitator should introduce the learning assessment as a means for participants to reflect upon the array of social issues they witnessed, experienced, or came to understand during their service-learning experience. (5 minutes)
2. Divide the group into pairs. The facilitator is encouraged to determine the pairs so that participants meet new people within the group and learn from diverse perspectives.
3. The facilitator will have participants write the primary social issue in a circle in the middle of their paper. Then, they should give the pairs five minutes to brainstorm the social issues connected to the primary social issue, which they will write in connecting circles to form a "social issue web." The facilitator will emphasize that participants should think about their academic discipline when constructing their social issue web. For example, if the service-learning experience was focused on homelessness, groups might brainstorm topics such as *mental health, education, access to housing, food insecurity, access to healthcare, criminalization of those living in homelessness*, et cetera. (5 minutes)
4. Next, the facilitator will reassign participants with a new partner. They will have 5 minutes to add six to eight sublevel topics to their webs. For example, from *criminalization of those living in homelessness*, pairs might mention *city ordinances, the role of race, local political climates*, et cetera. The facilitator should encourage participants to think about root causes and cause/effects when adding sublevels to their webs. (5 minutes)
5. The facilitator should reassemble the entire group and collectively create a social issue web representing the perspectives of all participants. As the facilitator draws the social issue web on the chart paper, participants can shout out answers. During the group creation of the social issue web, participants are able to learn from each other and fill in gaps, explain their perspectives, and pose questions. (10 minutes)
6. The facilitator will then lead a debrief about the creation of the social issue web as it relates to the service-learning experience. (10 minutes)

   - What strikes you about the social issue web we have collectively created?
   - What narrative seems to be most dominant in our web?
   - What narrative seems to be lacking or ill defined?
   - When did you see leadership being enacted in your community organization?
   - What themes of leadership are evident in our web?
   - How did this activity solidify, alter, or challenge your understanding of our primary social issue?
   - How does this activity solidify, alter, or challenge your understanding of leadership?
   - What area of the social issue web compels you to learn more?

Facilitator Notes:

- Facilitators can lead the activity as a "preflection" brainstorming session. This would allow the facilitator to get a baseline understanding of participants' knowledge about social issues.

- This activity could also be completed twice during the service-learning experience—once prior to the service experience and once at the conclusion of the program. This would allow the facilitator and participants to see their increased knowledge throughout the program. It could also provide space to debunk stereotypes that existed among participants and how the service-learning experience transformed their perspectives. For example, participants may enter a service-learning experience with the preconceived notion that all people living in homelessness are addicted to drugs or alcohol. After completing the service experience, the participant would have a more sophisticated understanding of the systems that impact people in poverty. Therefore, the second social issue web may include items such as access to treatment, funding for rehabilitation programs, role

of family and support networks, and mental health implications. Completing two social issue webs allows participants to dig deeper to analyze the root causes and connected systems related to social issues.

- The activity could also be adapted if the group is working with multiple social issues or different community organizations. In step 2, the facilitator would assign pairs within the same service teams. In step 3, participants would develop a separate web for each social issue. This adaptation would foster participants' learning about their peers' service-learning experiences and the community needs they addressed.

Reference:

Dugan, J. P., & Komives, S. R. (2010). Influences on college students' capacities for socially responsible leadership. *Journal of College Student Development*, *51*(5), 525–549.

CHAPTER 7

Self- and Peer-Assessments

Self-assessment refers to the involvement of learners in making judgments about their own learning, particularly about their achievements and the outcomes of learning (Boud & Falchikov, 1989). Research suggests using self-assessment as an instructional strategy to promote skill building, responsibility for one's own learning, and problem-solving capacities (Sluijsmans, Dochy, & Moerkerke, 1999). In higher education we most frequently see this practice in association with structured self-assessments or instruments, more commonly referred to as personality tests, questionnaires, and inventories. Thousands of them are available online, appearing on Buzzfeed, Facebook, and other popular websites, such as HumanMetrics and Queendom. Comparatively, peer-assessments are appraisal activities where students evaluate their peers and make observations of one another along established metrics (Bright et al., 2016). Benefits of this instructional strategy include empowering students to take partial ownership in the educative process and enhancing engagement, fostering accountability among students, and developing comparative representative evaluations of the performance of other learners or group members (Bryant & Carless, 2010; Cestone, Levine, & Lane, 2008; Malone, 2011; Topping 2009).

SELF- AND PEER-ASSESSMENTS IN LEADERSHIP EDUCATION

Much of what we aim to accomplish as leadership educators is the development of students' skills, behaviors, and dispositions related to some aspect of leadership or followership (Guthrie & Jenkins, 2018). Accordingly, the intentional use of assessment instruments provides participants opportunities for enhanced self-awareness and improved insight about their own leadership performance (Kılıç, 2016; Saito & Fujita, 2004). Moreover, when leadership educators empower students to use these learning tools, they are also providing opportunities for students to develop skills for providing feedback to others—a crucial leadership skill (Cameron & Caza, 2005; DeRue & Wellman, 2009; Goleman,

Boyatzis & McKee, 2013; Kouzes & Posner, 2017). Popular assessment instruments used in leadership education include the Leadership Practices Inventory (Posner, 2004), StrengthsFinder (Asplund, Lopez, Hodges, & Harter, 2007; Rath, 2007), and the Emotionally Intelligent Leadership Inventory (Shankman, Allen, & Miguel, 2015). Some popular leadership theory textbooks also include self-assessments to reinforce content (e.g., Followership Questionnaire) such as *Leadership: Theory and Practice* (Northouse, 2019), which includes an assessment instrument at the end of each chapter.

For a list and annotated bibliography of "Widely Used Self-Assessment instruments in Leadership Education", see *The Role of Leadership Educators: Transforming Learning* (Guthrie & Jenkins, 2018, p. 255–258).

References:

Asplund, J., Lopez, S. J., Hodges, T., & Harter, J. (2007, February). *The Clifton StrengthsFinder 2.0 technical report: Development and validation*. Retrieved from https://strengths.gallup.com/private/Resources/CSFTechnicalReport031005.pdf

Boud, D., & Falchikov, N. (1989). Quantitative studies of self-assessment in higher education: A critical analysis of findings. *Higher Education, 18*, 529–549.

Bright, D. S., Caza, A., Turesky, E. F., Putzel, R., Nelson, E., & Lutchfield, R. (2016). Constructivist meta-practices: When students design activities, lead others, and assess peers. *Journal of Leadership Education, 15*(4), 75–99.

Bryant, D. A., & Carless, D. R. (2010). Peer assessment in a test-dominated setting: Empowering, boring or facilitating examination preparation? *Educational Research for Policy and Practice, 9*(1), 3–15.

Cameron, K. S., & Caza, A. (2005). Developing strategies and skills for responsible leadership. In J. P. Doh & S. A. Stumpf (Eds.), Handbook *on responsible leadership and governance in global business* (pp. 87–111). Northampton, MA: Edward Elgar.

Cestone, C. M., Levine, R. E., & Lane, D. R. (2008). Peer assessment and evaluation in team-based learning. In L. Michaelsen, M. Sweet, & D. X. Parmelee (Eds.), *New directions for teaching and learning, No. 116: Team-based learning: Small group learning's next big step* (pp. 69–78). San Francisco, CA: Jossey-Bass.

DeRue, D. S., & Wellman, N. (2009). Developing leaders via experience: The role of developmental challenge, learning orientation, and feedback availability. *Journal of Applied Psychology, 94*(4), 859–875.

Goleman, D., Boyatzis, R. E., & McKee, A. (2013). *Primal leadership: Learning to lead with emotional intelligence.* Boston, MA: Harvard Business School Press.

Guthrie, K. L., & Jenkins, D. M. (2018). *The role of leadership educators: Transforming learning.* Charlotte, NC: Information Age.

Kılıç, D. (2016). An examination of using self-, peer-, and teacher-assessment in higher education: A case study in teacher education. *Higher Education Studies, 6*(1), 136–144.

Kouzes, J. M., & Posner, B. Z. (2017). *The leadership challenge: How to make extraordinary things happen in organizations* (6th ed.). Hoboken, NJ: John Wiley & Sons.

Malone, D. (2011). Empirical evidence of the fairness and quality of peer evaluation. *Academy of Educational Leadership Journal, 15*(2), 129–140.

Northouse, P. (2019). *Leadership: Theory and practice* (8th ed.). Thousand Oaks, CA: SAGE.

Posner, B. Z. (2004). A leadership development instrument for students: Updated. *Journal of College Student Development, 45,* 443–456.

Rath, T. (2007). *Strengthsfinder 2.0.* New York, NY: Gallup Press.

Saito, H., & Fujita, T. (2004). Characteristics and user acceptance of peer rating in EFL writing classrooms. *Language Teaching Research, 8,* 31–54.

Shankman, M. L., Allen, S. J., & Miguel, R. (2015). *Emotionally intelligent leadership for students. Inventory* (2nd ed.). San Francisco, CA: Jossey-Bass.

Sluijsmans, D., Dochy, F., & Moerkerke, G. (1999). Creating a learning environment by using self-, peer- and co-assessment. *Learning Environments Research, 1,* 293–319.

Topping, K. J. (2009). Peer assessment. *Theory into Practice, 48,* 20–27.

STRENGTHS-SPOTTING
Rachel Pridgen and Abigaile VanHorn

Self- and Peer-Assessments, Curricular Instructional

The Clifton Strengths for Students assessment (Gallup, 2017) is an effective tool for identifying individual talents and understanding how one might develop those talents into strengths. This learning activity provides a meaningful initial involvement in strengths-based development. It will help participants identify and understand their unique strengths, so they can begin to effectively apply their strengths in their daily lives.

Learning Outcomes:

Participants will have opportunities to:

- identify and describe their top five strengths.
- explain how their top five strengths manifest in their daily lives.
- discuss their strengths with others.

Setting Up the Activity:

- Group size: 2–40 participants
- Materials: Signature Themes Report, highlighter, writing utensil
- Time: 40 minutes

Instructions:

1. Strengths-Spotting: In-class Conversations

   Think, Pair, Share

   - **Think:** During the first meeting, ask participants to:

     o Read through your Signature Themes Report
     o Highlight things that resonate with you
     o Cross out points with which you disagree
     o After reading the theme description, is there anything you would add or subtract?

   - **Pair:** Each participant will find a classmate whom they do not know well. Each participant will take a turn sharing their strengths and their initial reaction to the report. *What did they agree/disagree with? What are some specific examples participants have seen their strengths?*
   - **Share:** As a group, discuss strengths and how they resonate for participants. *This is a great way*

for participants to become familiar with many of the other Gallup talent themes.

2. Strengths-Spotting: Out of Class Conversations

    - At the end of the in-class activity, participants will identify three individuals. One who is a relative, one who is a nonrelative, but someone known for a significant amount of time (2–5 years), and a classroom peer.
      - Questions to ask each "Strengths-Spotter— Out of Class Conversations"
        * Where and when have you seen me at my best using these talents?
        * I highlighted these areas that most resonate with me. Where have you observed these talents?
        * I crossed out these statements as they do not resonate with me or I disagree with them. Do you agree/disagree with my assessment? Why/Why not?

    Following Think, Pair, Share:

    - * What did you think about the descriptions of your top five talent themes? What did you agree/disagree with?
      * What components would you add/subtract to your Talent?
      * Who has the same talent as someone else in the class (e.g., achiever, maximizer, WOO); how does your Clifton Strengths for Students explanation compare for that Talent to each other?
      * Knowing that they are different, how does that manifest for you personally and comparatively?

3. Following "Strengths-Spotting—Out of Classroom Conversations" Assignment:

    - How did your conversations go? How did the conversations change based on how long the person has known you?
    - What surprised you of the conversation? Did anything disappoint you?

Facilitator Notes:

- This learning activity is highly adaptable to various teaching environments or coaching scenarios. Depending upon time and schedule, facilitators may choose to pare down the activity to focus on the participants' top one or two strengths. Facilitators may choose to alter the order in which participants seek feedback from others and share insights.

The Think portion of the in-class activity is based upon question prompts at the end of each theme insight description in *Clifton Strengths for Student Insight and Action-Planning Guide.*

References:

Clifton Strengths for Students Insight and Action-Planning Guide. Retrieved from https://students.usask.ca/documents/secc/Strengths%20Insight%20and%20Action%20Planning%20Report.pdf

Gallup. (2017). *Clifton Strengths for students: Your strengths journey begins here.* New York, NY: Gallup Press.

LEADERSHIP YOU ADMIRE
Jennifer Batchelder

Self- and Peer-Assessments, Cocurricular Instructional

This learning activity asks participants to reflect on personal contacts (mentor, friend, faculty/staff, family, etc.) to describe how others demonstrate leadership. Participants are then asked to shift perspective and reflect on how those leadership abilities apply to themselves through self-assessment. This activity is a modified version of a staff training facilitated by Michael Davila.

Learning Outcomes:

Participants will have opportunities to:

- recognize their accomplishments in their leadership journey.
- identify areas of personal growth and development.

Setting Up the Activity:

- Group size: 2–26 participants
- Time: 15–20 minutes
- Materials: Paper, writing utensil

Instructions:

1. Ask participants to reflect on the people they admire. This can include mentors, friends, faculty/staff, family members, and others. In particular, encourage them think about those who they feel demonstrate leadership. (1 minute)
2. Have participants write the header "Leadership I Admire in Others." Underneath header, instruct them to make a list of about 10 things they admire in others' leadership. These may include skills,

behaviors, abilities, accomplishments, and other characteristics. (5 minutes)

3. Next, invite participants to take one more view of their lists. Ask them to cross out the word "Others" in the title of their header and write above this the word "Myself" to give the list a new perspective on "Leadership I admire in Myself." Give them a moment to silently reflect on the list. (1 minute)

4. Bring the group back and discuss aspirations and accomplishments from their lists. As the participants review their lists, they may see reflections of themselves. Participants may identify things they have not accomplished yet, and they may see things they do not believe align with their own ideas of leadership. Give them some time to reflect and assess their own leadership development for each of the items on the list. (5 minutes)

5. Facilitate a group discussion using following debriefing questions. (5–10 minutes)

- How did you feel when we replaced "Others" with "My?"
- Was the list reflective of leadership within yourself?
- Did the list create any aspirations of your own leadership development?
- Can you identify any additional aspirations to add to this list?
- In what ways will you work toward achieving the items on your list?
- Do you see the role of follower show up in your list on leadership?
- What do followers contribute to accomplishing the items on your list?

Facilitator Notes:

- To help facilitate the discussion, be sure you are being conscious of the participants' responses to the instructions. Take note of how participants respond to the shift of admiring others to a list of admiring themselves. Some will be inspired and may respond with "aha" moments, while others will be challenged to see themselves in the list. During the second reflection, pay attention to participants who are challenged as they may need extra support in identifying different ways they can work toward developing those areas of leadership.
- One perspective of this activity is how participants may focus on traits-based leadership rather than the process of leadership. To challenge these notations, review Chapter 2 of Northouse (2019) and Burns (1978) definition of leadership, which incorporates leadership as relational between leaders and followers. With this in mind, you can also consider the importance of the role of follower. These concepts

will help you to understand the difference between traits and the relational process and incorporate the role of followers as you facilitate this activity. Further, with your participants, you could also choose one of the many definitions of leadership (or perhaps one your organization uses) and have participants relate the items on their list to the components of the definition. To further the discussion, include questions about the relational process to accomplish the items on the list. A great model to support this conversation would be the relational leadership model by Komives, Lucas, and McMahon (2013).

References:

Burns, J. M. (1978). *Leadership*. New York, NY: Harper & Row.

Komives, S. R., Lucas, N., & McMahon, T. R. (2013). *Exploring leadership: For college students who want to make a difference* (3rd ed.). San Francisco, CA: Jossey-Bass.

Northouse, P. G. (2019). *Leadership: Theory and practice* (8th ed.). Thousand Oaks, CA: SAGE.

VIRTUAL VALUES SORT
Vivechkanand S. Chunoo

Self- and Peer-Assessments, Technology Enhanced

The virtual values sort is an online learning activity where participants self-evaluate the relative importance of 30 predefined values into six categories of importance. This forced sorting process requires participants to carefully consider what is important to them. Discussions following the virtual values sort help participants make meaning of their results, articulate that meaning making to others, and consider how values shape their leader identities and leadership development.

Learning Outcomes:

Participants will have opportunities to:

- clarify their personal values.
- reflect on how personal values influence their leader identity.
- articulate the impact of personal values on their leadership practice.

Setting Up the Activity:

- Group size: 20–30 participants
- Time: 45 minutes

- Materials: Print outs participants might want to aid discussion, technology (if participants request it), chairs

Instructions:

The virtual values sort activity is a modification of the traditional values card sort activity. One of the major benefits of performing this exercise online is it can be done in a shared learning space synchronously, or independently by participants asynchronously. The primary method for this activity is a values sort; "a collection of 30 Value Cards that are sorted into six different columns ranging from Least Important to Most Important" (Project Zero Tools, n.d.). For the virtual values sort, the website (http://thegoodproject.org/toolkits-curricula/the-goodwork-toolkit/value-sort-activity/) maintained by The Good Project and sponsored by the Harvard Graduate School of Education (Harvard Project Zero, 2017) is a good resource.

1. Introduce the values card sort as an activity of values clarification which may help participants understand who they are as people, as leaders, and why they approach leadership in a particular way. (approximately 5 minutes when done synchronously; can also be delivered via learning management software)
2. Provide participants with a link to the virtual value sort (http://thegoodproject.org/toolkits-curricula/the-goodwork-toolkit/value-sort-activity/) and allow them to complete the activity. Instructions are found on the website, but they can also be reviewed together if appropriate. Remind participants to hit the "submit" button when finished. (10 minutes)
3. Once participants have completed the activity, divide them evenly into groups of 3–5 people. Have them discuss some of the following questions: (15 minutes)

   - What four cards were in your "Most Important" pile?
   - Was it difficult to come up just four "Most Important" values? If so, why?
   - Did any of your "Most Important" values surprise you? If so, which ones?
   - If those four values were everything a stranger knew about you, what kind of person would they think you are? Does that match the kind of person you think you are?
   - If those four values were everything a follower knew about you, what kind of leader would

they think you are? Does that match the kind of leader you think you are? (Note: this step can also be completed in discussion board groups if being conducted in a primarily online learning environment)

4. Once participants have completed their small group discussions, reorganize everyone into a large discussion group. You may choose to ask a few volunteers to describe their small group conversation. The facilitator may also ask of the larger group: (15 minutes)

   - How do you think your four "Most Important" values uncovered by the virtual values sort show up in your leadership? How might they influence what you do, what you say, and how you say it in leadership contexts?
   - Chances are you had different "Most Important" values than the other people in your group and the larger group overall. How might understanding the values of those around you change your approach to cooperation, collaboration, and leading across different values?
   - Based on this activity and the conversations we had today, is there anything you would like to do differently to more closely align your values with your approach to leading? What might those things be and how would you change them?

Facilitator Notes:

- Facilitators should be prepared to manage the emotionality of participants when thinking about and talking about their values orientations. These kinds of conversations can bring up a wide range of emotional responses in participants, sometimes in unpredictable ways. Some participants may need additional support as they manage the relationship between their values and their personal histories. Be mindful of participants who may attempt to derail the conversation toward personal traumas and/or challenging circumstances, and respectfully redirect toward the learning objectives. Reach out, or refer as appropriate, to participants who may be dealing with significant hardships which arise through discussion.

References:

Harvard Project Zero. (2017). *About us, The Good Project*. Retrieved from http://thegoodproject.org/about-us/

Project Zero Tools. (n. d.). *PZ tools*. Retrieved from http://www.pztools.org/valuesort/

HUMILITY EXERCISE:
SELF- AND PEER-ASSESSMENT
Matthew Sowcik and Austin Council

Self- and Peer-Assessments, Followership Focused

According to Tangney (2000) there are a variety of outcomes that occur when an individual possesses humility, some of which include (a) an accurate assessment of one's capabilities and accomplishments; (b) the ability for one to recognize one's mistakes; and (c) an openness toward different perspectives. Despite early definitions characterizing humility as a weakness or deficiency, many scholars have recently suggested that humility is accuracy (Tangney, 2000) and even more an ability for one to have a proper perspective of themselves, their relationship with others and their relationship with the larger environment. This learning activity addresses humility through the use of self and peer assessments in the context of a partner activity challenge.

Learning Outcomes:

Participants will have opportunities to:

* exercise a willingness to admit mistakes.
* develop a proper perspective of their relationship with others, including a willingness to consider feedback and openness to different perspectives.

Setting Up the Activity:

* Group size: 2–200 participants
* Time: 35 minutes
* Materials: Each participant will need one self-assessment handout, one peer-assessment handout, and each pair will need one maze handout.

Instructions:

1. Prior to activity, print out copies for participants. Each participant will need one self-assessment handout, one peer-assessment handout, and each pair will need one maze handout.
2. To begin activity, ask each participant to complete the self-assessment handout. (5 minutes)
3. Ask participants to get into pairs (if there is an odd number have one group of three). Once in pairs, ask participants to self-select which member will be Team Member "A" and who will be Team Member "B" (this will help giving the rest of the directions).
4. Ask Team Member "A" to place the maze handout in front of them, take out a pen/pencil and close their eyes.
5. "Team Member "A" will need to get through the maze and Team Member "B" will need to help them through the maze being their eyes. Team Member "B" can communicate however they would like to Team Member "A" but cannot touch Team Member "A," the pen/pencil, or the paper. The only way they can provide guidance is through communicating with the other team member.
6. Teams should engage in the maze activity. (10 minutes)
7. After maze activity is completed, ask both team members to fill out the peer-assessment handout. Remind participants to be as honest in providing feedback. (5 minutes)
8. Ask both participants in the pair to share their ratings of the other person. (5 minutes)
9. Debriefing has three areas: (10 minutes)

* Self and peer-assessments: Understanding strengths and weaknesses

   o Was there a difference between your initial self-assessment ratings and the ratings that your teammate rated you after the exercise? Is there any value in the feedback you received from your teammate? Why did this difference exist? What can you take away from this feedback that will change your perspective moving forward?
   o How did your strengths help you to be successful on this exercise? Do you think your areas of needed development (weaknesses) got in the way of you being successful? What is one area that you could improve on that would lead you to be more successful on a similar task in the future?

* Perspective

   o How important is it to see the task through the other person's perspective?
   o Did the Team Member "B" get out of their seat or move to see and communicate from the perspective of Team Member "A"? How did (or would have) this help or hurt the process of leading the other person through the maze?
   o Who was the leader in this exercise? Why did you suggest this person was the leader? What does it say about our preconceived notions of leadership? Can you make an argument that the other person was, in fact, the leader?
   o How important was the other person in successfully completing the maze? How import-

ant was it to know the strengths of the other person?

- Taking feedback and learning from mistakes

  o How was feedback given and received during the maze exercise? What mistakes did you make during the exercise that can help you do the exercise more effectively next time? What happened after those mistakes for you to keep going and learn from them? How can this apply to other leadership situations?
  o How difficult was it to give the other person honest feedback after the maze exercise? What does the other person have to gain from getting the honest feedback? How could your feedback about their strengths and opportunity areas help them be more successful on this task the next time?
  o Based on your experiences from the exercise, how is giving and receiving feedback import-

ant in the leadership process? What benefits would occur in the leadership process if the leader admitted mistakes to her or his followers?

Facilitator Notes:

- It takes time to reflect on this experience. After the debriefing, the facilitator may want to include some of the questions above in a reflective homework assignment.
- If there is an uneven number (a group of three), have only one person with their eyes closed working through the maze and the other two participants providing direction. The larger group size can be included in the debriefing.

Reference:
Tangney, J. P. (2000). Humility: Theoretical perspectives, empirical findings and directions for future research. *Journal of Social and Clinical Psychology, 19*(1), 70–82.

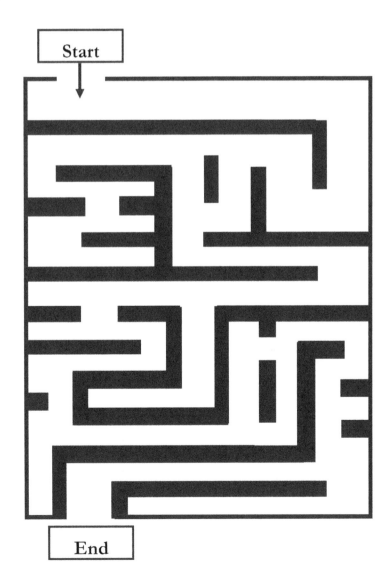

Self-Assessment Handout

The following is a list of 10 important leadership competencies. Please rate yourself on each of the competencies by putting an "X" in the box that corresponds with your rating. Then in the final column, force rank each competency according to how well you demonstrate that competency in your leadership. For example, the competency you demonstrate most effectively (or most often) give that competency a 10, for the competency you have the second greatest skill demonstrating give that a 9, continuing until you get to the competency that you have the very least amount of skill demonstrating (give that a 1).

Competency	A Below Average Demonstration of This Competency	An Average Demonstration of This Competency	An Above Average Demonstration of This Competency	Please Rank Here
1. **Innovative**: The ability to produce new ideas and insights into a situation.				
2. **Optimistic**: Have a positive attitude and advancing a positive outlook on goals.				
3. **Resilient**: Continuing to move forward despite setbacks or obstacles on the task.				
4. **Empathetic**: Being able to understand another person's feelings and perspectives.				
5. **Communication**: Being able to send clear messages that are easily understood by others.				
6. **Listening**: Actively seeks out others feedback and takes time to hear others' perspectives.				
7. **Adaptable**: Easily takes suggestions and is willing to change strategy to accomplish a goal.				
8. **Decision Making**: Analyzes different problems, evaluates information, and makes well-informed, effective, recommendations to advance toward the goal.				
9. **Emotional Self-Awareness**: Has an awareness of one's emotions and the impact they are having on others.				
10. **Planning**: Proving a clear and coherent plan, including different strategies, prior to jumping into the goal.				

Peer Assessment Handout

The following is a list of 10 important leadership competencies. Please rate the partner you just completed the exercise with, on each of the competencies, by putting an "X" in the box that corresponds with your rating. For the final column, force rank each competency according to how well that individual demonstrate this competency during the exercise. For example, the competency your partner demonstrated most effectively (or most often) during the exercise give that a 10, for the competency they demonstrated second most effectively give that a 9, continuing until you get to the competency that they showed the very least amount of skill demonstrating (give that a 1).

Competency	A Below Average Demonstration of This Competency	An Average Demonstration of This Competency	An Above Average Demonstration of This Competency	Please Rank Here
1. **Innovative**: The ability to produce new ideas and insights into a situation.				
2. **Optimistic**: Have a positive attitude and advancing a positive outlook on goals.				
3. **Resilient**: Continuing to move forward despite setbacks or obstacles on the task.				
4. **Empathetic**: Being able to understand another person's feelings and perspectives.				
5. **Communication**: Being able to send clear messages that are easily understood by others.				
6. **Listening**: Actively seeks out others feedback and takes time to hear others' perspectives.				
7. **Adaptable**: Easily takes suggestions and is willing to change strategy to accomplish a goal.				
8. **Decision Making**: Analyzes different problems, evaluates information, and makes well-informed, effective, recommendations to advance toward the goal.				
9. **Emotional Self-Awareness**: Has an awareness of one's emotions and the impact they are having on others.				
10. **Planning**: Proving a clear and coherent plan, including different strategies, prior to jumping into the goal.				

LUCK OF THE DRAW DISCUSSION GROUPS: USING SELF-ASSESSMENT TO PROMOTE LIFELONG LEADERSHIP LEARNING
Beth Hoag

Self- and Peer-Assessments, Curricular Learning Assessment

This activity uses the Illinois Leadership Inventory (ILI) to engage participants in guided self-reflection on leadership competencies. After completing the inventory, the participant receives a series of recommendations for further leadership learning. The ILI provides a framework teaching concepts such as the importance of self-reflection and feedback, lifelong leadership learning, integrative learning, and goal setting.

Learning Outcomes:

Participants will have opportunities to:

- engage in reflective practice and self-assess leadership competency areas.
- discuss past leadership experiences with their peers.

Setting Up the Activity:

- Group size: 10+ participants
- Time: 50–60 minutes
- Materials: Playing cards (one per participant), ILI Worksheet

Instructions:

1. Prior to the Activity: In order to maximize the use of time and participant learning for this activity, instruct participants to complete the *Illinois Leadership Inventory (ILI): Personal/Self Level* prior to coming to class. For a link, instructions to complete, and background information related to the ILI, please see Table 7.1.
2. Set-Up: Prior to class ensure that you have enough playing cards for each participant. If you have a small class size, limit the number of the card options so participants will be able to find a partner for each discussion group. As participants enter class, provide them with a card.
3. Introduction: Discuss how leadership development is an ongoing process that involves self-reflection and a commitment to continued learning. Leadership development is never finished and it is important to develop foundations and skills for lifelong learning. A goal of higher education and

leadership development is to develop a foundation of skills and disposition for life-long learning such as curiosity, initiative, independence, transfer, and reflection (Association of American Colleges and Universities, 2009). Discuss the importance of reflection and metacognition for leadership development. Reflection "is making meaning of knowledge and experiences to learn and grow" (Guthrie & Jenkins, 2018, p. 110). Frame reflection as an ongoing process that requires the learner to integrate past experiences with future goals. State that the goal of today is to engage in *critical reflection* of their past leadership experiences, accomplishments, and feelings and develop conclusions and an action plan for future learning (Harvey & Jenkins, 2014). (10 minutes)

4. Self-Reflection: Handout the ILI worksheet and ask participants to review their results from the ILI for each competency. Have them choose one recommendation that interests them the most from each competency and respond to the questions on their worksheet. (10 minutes)

   - Before taking this assessment, have you ever reflected on your abilities in these areas? Explain. (Ongoing)
   - Were the results what you expected? Did anything surprise you? (Provides Feedback, Critical Thinking)
   - Choose one competency that you want to learn more about or enhance your abilities. Why did you choose it? (Ongoing)

5. Discussion Groups: Transition participants from the individual reflection activity to a reflective discussion. State that learning is a relational process and by telling our stories and listening to others, we often gain greater clarity of our own thoughts and experiences (Guthrie & Bertrand Jones, 2012). Have participants pull out the card they received at the beginning of class and inform them they will form groups based on their card. (20–30 minutes)

   - Instruct participants to find someone with the opposite color card they have and to discuss the following questions:
     - Which of the competencies do you feel is a strength of yours? Explain why and give an example. (Promotes Critical Thinking and Connected to an Experience)
     - For each competency, the ILI asked you to describe a time that you demonstrated that competency. Tell your partner one example you provided. (Contextual, Ongoing, Connected to an Experience)

- Instruct participants to find someone with the same suit card that you have and discuss the following questions.
  - Choose recommendations and share them with your partner. Why did you choose them? Brainstorm together other resources or activities that could enhance your knowledge/skills in this competency. (Promotes Critical Thinking)
  - Which of these competencies do you value the most? Which do you value the least? Explain why. (Values Clarification)
- Instruct participants to find everyone with the same # card and discuss the following questions.
  - How can you use this assessment to become a better leader? (Ongoing)
  - What leadership skills will you need in your future career? (Ongoing, Contextual)

6. Debrief: Ask participants to return to their seats and spend time debriefing the discussion group experience. (5–10 minutes)

Facilitator Notes:

- The Illinois Leadership Inventory (ILI) was created to help participants at the University of Illinois reflect on and assess their leadership abilities. Although the tool was designed for Illinois students based on the Illinois Model of Leadership, it is publically accessible. For more information about the Illinois Model of Leadership visit: http://leadership.illinois.edu/about/core-competencies.
- The ILI is divided into four modules: Personal/Self, Interpersonal/Team, Organization, and Community/Society. Each module asks participants to self-reflect on 4–6 leadership competency areas. For each competency, the user is asked five questions on a Likert scale from *Never* to *Almost Always* and asked to describe a time them demonstrated that competency in an open-response format. Upon completing the assessment, users will receive their results for each competency and be classified as beginner-developing-expert. Users will also receive a list of recommendations, that can be downloaded in a PDF format, to further their learning in each area. Typically there are four recommendations based on their

skill level including podcasts, TEDtalks, books, journals, et cetera.
- Directions to complete the ILI:
  - Visit www.leadership.illinois.edu/ili and click the Log in button at the top right.
  - Choose the "Create a new account" tab and use your email address as the username and enter your email. An email will be sent to your to verify your account. Click on the link provided and set up your account and create a password.
  - Select "Start" under the "Personal/Self Module" on the bottom left.
  - Under the "Self-Review" portion on the bottom left click "Start Self Review."
  - Choose "Other" to indicate that you are not an Illinois Student, and decide if you wish to consent to the research study.
  - Click "Start Self-Review" at the bottom center.
  - There will be six questions asked for each competency including one open-ended response. Answer the questions honestly without over-thinking.
  - At the end of the inventory, you will receive a summary of your results for each competency and provided with a set of recommendations for further leadership learning.
  - Review the recommendation prior to coming to class and to download a PDF copy of your results. Bring a printed/digital copy of these results to class.

References:

Association of American Colleges and Universities. (2009). *Foundations and skills for lifelong learning VALUE Rubric*. Retrieved from https://www.aacu.org/value/rubrics/inquiry-analysis

Guthrie, K. L., & Bertrand Jones, T. (2012). Teaching and learning: Using experiential learning and reflection for leadership education. In K. L. Guthrie & L. Osteen (Eds.), *New directions for student services, No. 140, Developing students' leadership capacity* (pp. 53–64). San Francisco, CA: Jossey-Bass.

Guthrie, K. L., & Jenkins, D. M. (2018). *The role of leadership educators: Transforming learning*. Charlotte, NC: Information Age.

Harvey, M., & Jenkins, D. M. (2014). Knowledge, praxis, and reflection: The three critical elements of effective leadership studies programs. *Journal of Leadership Studies, 7*, 76–85.

Directions: After completing the inventory, review your recommendations for each competency. Choose one recommendation from each competency that interests you the most.

Competency	Description	Choose One Recommendation That Interests You
Self-knowledge	Possesses an accurate sense of one's current interests, values and goals in life; Can describe one's personality, interests, strengths, and weaknesses	
Self-management	Manages one's self and actions with a healthy attitude and productive relationships; Consciously identifies one's goals and works towards them; Starts work on one's goals and plan; Proposes new ideas or actions after consideration of options	
Reflection	Considers past experiences and current situations to inform current and future actions; Utilizes past mistakes and actions as learning opportunities to improve skills	
Empathy	Understands the perspectives of others, without necessarily agreeing with them; Recognizes and acknowledges the emotional context of interactions	
Openness	Values new experiences & people; Maintains strong sense of personal values while being responsive to new ones	
Integrity	Acts to do the "right" thing consistently; Possesses a strong personal character	

Before taking this assessment, have you ever reflected on your abilities in these areas? Explain:

Were the results what you expected? Did anything surprise you?

Choose one competency that you want to improve in this semester. Why did you choose it and how will you work to improve in this area?

IN MY FEELINGS: INDIVIDUAL AND COLLECTIVE CAPACITIES FOR EMOTIONAL INTELLIGENCE
Erica Wiborg

Self- and Peer- Assessments, Cocurricular Learning Assessment

This learning activity is designed to facilitate reflection and application of the results in the *Emotionally Intelligent Leadership for Students: Inventory* (Shankman, Allen, & Miguel, 2015). Although this activity can be facilitated in either cocurricular or curricular settings, this specific activity is designed for cocurricular leadership learning with groups, community organizations, employment, advocacy groups, or leadership programs. In addition to identifying the capacities participants most and least often utilize, they will be able to connect within their community to identify learning goals individually, as well as collectively.

Learning Outcomes:

Participants will have opportunities to:

- interpret their strengths in relation to the Emotionally Intelligent Leadership (EIL) capacities, as evidenced by their ability to apply these capacities to their current context.
- develop collaborative working relationships, as evidenced by their ability to engage in collective action planning.

Setting Up the Activity:

- Group size: Any size group (some activities might be with groups smaller than 10)
- Time: 60 minutes
- Materials: EIL Inventory (one per participant), assorted colorful writing utensils, large poster paper. Participants should bring their completed Emotionally Intelligent Leadership for Students: Inventory (EIL-I)

Instructions:

1. Emotions Warm-Up (15 minutes)

   - Prompt participants to draw how they currently feel at this point in the semester in a given context. This context could be an organization, office/department, about a previous event, in a partnership, etc.
   - Ask participants to pair up with someone to share their drawing.

- Debrief process by asking what it was like to draw a feeling/feelings. Was it difficult? Was it easy? What did you learn about the emotions you are feeling when you were prompted to draw them?
- Transition by introducing the importance of understanding emotions of self and others engaged in the leadership process, and how these change depending on the context (setting + situation).

2. Overview of Emotionally Intelligent Leadership (5 minutes)

   - While participants may have read the descriptions in the inventory packet, be sure to briefly introduce EIL (Shankman, Allen, & Haber-Curran, 2015) and describe the three facets: (a) consciousness of self; (b) consciousness of others; and (c) consciousness of context. Identify that these facets are strengthened as we build off all three in our leadership practice. Add that there are 19 capacities to develop and utilize at various points as needed in a situation and depending on the setting. Encourage participants to use the EIL-I as a reference tool for identifying capacities they most often consider or utilize, and which ones are not often thought about.

3. Individual: Concentric Circle Meaning Making (20 minutes)

   - Instruct participants to grab their inventory and create a concentric circle by splitting the group in half with the inside circle facing out while the outside circle faces in. Each person should connect across from another. Explain that they will hear a question about their EIL-I and they will share with their partner.
   - Provide enough time for both participants to share before asking the next question. Prior to asking the next question, request one of the circles to move (i.e. inside circle, move two people clockwise). At each cycle make sure participants are moving and talking with a different person. Question prompts include:
     - What was surprising for you in the results of your inventory?
     - What was reaffirming for you in the results of your inventory?
     - What was unfamiliar and new for you in the results of the inventory?
     - Share which facet (e.g., consciousness of self, consciousness of others, or consciousness of context) you are most skilled in. How does

this facet connect to your overall capacity for emotional intelligence?

4. Collective: Action Planning (20 minutes)

    • Utilizing either a dry-erase board or large poster paper, have the capacities organized by facet written out. Direct participants to page 9 in their inventory; write their name on the board next to the area of strength they utilize the most often, as well as the area of development. After everyone has added their two areas, ensure everyone has had time to analyze the makeup of the collective capacity of the group.
    • Debrief on opportunities for success, challenge, and learning.
    • Wrap up by describing the constant process of building skills and capacity will continue, as well as shift depending on context. Provide a brief example where a setting or situation shifted in a group. End by reaffirming the value of the collective capacity of the group in responding to contextual influences.

5. At the end of the *Individual: Concentric Circle Meaning Making* debrief on building connection and

gauge what surprises came up or what might have been unfamiliar.

• One theme that may come up is how participants were able to talk to someone who was very skilled at a capacity they were not skilled in. Identify the value of having a team or group with a diverse set of skills to build the collective capacity of the group.
• During the *Collective: Action Planning* debrief consider the following questions:
    ○ Are there any other skills not listed in the 19 you feel we need to add to either our strengths or areas of development? What do we notice about our group?
    ○ How do these themes affect our hopes and expectations as a group?
    ○ What can we do to learn and challenge each other to build our development areas?

References:

Shankman, M. L., Allen, S. J., & Haber-Curran, P. (2015). *Emotionally intelligent leadership: A guide for students* (2nd ed.). San Francisco, CA: Jossey-Bass.

Shankman, M. L., Allen, S. J., & Miguel, R. (2015). *Emotionally intelligent leadership for students: Inventory* (2nd ed.). San Francisco, CA: Jossey-Bass.

CHAPTER 8

Role-Play

Role-play, simulation, and games are widely considered as effective instructional strategies to promote student engagement (Booth, 1993; Cherney, 2008; Stevens, 2015). The primary advantage is that "students are active participants rather than passive observers" (Svinicki & McKeachie, 2014, p. 210). Moreover, these instructional strategies are effective in achieving a broad range of learning outcomes (Rao & Stupans, 2012), including knowledge acquisition (Eitington, 2001; Lauber, 2007; Taylor, 1999; Van Ments, 1994), communication skill development (Nestel & Tierney, 2007), and emotional development (Roberts, Wiskin, & Roalfe, 2008). Role-play—where learners act out or improvise assigned roles (based on their conceptions) in case scenarios or unstructured situations (McKeachie, 1986)—is an effective active learning strategy that enhances students' motivation to learn, promotes retention of material, encourages working in groups, and can potentially generate student enthusiasm and interest (Beidatsch & Broomhall 2010; Bonwell & Eison, 1991; Frederick 2000). One principal utility of role-play is that it can be implemented by instructors as a way to increase practice of skills within the confines of a college classroom among peers and prior to implementing the skills in professional environments (Sorbet, 2019). Case in point, "if students are to learn how to think more effectively, they need to practice thinking" (Svinicki & McKeachie, 2014, p. 211)—role-play presents opportunities to do so in a safe environment.

ROLE-PLAY IN LEADERSHIP EDUCATION

There is substantial support for the use of role-playing, games, and simulation in the leadership education literature (e.g., Allen & Hartman, 2008; Gibson, 2003; Guthrie & Jenkins, 2018; Sogurno, 2003). Among their qualities, they offer students learning experiences along cognitive, social, emotional, and intellectual dimensions (Guthrie, Phelps, & Downey, 2011). Moreover, these instructional strategies provide students opportunities to practice varying leadership styles,

skills, behaviors, situations, dispositions, and attitudes while exerting some control of the practical consequences (Guthrie & Jenkins, 2018). In particular, role-play activities provide opportunities for learners to engage in a variety of leadership situations and take on roles they are unlikely to encounter elsewhere. As well, role-play can be adapted by assigning students to play the roles of any important content knowledge, theory, model, behavior, trait, approach, historical figure, or leader/follower role—to allow for deeper learning and engagement in material (Guthrie & Jenkins, 2018). Exemplary leadership role-play learning activities provide equal opportunities to rich dialogue around a certain scenario or decision-making process and place students in specific behavioral roles that either help or hinder organizational processes.

For a list of best practices in using simulations and role-plays see *The Role of Leadership Educators: Transforming Learning* (Guthrie & Jenkins, 2018, pp. 274–275).

References:

Allen, S. J., & Hartman, N. S. (2008). Leadership development: An exploration of sources of learning. *SAM Advanced Management Journal, 73*(1), 10–19.

Beidatsch, C., & Broomhall, S. (2010). Is this the past? The place of role-play exercises in undergraduate history teaching. *Journal of University Teaching & Learning Practice, 7*(1), 1–20.

Bonwell, C. C., & Eison, J. A. (1991). *Active learning: Creating excitement in the classroom.* Washington, DC: George Washington University ERIC Clearinghouse on Higher Education.

Booth, A. (1993). Learning history in university: Student views on teaching and assessment. *Studies in Higher Education, 18*(2), 227–235.

Cherney, I. D. (2008). The effects of active learning on students' memories for course content. *Active Learning in Higher Education, 9*(2), 152–171.

Eitington, J. E. (2001). *The winning trainer winning ways to involve people in learning* (4th ed.). Boston, MA: Butterworth Heinemann.

Frederick, P. J. (2000). Motivating students by active learning in the history classroom. In A. Booth & P. Hyland (Eds.), *The practice of university history teaching* (pp. 101–111). Manchester, England: Manchester University Press.

Gibson, K. (2003). Games students play: Incorporating the prisoner's dilemma in teaching business ethics. *Journal of Business Ethics, 48*(1), 53–64.

Guthrie, K. L., & Jenkins, D. M. (2018). *The role of leadership educators: Transforming learning.* Charlotte, NC: Information Age.

Guthrie, K. L., Phelps, K., & Downey, S. (2011). Virtual environments: A developmental tool for leadership education. *Journal of Leadership Studies, 5*(2), 6–13.

Lauber, L. (2007). Role-play: Principles to increase effectiveness. In M. L. Silberman (Ed.), *The handbook of experiential learning* (pp. 185–201). San Francisco, CA: Wiley.

McKeachie, W. J. (1986). *Teaching tips: A guidebook for the beginning college teacher.* Lexington, MA: DC. Heath & Co.

Nestel, D., & Tierney, T. (2007). Role-play for medical students learning about communication: Guidelines for maximising benefits. *BMC Medical Education, 7,* 3.

Rao, D., & Stupans, I. (2012). Exploring the potential of role play in higher education: Development of a typology and teacher guidelines. *Innovations in Education and Teaching International, 49*(4), 427–436.

Roberts, L. M., Wiskin, C., & Roalfe, A. (2008). Effects of exposure to mental illness in role-play on undergraduate student attitudes. *Medical School Education, 40*(7), 477–483.

Sogurno, O. A. (2003). Efficacy of role-playing pedagogy in training leaders: Some reflections. *Journal of Management Development, 23*(4), 355–371.

Sorbet, S. R. (2019, February 11). Role play gives students valuable pre-practicum experiences. *Faculty Focus.* Retrieved from https://www.facultyfocus.com/articles/effective-teaching-strategies/role-play-gives-students-valuable-pre-practicum-experiences/

Stevens, R. (2015). Role-play and student engagement: Reflections from the classroom. *Teaching in Higher Education, 20*(5), 481–492.

Svinicki, M. D., & McKeachie, W. J. (2014). *McKeachie's teaching tips: Strategies, research, and theory for college and university teachers* (14th ed.). Belmont, CA: Wadsworth Cengage Learning.

Taylor, H. (1999). *Role-play cases for teaching interviewing skills in information systems analysis.* Paper presented at the HERDSA Annual International Conference. Retrieved May 23, 2009, from http://www.herdsa.org.au/wp-content/uploads/conference/1999/pdf/TaylorH.PDF.

Van Ments, M. (1994). *The effective use of role play.* London, England: Kogan Page.

LEADERSHIP BEHAVIORS AND FAST FOOD
Daniel M. Jenkins and Amanda Cutchens

Role-Play, Curricular Instructional

This learning activity emphasizes experiential learning techniques that influence reflective judgment while allowing participants to apply leadership theories learned in class to "real" situations. Prior to facilitating this role play, we recommend reviewing the "Best Practices in Using Simulations and Role-Plays" (Guthrie & Jenkins, 2018, pp. 274–275).

Learning Outcomes:

Participants will have opportunities to:

- understand the experienced differences and similarities among task-related and relationship-oriented attitudes and behaviors.
- explore the behavioral approach to leadership (Northouse, 2019).

Setting Up the Activity:

- Group size: 3 role players; no limit on peer observers
- Time: 30–40 minutes
- Materials: Scenario handouts for role players; copies of Leadership Behavior Questionnaire (Northouse, 2019, p. 88–90)

Instructions:

1. Pass out a Leadership Behavior Questionnaire for all participants to complete.
2. Give the participants time to complete the questionnaire. (15 minutes) While they are doing so, ask for or select three strong participants with improvisational acting experience. Explain to the three participants that one of them will play the role of a new employee at an walk-up eatery (choose an eatery participants are familiar with or let them come to a consensus—the key here is that the eatery will be wholly familiar to the participants, allowing them to infuse humor and really get into their roles) in the food court who is responsible for marketing the cuisine to participants. Their position is called "Food Dude." They have undergone a 6-week training program at the eatery's headquarters and are now working full time. This particular location of the eatery has been operating for just 4 weeks and the sales are worse than all other locations. The regional manager—the "Sauce Boss"

(played by two other participants in two separate interactions)—is meeting with the Food Dude to discuss their progress.

3. While your participant actors are preparing for the role play, explain to the remaining participants that they are about to observe two scenarios. Ask them to jot down observations as to the effectiveness or ineffectiveness of the leadership behaviors they notice in each scenario and to respond to the questions on the Participant Observation Handout.

4. Run Scenario 1 (5 minutes) and then allow time (10 minutes) for participants to respond on the handout. Then, run Scenario 2 (5 minutes).

5. Debrief:

    • Ask participants about their feelings related to the scenario, what leadership behaviors were present in the activity, what they learned from the experience, and how this scenario relates to a real-world experience. Best practice is "Six Phases of Debriefing" (Guthrie & Jenkins, 2018, pp. 166–169).

(Handout) Participant Observation

As you observe each scenario, jot down feedback as to the effectiveness or ineffectiveness of the leadership behaviors you notice. Additionally, consider:

• What leader behaviors were appropriate or inappropriate?
• What was effective in each interaction?
• What aspects of the task-related approach were effective? Ineffective?
• What aspects of the relationship-oriented approach were effective? Ineffective?
• Was anything over the top?
• Where could the leaders have improved?
• What worked best?
• What was the purpose of this activity?

(Handout) Scenario

• **Food Dude:** You are a new employee at a walk-up eatery in the food court. You were hired with the task of marketing the eatery to your fellow participants. Today your regional manager—the Sauce Boss—is going to meet with you to discuss your progress.

• **Sauce Boss #1:** You are a task-oriented leader. Come in and meet with your employee and emphasize what the employee is *not* currently doing. Focus on the situation at hand and set the new direction for your employee right off the bat—they need guidance! Set high-performance standards and state

them explicitly. When talking to your employee, emphasize their strengths when directing them for future action. Be willing to implement risky changes in order to meet specific tasks. Be sure to offer hands-on guidance and initiate tough questions with the employee like "so why do you think sales are down?" or "what do you think you can do differently to increase sales?" or "you know we're the lowest grossing [insert eatery name here]."

• **Sauce Boss #2:** You are a relationship-oriented leader. Establish rapport with your employee immediately and talk about how they're integral to the vision of the eatery and are aligned for success in their current role selling tasty cuisine. Emphasize your openness to the employee's opinions and explicitly ask for their views. Try and appeal to their emotions and reassure them that they can call on you for help at any time. Inquire if there are any extenuating circumstances, personally or professionally, that are inhibiting their ability to market effectively. Shower them with praise, emotional support, and encouragement. No *really*, go all out here, but, make sure to promote the principles and values of the eatery. And lastly, remember—you are a servant leader as well—remind your employee that your role as the regional manager is a supportive one. You're there to achieve *their* goals, not your own.

• **Acting Notes:** Think for a how you would behave if you were placed in this role in real life. To make this fun, overemphasize the emotions (frustration, joy, etc.) of your character. Remember—a good role player is both a scriptwriter and an actor!

Facilitator Notes:

• Challenges may arise from participants' understanding or misunderstanding of key terminology or theories to be explored in role play. This may be rectified through additional readings, reflective journaling supplemented by a leadership theories textbook, including discussion on these topics and/or interactive discussion prior to the activity.

• It is highly recommended that a structured briefing period occurs with those taking on roles in the scenario. Feel free to meet participants in a secluded area of the activity space. Participants should be informed of their roles and allowed to ask questions. Give participants a few minutes to get into their roles.

References:

Guthrie, K. L., & Jenkins, D. M. (2018). *Role of leadership educators: Transforming learning.* Charlotte, NC: Information Age.

Northouse, P. G. (2019). *Leadership: Theory and practice* (8th ed.). Thousand Oaks, CA: SAGE.

Resources:

Allen, S. J., & Hartman, N. S. (2009). Sources of learning in student leadership development programming. *Journal of Leadership Studies*, 3(3) 6–16.

Sogurno, O. A. (2003). Efficacy of role-playing pedagogy in training leaders: some reflections. *Journal of Management Development*, 23(4), 355–371.

A "STARRING ROLE" IN PROCESSING DIVERSITY AND INCLUSION

Jason Headrick

Role-Play, Cocurricular Instructional

This learning activity allows participants to look at diversity and inclusive leadership through the role of a casting director and actors who are trying to get their "big break." This real-world role play permits participants to see prejudice and bias in action, while also setting the foundation for further discussions on diversity and inclusion and understanding others through leadership development.

Learning Outcomes:

Participants will have the opportunity to:

- discover affective connections to identify parallels into diversity and inclusion concerns in society and in their own life.
- demonstrate and integrate their understanding of empathy, inclusion, and diversity through class discussions, journals, and their personal leadership plans and philosophies.

Setting Up the Activity:

- Group size: 20–30 participants of diverse identities
- Time: 30–60 minutes
- Materials: Facilitators need to prepare color-coded identity cards. Each card will have instructions for how participants are to navigate the role play scenario (outlined below) and each color helps them to be identified by their peers in the activity.

  o Yellow: You are a very timid person. You like to talk to people, but you are afraid to start the conversation. DO NOT approach anyone. Let others come to you.
  o Orange: You have strong issues with people who are blue. You will NOT work with them, talk to them, or associate with anyone who is blue. If a person who is blue talks to you or comes near you, make an excuse to leave or refer them to someone else.
  o Blue: You are an outgoing person and you want to try and talk to everyone. You are very welcoming. It is also your desire to connect people.
  o Red: You are a nice person, but you have a slight issue with orange people. You will work with them, but you question everything they say and don't trust them. You always want to be nice, but you hold a grudge against orange so you would never be left one-on-one with them, so you will always pull someone in.
  o At the bottom of each card (Suggested): To move along discussion with your peers, talk about the types of movies or TV shows you want to act in/ are looking for actors for. What's your favorite TV/ movie character? Have you done any acting before?

Instructions:

1. Begin the activity by scaffolding class discussion/ readings and setting the scene for the activity. Assign three participants as casting agents and inform the participants that the agents will be in class casting for an upcoming movie about leadership. For added effect, bring in three outside individuals to add an element of legitimacy. (5 minutes)
2. Instruct participants that they will be given directions on a unique card so they know how to "act" in the audition. You may assign an activity observer to get an outside perspective through taking notes and documenting what occurs. (5 minutes)
3. Distribute the color-coded identity cards to participants and instruct them to turn these over at the same time, but not share the information with others. They are to read the character description on the card and be "in character" for the audition portion. Their objectives as an "actor" are to interact with each of the casting agents and other actors in order to be hired for the movie. Their identity card must be in their hands and visible for the activity. (5 minutes)
4. Spread the casting agents out across the room. Each casting agent has also been assigned a color-coded identity card. You may want to provide them with a ribbon or color-coded designation as long as it is visible to everyone in the activity.
5. Restate the objectives of networking with all casting agents and fellow actors and announce the beginning of the audition process. Observe and initiate as needed. Announce to participants when there are five minutes remaining. (10–20 minutes)

6. You have two options (or can be combined): (a) Allow participants to freeze where they are in the role play and engage in a debrief session; or (b) Allow participants to gather in color-coded groups and discuss their experiences from the activity before discussing as a class. (10–20 minutes)
7. Debrief. Depending on your direction from #6 above, the debrief can help arrive at the "heart and soul" of your activity (Qudrat-Ullah, 2004). Using a discussion frame (Davis, 2009; Rao & Stupans, 2012), participants are asked the following questions, but other approaches you are more comfortable with may be used:

- How did this activity make you feel? How does this translate over to what others experience?
- What happened in the activity? What did we see happening to others? How could this impact your future as a leader or working in a group?
- How does this relate to the real world?
- Did this parallel with your own beliefs or values, or not?
- What if you saw this happening in a group you are working with? Among your friends? Among your family?
- Share some things you have learned from this activity.

Facilitator Notes:

- Facilitators should be willing to share your own related experiences to help participants process during debrief. Be aware of the participants in your group and recognize this activity may hit close to home for participants because of identities. For added reflection, assign a reflective journal assignment to help participants process the activity and scaffold the topics and how it ties back into leadership and leadership development.

References:
Davis, B. G. (2009). *Tools for teaching*. San Francisco, CA: John Wiley & Sons.
Qudrat-Ullah, H. (2004). Improving dynamic decision making through debriefing: An empirical study. In *Proceedings IEEE International Conference on advanced learning technologies* (pp. 1–15). Finland: ICALT.
Rao, D., & Stupans, I. (2012). Exploring the potential of role play in higher education: development of a typology and teacher guidelines. *Innovations in Education and Teaching International*, 49(4), 427–436.

UNCOVERING CHALLENGES WORKING THROUGH TECHNOLOGY
Kirstin C. Phelps

Role-Play, Technology Enhanced

The following role-play will encourage participants to explore the dynamics of engaging with others in technology-enhanced contexts. Participants will uncover assumptions around familiarity and accessibility with technology, as well as identify leadership best practices to support group processes online. Debriefing the experience will help connect environmental (i.e., distractions, colocation of team members), personal (i.e., prior experience, familiarity with technology), and group dimensions that had an impact on task process, completion, and group outcomes.

Learning Outcomes:

Participants will have opportunities to:

- appreciate challenges and opportunities to engage in technology-enhanced group environments.
- uncover assumptions, limitations, and opportunities of working within technology-enhanced environments.

Setting Up the Activity:

- Group size: Groups of 6 participants, total size varies on room size.
- Time: 1 hour 15 minutes
- Materials: Internet-enabled/connected device, scenario/group task that is meaningful to the class or university context with a clear scope and deliverables, Editable Google Docs (GDocs) with sharable links, PowerPoint slides (2) displaying a) description of the task/scenario and b) list of groups and their group GDoc link

  ○ Team Envelopes (1 per team) containing slips of paper describing the following team roles:
  * *Role 1—Formal leader*: You are the formal leader of the group. It is your responsibility to ensure the task is completed within the allotted time.
  * *Role 2—Team member/multitasker*: You will be given an article you must read while contributing to the group task.
  * *Role 3—Team member/late joiner*: Wait 3 minutes after the start of the scenario before you join your group and start contributing to the Google Doc.

* *Role 4—Colocated team member*: Participate in the group process as a team member to support completion of the task. You will be physically able to work with the other colocated team member.
* *Role 5—Colocated team member*: Participate in the group process as a team member to support completion of the task. You will be physically able to work with the other colocated team member.
* *Note*: If you have more than 5 people per group, add: *Role 6—Slow connection. You must wait 5 seconds before responding to or answering to the group.*

• Short 2–3-page article (printed out) on a leadership or class-related concept, to be given to all participants playing role: *Role 2: Team member—Multitasker.*

Instructions:

Prior to the session:

1. Prepare the group task/scenario, such as creating a plan for an organizational event, writing a 1–2-page document to promote the university, finding materials (journal articles, multimedia, or popular press publications) relevant to a specific leadership theory or class topic, or something similar with clear deliverables.
2. Prepare group envelopes (1 per group), containing slips of paper for each role.
3. Create an editable Google Docs with a sharable link for each group, copying the chosen task/scenario to the top of the GDoc, along with the group number. For more information, visit the user guide at https://gsuite.google.com/learning-center/products/docs/get-started/#!/
4. Remind participants to bring their internet-enabled device to class for the session.

During the session:

5. Introduction (15 minutes)

   • Share the group task with participants by reviewing the task/scenario on the PowerPoint slide.
   • Have participants count off to form groups of five members; that is, count off by 5 for a class of 25 participants.
   • Pass out a Group Envelope to each group, having members choose a role at random by each taking a slip of paper. Participants should not share their role description with other members.

6. Provide directions:

   • Individuals should spread out around the room so they are working independently from their group. Take your device with them to access the GDoc.
   • Group members playing roles #4 and #5 (colocated team members) should sit together.
   • Group members playing roles #2 should come to the front to collect their article.

7. Answer any questions. Remind participants they have 30 minutes to work and there will be reporting out time afterwards on their progress.
8. Have participants arrange themselves throughout the room and begin the timer.
9. Display the group numbers and their associated Google Docs URLs on the PowerPoint.
10. Group Work Time (30 minutes)

    • While struggle is appropriate, keep an eye out for any participants who are having difficulties beyond what should be expected in the role play. Provide reminders to participants at the 5-minute, 3-minute, and 1-minute mark to complete their work.

11. Debrief Activity (30 minutes)

    • Call participants back to their seats and spend 5–10 minutes reviewing each group's GDoc and asking for any observations or comments on process from group members.
    • Spend the remaining time responding to the following debriefing questions.

12. Activity Debriefing Questions:

    • By a show of hands, how many people have used GDocs (or other collaborative applications) before? How many people were comfortable working in this fashion? How many people felt they contributed appropriately to the group? How many people felt other members of their group contributed appropriately?
    • What environmental factors made collaboration difficult? Why and how?
    • What technological factors made collaboration difficult? Why and how?
    • What personal factors made collaboration difficult? Why and how?
    • What would have made this process better? Easier? More effective?
    • What were things group members did or said (formal leader or otherwise) that helped the group in this situation?

- If you could redo this activity, what changes would you make to improve the process?
- How would these changes apply in real life group situations, working through technology?
- What are some key takeaways for supporting group processes in technology-enhanced/online contexts?

Resources:

Endersby, L., Phelps, K., & Jenkins, D. (2017). The virtual table: A framework for online teamwork, collaboration, and communication. *New Directions for Student Leadership, 153*, 75–88.

Hambley, L. A., O'Neill, T. A., & Kline, T. J. (2007). Virtual team leadership: The effects of leadership style and communication medium on team interaction styles and outcomes. *Organizational Behavior and Human Decision Processes, 103*(1), 1–20.

Huffaker, D. (2010). Dimensions of leadership and social influence in online communities. *Human Communication Research, 36*, 593–617.

Orlikowski, W. J. (1992). The duality of technology: Rethinking the concept of technology in organizations. *Organization Science, 3*(3), 398–427.

ARCHITECTS, INVENTORS, CREATORS: EXPLORING FOLLOWER BEHAVIOR IN GROUPS

Maritza Torres

Role Play, Followership Focused

This learning activity uses Kellerman's (2008) follower typology in order to showcase the varying levels of follower behavior in groups. Participants will be able to identify each behavior and experience the outcomes of an intended goal based on the levels of engagement. At the end of the activity, debriefing questions will be provided in order to connect the activity to Kellerman's (2008) typology and personal and/or professional situations and experiences.

Learning Outcomes:

Participants will have opportunities to:

- identify and define the five behaviors of Kellerman's (2008) typology.
- observe how Kellerman's (2008) follower typology behaviors influence a group's outcome and intended goals.

- discuss strategies on how to work with Kellerman's (2008) follower typology behaviors in a group setting.

Setting Up the Activity:

- Group size: 15–25 participants
- Time: 30–60 minutes
- Materials: Index cards, Play-Doh, Legos, or anything that can be used to build

Instructions:

1. Divide the class into groups of five and in each group provide an index card with the one of the five levels of follower engagement behaviors to four members of the group. (5 minutes)

   - Kellerman (2008) Follower Typology

     o *Isolates:* completely unengaged.
     o *Bystanders:* observe but do not participate in the activity. This individual listens to group discussion but disengaged when it is time to make a decision or will claim to be neutral.
     o *Participants:* Partially engaged and willing to challenge and support the leader in a group.
     o *Activists:* Change agents and feel strongly about the leader and policies, but act on their own beliefs.
     o *Diehard:* EXTREMELY engaged. Committed to supporting or not supporting the leader. They are dedicated to the group goal and are willing to risk their lives for it.

   - The fifth card can be labeled as "leader or manager" (depending on the prompt). You can either use a definition you discussed or allow the participant to pick one of their own that was discussed.

2. Provide the following instructions: "You are a group of architects and have been tasked with creating a new university. Each group is responsible for creating their ideal university. You will have 15 minutes to come up with the name, course offerings, mission statement, and a visual model of the institution. You will work in groups based on the follower engagement behavior that is on your card. When you are done, each group will present their ideal university to the class." (10–15 minutes)

3. Have each group "pitch" their university. (5 minutes)

4. Make sure to address the following debrief questions. (dependent on group size, 20–25 minutes)

- What behaviors did you observe in your group?
- How did it feel having to play the role of your respective behavior?
- What experiences have you had in which you encountered individuals exhibiting one of the five follower engagement and behaviors?

Facilitator Notes:

- Make sure to make this activity fun and light-hearted. Other examples for groups to create are a new toy or study tool.
- Be ready to provide more time in case the participants take a while to start the activity and prepare their pitch.
- Use aspects of leadership literature to apply the "leader" role back to class materials and discussion. Feel free to use your own definition of leader for this index card or let the person in the role use one of the definitions discussed in class.
- You can adjust time frames and group sizes if needed.

Reference:

Kellerman, B. (2008). *Followership: How followers are creating change and changing leaders.* Boston, MA: Harvard Business Press.

CONSCIOUS SELECTION AND REVIEW OF ROLE-PLAYING ACTIVITIES
Michaela Shenberger

Role-Play, Curricular Learning Assessment

Facilitators and participants will work as a team to assess a role-playing activity in three stages: activity selection, during facilitation, and postfacilitation. This activity can be applied to any role-playing activity; however, it was created and written specifically with student leadership in a curricular setting in mind. This learning activity can be applied to a precreated role-playing activity as well as an original creation.

Learning Outcomes:

Participants will have opportunities to:

- learn different forms of and language around providing constructive feedback, especially with dynamics of power and authority at play.

- be empowered to engage in dialogue with their instructor, in relation to their leadership education.
- feel a sense ownership over their curriculum and their overarching leadership education.

Setting Up the Activity:

- Group size: Any size group
- Time: 1 hour 10 minutes

Instructions:

Activity Selection: Prior to selecting and facilitating an activity, the instructor will reflect and work through the following questions. (30 minutes)

1. Instructors should consider the following questions in relation to the potential role-playing activity:

   - What are the overarching learning outcomes of this course? What are the learning outcomes of this particular class facilitation?
   - What is your intention/hopes in relation to including a role-playing activity in the class facilitation?
   - What are the original learning outcomes and intent of this activity?
     - Do these outcomes/intentions align with the outcomes of the overarching course? How about this particular class facilitation?
     - Does this activity's intention/outcomes align with your intentions/hopes? If so, how? If not, how will it be adjusted?
   - Who was the original audience this activity was designed for?
     - Who is the audience for your facilitation of this activity? Is there alignment? If not, what has been/will need to be adjusted to ensure alignment?
   - Is the language used in the activity inclusive and accessible to the audience?
   - Does this activity have any potential to be triggering for any of your participants? If so, how do you plan on addressing/adjusting it?
   - Does this activity provide all participants with the opportunity to display different elements of leadership? If not, which particular roles provide this opportunity? How will those outside these roles grow in their leadership development? Consider the audience of the activity as well, if there is one.
     - Does this role-play activity have the potential to directly display participants' completion of the course's/class facilitation's learning out-

comes? If so, which learning outcomes and how?

- Does this activity have transferable elements into participants' real lives? Is technology considered?
- Does this activity provide a debriefing space? What are potential areas of the activity that may require additional debriefing?
  - Within the facilitation time available, can both the activity and debriefing be completed? Is there space to add more time to debriefing if needed? If there is not enough time, when will debriefing take place? Is this time guaranteed? Will time between the activity and debriefing help or hinder participants' learning/development?

2. If upon reflection of these questions, the instructor decides the role-playing activity no longer fits their needs or the learning outcomes for participants, they may decide not to go further with the assessment. However, if the activity does seem to fit, they should continue to the next stage.
3. During Role-Playing Activity Facilitation: This aspect of the assessment will take place during an actual facilitation of the role-playing activity.
4. Prior to the facilitation activity the instructor should inform participants this activity is up for review and their input will be considered.
5. Instructor should conduct the role-playing activity as instructed by the activity instructions, including the debrief portion of the activity.
6. During the facilitation of the activity, the instructor should consider the following:

- Did the directions need to be explained multiple times?
- Are all participants engaged and participating in this role-playing activity? If not, who is not and why?
- How is leadership being defined or explored by participants? Is this role-playing activity reinforcing any potentially harmful leadership ideas (in relation to positionality, gender, race/ethnicity, etc.)?
- Are participants using the knowledge/understanding they obtained in this course during this role-playing activity? How can you tell?
- Are they referencing specific course material such as textbooks? Is the language/vocabulary they are using from the coursework?
- Are the expressed learning outcomes for this activity being achieved?
- During the role-playing activity's debrief, are participants actively participating?

- Is the format an open free-flowing discussion or more question/response based? Does this format reflect how these participants generally engage best in the course? Are participants asking questions of each other and the instructor?
- Are participants self-assessing in relation to the activity's learning outcomes? What about in relation to the overarching class facilitation and course learning outcomes?

7. Postfacilitation: Following the facilitation of the activity space will be created for feedback from participants, prior to the final decision being made in relation to the continuation of using this activity. (40 minutes)
8. Provide participants with a copy of the Role-Playing Activity Feedback Worksheet, ask them to complete it, they can do so anonymously. (10 minutes)
9. Once completed, open the space for feedback on the activity. This could take the form of open discussion or a question/response. Potential prompting questions include:

- What did you think of the role-playing activity?
- What did you learn from that activity?
- Where are some areas of improvement? Areas of confusion?
- If you could change something about the activity what would it be?
- Should this activity continue to be used?

10. Following the debriefing conversation with participants, the instructor should review all of their notes in conjunction with participants' feedback to make a decision on the continued use of this role-play activity. (30 minutes)

Facilitation Notes:

- The portion of this assessment involving participant feedback, requires the environment of the two-way conversation between participants and instructor about leadership education be in place. Start building this trust/dynamic early in the space.
- When possible, having more than one perspective on the selection and observation of a role-playing activity can be helpful and insightful.
- Let participants know what is decided about the activity and why. This allows them to understand their feedback has an impact on their leadership education and others.
- Considering asking for feedback on other activities within the curriculum as well.

(Handout) Role-Playing Activity Feedback

I think the purpose of the role-playing activity was:	
What did I learn during the role-playing activity?	
Positive things about the role-playing activity	Negative things about the role-playing activity
Questions/feedback I still have about the role-playing activity:	
Should this activity continue to be used? Why? Why not?	

EMPATHIC LISTENING TRIADS
Gayle Spencer

Role-Play, Cocurricular Learning Assessment

With the continued use of social media, participants may be less confident in their interactions with others, particularly listening for understanding. This learning activity allows participants to practice empathic listening skills, while also observing and giving feedback to others.

Learning Outcomes:

Participants will have the opportunity to:

- practice skills to more effectively empathically listen to others.
- understand/comprehend the importance of empathically listening.
- understand methods for effective listening.

Setting Up the Activity:

- Group size: 2–100 participants
- Time: 23–32 minutes
- Materials: One activity sheet per participant (included after instruction sheets)

Instructions:

1. Give a brief lecture about the five different levels of listening as well as skills you can use to be an empathic listener. Might be helpful to share on PowerPoint or board:

   The listening levels are:

   - Ignoring
   - Pretending to listen
   - Selective hearing
   - Active listening
   - Empathic Listening

   The techniques to use are:

   - eye-to-eye contact and looking interested;
   - encouraging statements;
   - clarifies for understanding;
   - relevant questions,
   - reflects back what is said, does not interrupt

2. Ask participants to get into groups of three. In each group, participants will each play one of the following roles:

   - Each person to tell a story (5–7 minutes)
   - Evaluation/feedback to the listener (5–7 minutes)
   - Individual reflection using the questions for discussion (5–7 minutes)

3. One participant needs to be the talker, who thinks about a story they would like to tell.

   - Possible stories could be:
     - You got a new job. Tell details of the job and how you feel about it, the boss, coworkers.
     - You broke up with a boy/girlfriend. Tell what happened, why, and how you felt about it.
     - Talk about how you feel about school this semester—the homework, your grades, your professors, the classes you like or dislike.
     - Talk about a challenge you are having with a roommate (e.g., does not help keep your apartment clean, plays loud music, leaves dishes in the sink and never washes or puts them away).
   - One participant is the listener, and will practice using the skills listed on the activity sheet.
   - One participant will observe, using the evaluation chart.
   - After 5–7 minutes, call time and ask the observer and listener to give feedback to the talker. After 3–5 minutes, ask the participants to switch roles and repeat the process. You will repeat the process two more times, so each participant has a chance to be in each of the three roles.

4. After each person has been in each role, individually, participants answer these questions. (5–7 minutes) If time allows, have them discuss the answers with their triad. (5–7 minutes)

5. Debrief as a large group using the following questions:

   - What difficulties did you experience in each of the roles—speaker, listener, and observer?
   - What barriers to effective listening emerged during this exercise?
   - What did you learn about the effectiveness of your empathic listening?
   - What applications can you used to more empathically listen in the future?
   - Why is it important to listening empathically?

Resources:
Brown, B. (2013). Brene Brown on Empathy. Retrieved from https://www.youtube.com/watch?v=1Evwgu369Jw

Cleveland Clinic. (2013). Empathy: The Human Connection to Patient Care. Retrieved from https://www.youtube.com/watch?v=cDDWvj_q-o8

Crawley, D. (2018). The Five Levels of Listening. The Compassionate Geek Blog. Retrieved from https://www.doncrawley.com/the-five-levels-of-listening-how-to-be-a-better-listener/

Live Bold and Bloom (n.d.). The Power of Empathic Listening. Retrieved from https://liveboldandbloom.com/06/self-improvement/empathic-listening

(Handout) Empathic Listening Triads

1 participant talks; 1 participant listens; 1 participant evaluates skills of listener

This exercise is intended for participants to practice their empathic listening skills and to also learn now to observe and give feedback to others about their listening skills.

Possible topics for participant talking:

1. You got a new job. Tell details of the job and how you feel about it, the boss, coworkers.

2. You broke up with a boy/girlfriend. Tell what happened, why, and how you felt about it.

3. Talk about how you feel about school this semester—the homework, your grades, your professors, the classes you like or dislike.

4. Talk about a challenge you are having with a roommate (e.g., doesn't help keep your apartment clean, plays loud music, leaves dishes in the sink and never washes or puts them away).

(Handout) Evaluation of the Listener

	Good	Needs Improvement
Eye-to-eye contact and looks interested		
Encouraging statements		
Clarifies for understanding		
Relevant questions		
Reflects back what they said		
Does not interrupt		
Validates—never discredits their feelings		
Appropriate feedback		
Problem solving if necessary (only if asked for)		
Does not insert their own experiences into the discussion		

Listening Triads: Questions for Discussion

1. What difficulties did you experience in each of the roles—speaker, listener, and observer?

2. What barriers to effective listening emerged during this exercise?

3. What did you learn about the effectiveness of your empathic listening?

4. What applications can you used to more empathically listen in the future?

5. Why is it important to listening empathically?

CHAPTER 9

Simulation

Simulations are structured, experiential activities that replicate complex problems or issues, require decision making, and challenge students to demonstrate a skill when it is not feasible to use a real-world setting (Bonwell & Eison, 1991; Curry & Moutinho, 1992; DeNeve & Heppner, 1997; Drew & Davidson, 1993; Faria & Dickinson, 1994; Keys & Wolfe, 1990; Palomba & Banta, 1999). Simulations may take several hours or even several days to accomplish (Bonwell & Eison, 1991). In any case, simulations provide realistic representations of real-world situations and deliver participants with a more global view of their organization (Faria & Dickinson, 1994; Keys & Wolfe, 1990; Van Velsor, Ruderman, & Phillips, 1989) and offer student opportunities for direct and authentic involvement in their learning as well as rapid feedback about performance, which has the power to draw in participants (Drew & Davidson, 1993; Faria & Dickinson, 1994; Keys & Wolfe, 1990).

SIMULATION IN LEADERSHIP EDUCATION

Among the instructional strategies that foster students' leadership experiences and in turn provide a better understanding of content, simulations are probably the most effective (Gopinath & Sawyer, 1999; Haro & Turgut, 2012; Zantow, Knowlton, & Sharp, 2005). This is because simulation allows students to make decisions through problem solving (Keys & Wolfe, 1990), gain exposure to complex decision making under conditions that approximate real life, and learn from their own mistakes and the mistakes of others (Haro & Turgut, 2012). Moreover, rather than passively learning about terms used to describe complex social and technical dynamics, students have opportunities to witness these dynamics unfold firsthand among their peers and within teams (Faria & Dickinson, 1994). Simulations in leadership education range from full-class organizational simulations (e.g., "The Organization Simulation," Bolman & Deal, 2014) to computer-simulated collaborative adventures (e.g., "Mount Everest," Harvard Business Publishing, 2017; Roberto & Edmondson, 2011). In any case, simulation activities give students opportunities to find ways of leading under conditions that replicate those in other arenas without having to contend with the consequences of costly mistakes (Guthrie & Jenkins, 2018).

For a list of "Best Practices in Using Simulations and Role-Plays" see *The Role of Leadership Educators: Transforming Learning* (Guthrie & Jenkins, 2018, pp. 274–275).

References:

Bolman, L. (2014). *The organization simulation*. Retrieved from http://www.leebolman.com/organization_simulation.htm

Bonwell, C. C., & Eison, J. A. (1991). *Active learning: Creating excitement in the classroom*. Washington, DC: George Washington University ERIC Clearinghouse on Higher Education.

Curry, B., & Moutinho, L. (1992). Using computer simulations in management education. *Management Education and Development, 23*, 155–167.

DeNeve, K. M., & Heppner, M. J. (1997). Role play simulations: The assessment of an active learning technique and comparisons with traditional lectures. *Innovative Higher Education, 21*(3), 231–246.

Drew, S. A. W., & Davidson, A. (1993). Simulation-based leadership development and team development. *Journal of Management Development, 12*(8), 39–52.

Faria, A. J., & Dickinson, J. R. (1994). Simulation gaming for sales management training. *Journal of Management Development, 13*(1), 47–59.

Gopinath, C., & Sawyer, J. E. (1999). Exploring the learning from an enterprise simulation. *The Journal of Management Development, 18*(5), 477–489.

Guthrie, K. L., & Jenkins, D. M. (2018). *The role of leadership educators: Transforming learning*. Charlotte, NC: Information Age.

Haro, S. P., & Turgut, G. (2012). Expanded strategy simulations: Developing better managers. *Journal of Management Development, 31*(3), 209–220.

Keys, B., & Wolfe, J. (1990). The role of management games and simulations in education and research. *Journal of Management, 16*(2), 307–336.

Palomba, C. A., & Banta, T. W. (1999). *Assessment essentials: Planning, implementing, and improving assessment in higher education*. San Francisco, CA: Jossey-Bass.

Roberto, M., & Edmondson, A. (2011). *Leadership and team simulation: Everest V2* (Software). Retrieved from https://cb.hbsp.harvard.edu/cbmp/product/7000-HTM-ENG

Van Velsor, E., Ruderman, M., & Phillips, A. D. (1989). The lessons of the looking glass: Management simulations and the real world of action. *Leadership and Organization Development Journal, 10*(6), 27–31.

Zantow, K., Knowlton, D. S., & Sharp, D. C. (2005). More than fun and games: Reconsidering the virtues of strategic management simulations. *Academy of Management Learning and Education, 4*(4), 451–458.

WHAT IF THERE IS NO "RIGHT" ANSWER? PREPARING FOR THE "GREY AREAS" OF ETHICAL DECISION MAKING

Sonja Ardoin

Simulation, Curricular Instructional

Exploring ethical decision making is critical to leadership learning because these decisions are the "bread and butter of leaders' work" (Cranston, Ehrich, & Kimber, 2014, p. 229). Ethical decision-making simulations can help leaders consider how they may react when facing a "grey area" where there is not a clear "right" decision to be made nor a straightforward way to proceed (Salas, Wildman, & Piccolo, 2009). The simulations described below allow participants to examine "right versus right situations" (Kidder, 1995, p. 6) in a higher education context where values may be in tension yet a collective consensus has to be made in order to respond and move forward.

Learning Outcomes:

Participants will have opportunities to:

- examine ethical dilemmas that create values tension in a "right versus right" situation.
- reconcile ethical dilemmas based on a collective consensus of their group.
- create a written plan of action and written response about how move forward from the incident.

Setting Up the Activity:

- Group size: 6–30 participants
- Time: 2 hours–2 hours 30 minutes
- Materials: List of consensus practices (electronic to show on screen, in hard copy, or written on a board), 2–4 hard copies of the simulation instructions for

each subgroup; each instruction sheet includes the assigned university, team composition, and a right versus right ethical dilemma (Kidder, 1995, p. 6) that addresses one or more of Kidder's four paradigms: truth versus loyalty; individual versus community; short term versus long term; and justice versus mercy, debriefing questions for subgroups (electronic to show on screen, in hard copy, or written on a board) and debriefing prompts/questions for the entire class.

Instructions:

1. Introduction of Simulation (5 minutes)

   - Welcome participants to the class or meeting and share that they will be engaging in a simulation activity in groups of [insert number]. Have participants rearrange themselves accordingly.

2. Review leadership theory or theories (Dugan, 2017) (10 minutes)

   - Review leadership theories and remind participants that theories can be layered depending on context, situation, and group dynamics.

3. Discuss the concept of consensus (5 minutes)

   - Lead participants in a quick discussion about the concept of consensus (Dressler, 2006; Urfalino, 2014).
   - Post a list of consensus practices in the room. Instruct participants to employ the concept of consensus in their decision-making process in the simulation.

4. Share the purpose of the simulations, instructions, and timeline (5 minutes)

   - Share the purposes of the simulation—to (a) examine ethical dilemmas that create values tension in a right versus right situation and (b) practice reconciling ethical dilemmas based on a collective consensus of a group.
   - Explain that each group will encounter a different simulation and, thus, have a different resolution because "an ecological interpretation of context" (Notman, 2014, p. 176) is key during ethical challenges. However, point out that all groups will need to arrive at consensus within the allotted time.
   - Share that you will provide time checks for the groups.

5. Facilitate the simulations (60 minutes–1 hour 30 minutes)

- Explain that each group is simulating the executive team of the respective university listed on their instructions sheet and their charge is to reconcile the ethical dilemma described on the sheet by responding to the prompts: How do you respond? What is your plan moving forward?
- Direct each group to create of a written plan of action and a written response about how to recognize and move forward from the incident as an effort to heed "stronger calls for accountability and transparency" (Cranston et al., 2014, p. 230). These tangible products of the simulation include:
  ○ Written plan of action: (1) a list of internal actions: how will you respond to and move forward from this incident with campus constituents: students, administrators, faculty, trustees/board, and (2) a list of external actions: how will you respond to the community, media, educational news outlets such as *Inside Higher Ed*, *The Chronicle*, et cetera.
  ○ Written response to the incident: (1) email text that will be sent out to the entire school/university community, and (2) text for a twitter post (240 characters) that will be sent out via the school/university twitter handle.
- Walk around to check on the groups, respond to questions, and provide participants with time checks.
- After the allotted simulation time, collect the written plan of action and responses and begin the debriefing processes.

6. Debrief with questions:

- Subgroup debriefing (10 minutes)
  ○ Subgroup members will share their perceptions of the consensus and creation processes they faced in the simulation, based on the posted debriefing questions:
    * How did you feel your assigned group role influenced your perspective on the simulation?
    * How would you assess your group's ability to reach consensus about ways to reconcile the dilemma? What were challenges the group faced in this process?
    * How did the creation process unfold? How did you feel about the finished products?

7. Large group discussion (20 minutes)/Q&A (5 minutes)

- Bring the subgroups together and share a synopsis of each simulation to showcase the myriad of ethical dilemmas faced in higher education. (5 minutes)
- Engage the entire class in discussion about the process of making decisions and creating responses in right versus right ethical dilemmas. (15 minutes)
  ○ Offer insights on how these simulated dilemmas were derived from real-life examples that occurred in higher education environments
  ○ Share how those institutional administrators responded in real life.

8. Allot time for questions at the end. (5 minutes)

Facilitator Notes:

- To modify these simulations for larger groups, increase the size of the executive team by adding members (such as the provost, the chief finance officer, etc.) and/or further complicate each ethical dilemma simulation by adding tasks to the written plan of action and/or written response.
- When creating the simulations for each group, utilize current ethical dilemmas.

References:

Cranston, N., Ehrich, L. C., & Kimber, M. (2014). Managing ethical dilemmas. In C. M. Branson & S. J. Gross (Eds.), *Handbook of ethical educational leadership*. New York, NY: Routledge.

Dressler, L. (2006). *Consensus through conversations: How to achieve high-commitment decisions* (1st ed.). San Francisco, CA: Berrett-Koehler.

Dugan, J. (2017). *Leadership theory: Cultivating critical perspectives*. San Francisco, CA: Jossey-Bass.

Kidder, R. M. (1995). *How good people make tough choices*. New York, NY: Harper.

Notman, R. (2014). The interplay of values. In C. M. Branson & S. J. Gross (Eds.), *Handbook of ethical educational leadership*. New York, NY: Routledge.

Salas, E., Wildman, J. L., & Piccolo, R. F. (2009). Using simulation-based training to enhance management education. *Academy of Management Learning & Education, 8*(4), 559–573.

Urfalino, P. (2014). The rule of non-opposition: Opening up decision-making by consensus. *Journal of Political Philosophy, 22*(3), 320–341.

DIVERSIFYING THE VISION OF LEADERSHIP
Jesse Ford

Simulation, Cocurricular Instructional

The purpose of this learning activity is to encourage a discussion around leadership and diversity of thought (Bordas, 2007). The intent is to showcase that while individuals have different views on leadership, they all have similarities in how leadership can impact the world. Through this process, participants will create a large vision board which displays a diverse view of what leadership is and how it is understood by the participants.

Learning Outcomes:

Participants will have opportunities to:

- formulate and identify characteristics to define personal thoughts, opinions, and ideas of leadership and leader identity (Komives, Longerbeam, Owen, Mainella, & Osteen, 2006).
- differentiate and examine the connections between personal leadership definitions and the diversity of thought within theory formation.
- synthesize knowledge and use creativity to construct views on how leadership is a multilayered and a diverse school of thought.

Setting Up the Activity:

- Group size: Any size
- Time: 35–65 minutes
- Materials: Large poster board, markers, one 4 x 4 sheet construction paper per participants, tape, timer

Instructions:

1. With the construction paper and markers provided, instruct participants to draw their personal thoughts and understanding of leadership in picture form only. (5–10 minutes)
2. On the reverse side of the construction paper, inform participants to write their description of the picture. (5–10 minutes)
3. Each participant should post one side of the paper (of their choosing) on the poster board. (5 – 10 minutes)
4. Invite participants to observe their peer's artwork on the poster board. (5–10 minutes)

5. Conclude the activity by facilitating the debriefing and allow participants to ask questions that may have come up during the activity. (15–25 minutes)
6. Debrief with questions (3–5 minutes):

   - What are some common messages from participant's drawings? What are some of the differences?
   - In three sentences, generate a new definition of leadership based on the diverse understandings of leadership using the participant's drawings. How did the diverse prospective changed your thoughts and understanding of leadership?
   - Find a partner in the room. Take time to discuss how you determined what were the most salient parts of the vision board that assisted you in generating your personal definition.
   - Using your newly generated leadership definition, creating a vision for a group, team, or community that you are a member of. How will your definition help you lead your group, team, or community?

Facilitator Notes:

Prior to the start of the activity:

- Arrive at the session 10–15 minutes early to set up set up the room.
- Gather and organize the supplies need for the session prior to the start of the activity.
- Find a place in the room to post the larger poster board and hang it prior the participants arriving.
- Think about possible questions that the group may have if you have prior experience with the participants.

Starting/during the activity:

- Encourage participant to fully engage and embrace their creativity.
- Before starting the activity, ask the participants to identify a few words, thoughts, or phases that come to mind when they think of the word leadership with the group. This is to get the participants thinking about things they have heard, seen, or learned about the word leadership.

Following the activity:

- Following the debriefing questions, be sure to leave time for participants to ask questions and insights from each other.
- Encourage participants to continue to have dialogue about their views on leadership beyond the session.

References:

Bordas, J. (2007). *Salsa, soul, and spirit: Leadership for a multicultural age.* San Francisco, CA: Berrett-Koehler.

Komives, S. R., Longerbeam, S. D., Owen, J. E., Mainella, F. C., & Osteen, L. (2006). A leadership identity development model: Applications from a grounded theory. *Journal of College Student Development*, 47(4), 401–418.

GAMIFIED TEST
Elizabeth Goryunova

Simulation, Technology Enhanced

Gamified instruction increases learners' motivation and engagement thus contributing to a positive learning experience. This learning activity utilizes said advantages of a gamified environment to test participants' cross-cultural cognitive awareness that contributes to leadership effectiveness in a global environment. Participants access a virtual learning center to play the game where they apply their critical thinking skills to a variety of cross-cultural scenarios in order to identify/learn the appropriate course of action/response.

Learning Outcomes:

Participants will have opportunities to:

- improve critical thinking skills assessing effectiveness of a cross-cultural interaction.
- increase cultural cognition related to interaction across cultures.
- enhance cross-cultural awareness.

Setting Up the Activity:

- Group size: Any size group as an asynchronous individual assignment or 23 participants or under as a synchronous in class group activity (limited by the number of free licenses)
- Time: 30–60 minutes
- Materials: Free version of gamified platform Virgo START can be requested at https://solargames-corp.com/en/. Free version allows 25 user accounts (23 participants, 1 administrator and 1 coach) with access to a Virtual Center with 3 virtual rooms and is limited to 10 simultaneous connections and 10 GB total memory.

Instructions:

1. Setting up the user accounts (5 minutes)

   - Facilitator sends email request to the provider, to create individual accounts for participants.
   - Credentials for access are instantly issued and emailed to individual learners

2. Setting up content for the game (25 minutes, one-time set up for the lifetime of test)

   - Facilitator enters test questions (grouped into 3 levels of complexity: low, medium, high) into the provider's template, marks correct answers and forwards the template to the provider by email. (20 minutes)
   - Facilitator specifies the time limit and the minimal acceptable score for the game. (5 minutes)

3. Administer the test (30 minutes)

   - Individual learners attempt test asynchronously, groups attempt test collectively.
   - As participants progress through the game, they are introduced to cross-cultural scenarios, one at a time, along with four possible responses/actions.
   - Learners apply critical thinking skills to evaluate scenario and select an appropriate response/action.
   - Learners complete the game and if desired make another attempt to improve their outcome.

4. Debrief with questions for each scenario:

   - What was the turning point, from where things went wrong?
   - How do you feel your solution changes the outcome?
   - What would you do differently if you were in this situation?
   - What have you learned that you can use in the future?

Examples:

- Cross-Cultural Scenario #1: American company is hosting in their headquarters a delegation of potential business partners from Japan. After the initial introductions, the guests were seated across the table from the hosts and offered a drink. Meantime, the hosts proceeded to take off their jackets and roll up their sleeves as a sign of "lets get down to business." The meeting was unsuccessful and the partnership was not established. What went wrong?

- The seating arrangements came across as distant to the Japanese who like to conduct business in a friendly atmosphere.
- The U.S. business men should have also offered the Japanese the chance to take off their jackets
- The removal of jackets was seen as unbusiness-like, inappropriate and in breach of professional conduct.
- Drinks are always left to after meetings in Japan.

- Cross-Cultural Scenario #2: American company assigns Emily as their representative in France. Emily speaks French and is excited for the opportunity. At an introductory meeting with French team, Emily initiates "small talk" with one of the team members: Mr. Lanvine. She introduces herself as Madame Briggs and asks Mr. Lanvine about his family and children. Monsieur Lanvine seems distance and unapproachable. Why?
  - Introducing oneself as monsieur/madame if you are a foreigner is considered arrogant in France.
  - As a new member of team Emily should have waited for Mr. Lanvine to approach her.
  - Asking personal questions in France is considered intrusive.
  - Chatting before meetings in not considered proper business conduct.

- Cross-Cultural Scenario #3: John has been assigned as a manager to a Riyadh, Saudi Arabia office of a United Kingdom engineering company. After a few months he has become increasingly frustrated by what he sees a less than effective Saudi team, their lack of competence and slow work pace. What should he do to try and bring the Saudi staff back into line?
  - Publicly reprimand a few of the Saudi staff to ensure the message gets across to them all. By doing so he will also establish who is boss.
  - Pick one member of the Saudi staff to explain his worries to. This staff member will then be used to relay John's opinions to the rest.
  - Speak to as many members of staff individually or in small groups, explaining his viewpoint and encouraging them to better their work practice and enthusiasm.
  - Report them to his manager, a Saudi national, and let him deal with them.

Resources:

Nah, F. F. H., Zeng, Q., Telaprolu, V. R., Ayyappa, A. P., & Eschenbrenner, B. (2014, June). Gamification of education: A review of literature. In *International conference on HCI in business* (pp. 401–409). Chaam, Netherlands: Springer.

Kapp, K. M., Blair, L., & Mesch, R. (2013). *The gamification of learning and instruction fieldbook: Theory into practice.* New York, NY: John Wiley & Sons.

Sailer, M., Hense, J. U., Mayr, S. K., & Mandl, H. (2017). How gamification motivates: An experimental study of the effects of specific game design elements on psychological need satisfaction. *Computers in Human Behavior, 69*, 371–380.

FINDING THE PATH: LEADERSHIP AND FOLLOWERSHIP AS A RELATIONSHIP
Jillian M. Volpe White

Simulation, Followership Focused

In this learning activity, participants must rely on each other to accomplish a task. During the debrief, the group should focus on building trust and developing the knowledge and skills to rely on and support other people. This activity is adapted slightly from the Florida State University Challenge Program.

Learning Outcomes:

Participants will have opportunities to:

- understand the relationship between leadership and followership in the context of completing a group task.
- recognize the importance of clear communication and developing trust when working as part of a team.

Setting Up the Activity:

- Group size: 10+ participants
- Time: 30–45 minutes
- Materials: boundary marker (outside—rope or cones; inside—masking tape or chairs), items to place in the space (these could include small cones, bean bags, pieces of pool noodles, stuffed animals, etc.), one blindfold per participant

Instructions:

1. Before participants arrive, section off a space using the boundary marker. The space should be able to accommodate half the group at one time with room to walk around objects which will be placed in the boundary. Scatter the items within the boundary. There should be enough items that is would be difficult to walk across the space without encountering some, but not so many that someone would be unable to maneuver without coming into

contact with an object. If possible, do not let the participants see the space in advance of the activity.

2. Have participants get into pairs. To begin, one person should put on the blindfold. The person who is not blindfolded should guide the blindfolded person to the edge of the boundary. Have pairs spread out around the edge of the boundary.

3. Explain that the boundary represents a situation the group may face. For example, their organization is planning a major event, and to successfully execute the event, they must guide their partner from one side of the boundary to the other. There are objects in the boundary which represent obstacles on the path to success.

4. The person who is blindfolded must cross the boundary without touching any of the objects. The person who is not blindfolded cannot enter the circle. They can only provide directions to their partner from outside the boundary. After making sure that people clearly understand the directions, tell the group they can begin.

5. As the people outside the boundary provide directions, make sure they do not cross into the space. If you see someone moving easily from one side of the space to the other, you can move some objects into their path. Once all participants have made their way across the space, tell the partners who were blindfolded they can remove their blindfolds and ask the other person to put on their blindfold.

6. Shuffle the items in the space. Once the partners have switched roles, invite them to guide their pair across the space. Once all partners have been guided across the space, invite everyone to remove their blindfolds, and facilitate a debrief discussion.

7. The debrief has two areas of emphasis. First, was it like to trust someone to give you directions? Second, what was it like to give directions to someone? Some people may react strongly to not having control whereas other people may have been comfortable listening for directions.

- Start by asking the group what they just experienced. Push them not to shift into interpretation, but to elaborate on what they were asked to do and their experience with giving or following directions. When many people were speaking at the same time, it may have been difficult to hear their partner. How did they make them feel? How did they compensate for this?

- Next shift into interpretation. How did their level of trust influence their ability to complete the task? What enabled them to reach their goal? If the group gives general responses like "team-

work," "communication," or "trust," ask them to say more about what they mean.

- Finally, ask the group to consider how this could be a metaphor for their experiences together. What aspects of this activity mirror a situation they have faced? How could the lessons they learned from this apply to their work together?

- Some other questions may include:

- How were you able to trust the directions from your partner? If you did not trust your partner, what could they have done to engender your trust?

- What does it mean to be a supportive follower? How did you see people practicing followership in this activity?

- What knowledge or skills do you need to develop in order to be a follower?

Facilitator Notes:

- There are some variations for this activity which can be substituted or combined.

  - *Collect the Objects:* Use the same directions as above, but divide the group into teams. Tell them the goal of the activity is that all the items inside the boundary are collected. The person who is not blindfolded cannot enter the boundary, but they must guide their partner to collect objects in the circle one at a time. *Do not say this is a competition*; groups often assume this which initially leads to competitiveness until someone realizes they can collaborate to be more efficient. The goal is to collect the objects as expeditiously (and safely!) as possible.

  - *Blindfolded Walk:* If you have access to an outdoor space or a space where a group can move more freely, have the group get in line. Ask everyone to put on their blindfold and place their hands on the shoulders of the person in front of them. Let the group know you will be tapping people to guide the group, and periodically you will switch the person who is guiding. You might begin with the person at the front of the line, but after a few moments, ask them to stop and put on their blindfold. Tap someone in the middle of the group. They will be in charge of giving directions, but they will remain where they are in line. At different points, you can switch who is giving directions, but they should remain in their place in the line, whether in the front, middle, or back. Time permitting, this is a good precursor to the other activities.

GAME ON! USING BARNGA TO FACILITATE CULTURAL AWARENESS IN LEADERSHIP EDUCATION
Amber Manning-Ouellette

Simulation, Curricular Learning Assessment

Created by Thiagarajan and Thiagarajan (2006), Barnga is a card game that encourages participants to confront cultural assumptions and intentionally reflect upon them. Utilizing the game as a simulation activity to deconstruct cultural assumptions, participants can relate their game experiences to how they might encounter cultural bias in leadership situations.

Learning Outcomes:

Participants will have opportunities to:

• build their cultural awareness in relation to leadership.
• confront cultural assumptions in leadership.
• intentionally reflect on culturally relevant leadership actions.

Setting Up the Activity:

• Group size: Participants should be divided into groups of 4–6 to play the Barnga simulation.
• Time: 55–60 minutes
• Materials: You will need a deck of playing cards for each group, copies of the Barnga instructions for the facilitator, and the game rules printed for each group. Barnga game rules and materials can be found online or by purchasing the text, *Barnga: A Simulation Game on Cultural Clashes* by Thiagarajan and Thiagarajan (2006).

Instructions:

1. Play *Barnga: A Simulation Game on Cultural Clashes* following game instructions. (35–40 minutes)
2. Facilitators should conceptualize debriefing through a two-stage process. (20–25 minutes) The initial stage's purpose is to initiate reflection on individual- and group-level dynamics and the second stage's purpose to process the connection to larger cultural systems in leadership processes.

   • Initial debrief: Individual-level reflection

     ◦ How did this experience feel?
     ◦ What individual challenges did you incur in playing the game?

     ◦ What was it like to experience silence in your position with the group?
     ◦ Did you feel uncomfortable during the game and what impact did that have on your experience?

   • Group-level reflection
     ◦ As a group, what were dynamics in your interactions during the game?
     ◦ What challenges did you incur through the game as a group?
     ◦ How does personal comfort play a role in our experience with others?
     ◦ If challenges occurred, how did the group work to resolve them or not?
     ◦ How does silencing one another impact the dynamics of a group setting?
     ◦ Were there emergent individuals that exercised leadership capacity during the game and if so, what did that look like?

   • Secondary debrief: Reflection questions on cultural assumptions and silence

     ◦ How does your experience in the game translate to navigating a new culture or experience?
     ◦ How does experiencing silence translate into navigating experiences (especially those outside of your comfort zone)?
     ◦ How does this simulation help you to understand cultural assimilation and/or assumptions?
     ◦ How does the experience translate into navigating social and cultural norms that we might experience on a daily basis?
     ◦ What might happen when we encounter "different" norms or "unwritten rules" in our world?
     ◦ How does your experience translate into navigating leadership experiences and cultural capital?
     ◦ What are examples of situations in leadership that might require you to consider cultural assumptions?

Facilitator Notes:

• Ensure you have enough space for participants to move around and separate into small groups at individual tables. Divide chairs and tables into the number of groups you will have for the activity with room to move around. Each table will need materials listed below. Please note challenges may be present for participants in regard to mobility across the classroom.

- The success of this learning activity is contingent on following the Barnga instructions as written, without any variation. It is critical to the simulation that no one speaks or writes during the game tournament. Having designated "observers" that watch interactions of participants during the simulation can help with reflection after the activity has commenced. Indicate to participants that there will be clear winners and losers in the game to initiate competition. Participants may ask for clarification on the game, but ambiguity is an essential part of the simulation. After you have taken away the "rules" at each table, begin the tournament. Players that "win" their table, will move to the next highest number table (if they are at the highest number table they will stay) and the player that "losses" their table will move to the next lowest table number (if they are at the lowest number table, they will stay). The tournament should consist of 4–5 rounds and then time for reflection.

Reference:
Thiagarajan, S., & Thiagarajan, R. (2006). *Barnga: A simulation game on cultural clashes*. Boston, MA: Intercultural Press.

ON CAMPUS SIMULATIONS AS LEADERSHIP DEVELOPMENT
Kathleen Callahan

Simulation, Cocurricular Learning Assessment

Using simulations that mirror real campus conflict or uncomfortable topics, helps participants put themselves in the position of having to meet issues head on. Participants can recall and apply knowledge and skills learned in leadership trainings or classes on campus to engage in dialogue around difficult topics in higher education.

Learning Outcomes:

Participants will have opportunities to:

- practice leadership skills such as mediation, conflict management, and effective communication, during controlled situations in the various environments.
- translate leadership knowledge on topics like mental health, personality types, and leadership development into active practice scenarios.

Setting Up the Activity:

- Group size: 7–10 participants per small group to have reflective discussion
- Time: 25–30 minutes (5 minutes for scenario and remaining time for discussion)
- Materials: None

Instructions:

1. Each leadership program will have different topic areas of interest, but below are two examples that leaders might encounter or observe. With each example below, tailor the wording to align with the participants you are working with—for the examples below, the participant who will be going through the simulation will be labeled as *leader*. Other than the leader, the other *actors* should be played by experienced participants (experienced employees, veteran student leaders) and/or staff.

    - Example 1: Personal Conflict *(needed: two actors and one leader as Resident Assistant)* 3–5 minutes for acting: Two of your freshmen residents are not getting along. They have each come to you separately to discuss how much they dislike each other. *Actor 1* says that their roommate is always having people over, going out a lot, talks all the time, and generally gets on their last nerve on a daily basis. *Actor 2* complains that their roommate is always in the room alone, eats alone, does not like to talk or engage with them, and is pretty sure the roommate hates them.

- Conflict between people is a constant issue in residence halls, organizations, teams, classes, and just about everywhere on a college campus. Conflict mediation is a skill set everyone can learn in order to communicate with one another to figure out why they are having issues. Many freshmen have never lived with someone outside of their family, therefore, being thrown into a new living situation may be difficult. Understanding difference, past experiences, and creating a community based on open communication is important for residential living as well as coexisting on a campus.
- Possible underlying issues and key issues: personality differences/types, lack of communication, need for roommate agreement or mediation, other situational factors such as being away from home might need to be addressed in this scenario.

• Example 2: Mental Health *(needed: two actors and one leader as organizational leader)* 3–5 minutes for acting: *Actor 1* comes to you, the *leader*, to let you know that a mutual friend and member of your organization seems to be experiencing high levels of anxiety and depression and has been engaging in uncharacteristic behaviors of partying and staying out all night over the last week. You know that this individual has a program they are in charge of for your organization, graduate school applications due, they have RA duty, and finals fall within the next week, and you just realized they missed the last organization meeting and the class you have together but you've been busy too so you didn't connect everything until now. You go to their room to talk with them.

- As mental health on college campuses is a major issue, leaders are having to address stress, anxiety, depression, and coping mechanisms with a healthy approach. Knowledge of campus and community resources along with creating a culture of wellness is critical for success.

- Possible underlying issues and key issues: Mental health, coping mechanisms, time management, other situational factors that should be explored, lack of communication, and emotional intelligence might be issues to address in this scenario.

2. Debrief (15–20 minutes for each scenario)

• After each scenario, facilitators will debrief, ask questions, and analyze successes and opportunities for growth within each scenario. Some questions that can be discussed: Looking back at the situation, how well was the situation handled? Are there any opportunities for growth? What do you think the intention of this scenario was? What issues came up? Could there have been any other underlying issues not addressed?

Facilitator Notes:

• *Actors' notes:* Often participants will act based on their past experiences with a particular topic, or with a current issue within the group (example: recently participants in the group have formed multiple subgroups, so the advisor may create a scenario based on how to address this issue). However, these topics can be scripted by program staff, advisor, or supervisor to ensure each issue is discussed thoroughly.

• *Facilitator notes:* Your position as facilitator will be to go through each scenario, the underlying issues involved, and to lead a dialogue with the group about anything that may have been touched on within each example. Tying in campus resources, relevant offices or community partners, and ensuring that participants understand that with most situations their job is not to solve a complex human problem, rather they should use their knowledge and skills to assist to the best of their ability.

Reference:

Evans, N. J., Forney, D. S., Guido, F. M., Patton, L. D., & Renn, K. A. (2016). *Student development in college: Theory, research, and practice* (3rd ed.). San Francisco, CA: Jossey-Bass.

Resource:

Roberts, D. C. (2007). *Deeper learning: Helping college students find the potential within.* San Francisco, CA: Jossey-Bass.

CHAPTER 10

Games

Educational games involve students actively participating in some sort of competition or achievement in relationship to a goal and provide opportunities for students to learn from the experience of play (Lopes, Fialho, Cunha, & Niveiros, 2013) and consider diverse viewpoints (Svinicki & McKeachie, 2014). Such games range in scale and modality where participants might play roles of individuals or groups in social or political situations to simulated worlds and environments (Svinicki & McKeachie, 2014) or occur in a prescribed setting where students constrained by a set of rules and procedures (e.g., Jeopardy, Family Feud, etc.) (Hsu, 1989). In any case, the chief advantage of games is that student participants are more likely "to be active participants rather than "passive observers" (Svinicki & McKeachie, 2014, p. 210), require students to make decisions, solve problems, and react to the results of their decisions, raise awareness, spark challenges, have normative implications, and are descriptive (Gibson, 2003).

GAMES IN LEADERSHIP EDUCATION

Students need to directly experience what it is like to be part of a system, particularly when educational programs represent a student's first exposure to particular leadership challenges (Lewis & Maylor, 2007). Accordingly, games in both traditional and virtual, that is, technology simulated, conditions and spaces accelerate leadership learning and offer an effective and creative approach for preparing leaders to take on new challenges (Carucci, 2009; Reeves & Malone, 2007; Reeves, Malone, & O'Driscoll, 2008). Examples range from conflict (e.g., the prisoner's dilemma, see Rapoport & Chammah, 1965) collaboration (e.g., massively multiplayer online role-playing games such as World of Warcraft, see Guthrie, Phelps, & Downey, 2011; Jenkins, Endersby, & Guthrie, 2015), and gamified learning environments (Goryunova & Jenkins, 2017) to team-based complex problem solving (e.g., The Collegiate Leadership Competition, see Allen, Jenkins, & Kri-

zanovic, 2018; Collegiate Leadership Competition, 2019).

For an in-depth review and additional resources related to the examples of games in leadership education mentioned above, see *The Role of Leadership Educators: Transforming Learning* (Guthrie & Jenkins, 2018, pp. 275–278).

References:

Allen, S. J., Jenkins, D. M., & Krizanovic, B. (2018). Exploring deliberate practice & the use of skill sheets in the collegiate leadership competition. *Journal of Leadership Education, 17*(1), 28–34.

Carucci, R. (2009). Companies rehearse a very different future: Connecting leadership capability and strategy execution through simulation. *Global Business and Organizational Excellence, 28*, 26–38.

Collegiate Leadership Competition. (2019). Collegiate leadership competition: With practice, leadership is available to all. Retrieved from https://collegiateleader.org/

Gibson, K. (2003). Games students play: Incorporating the prisoner's dilemma in teaching business ethics. *Journal of Business Ethics, 48*(1), 53–64.

Goryunova, E., & Jenkins, D. M. (2017). Global leadership education: Upping the game. *Journal of Leadership Education, 16*(4), 76–93.

Guthrie, K. L., Phelps, K., & Downey, S. (2011). Virtual environments: A developmental tool for leadership education. *Journal of Leadership Studies, 5*(2), 6–13.

Hsu, E. (1989). Role-event gaming simulation in management education: A conceptual framework and review. *Simulation & Gaming, 20*(4), 409–438.

Jenkins, D. M., Endersby, L., & Guthrie, K. L. (2015). Leadership education 2050: Changing the spaces and faces of experience. In M. Sowcik, A. C. Andenoro, M. McNutt, & S. E. Murphy (Eds.), *Leadership 2050: Critical challenges, key contexts, and emerging trends* (pp. 127–139). Bingley, England: Emerald.

Lewis, M. A., & Maylor, H. R. (2007). Game playing and operations management education. *International Journal of Production Economics, 105*, 134–149.

Lopes, M. C., Fialho, F. A. P., Cunha, C. J. C. A., & Niveiros, S. I. (2013). Business games for leadership development: A systematic review. *Simulation & Gaming, 44*(4), 523–543.

Rapoport, A., & Chammah, A.M. (1965). *Prisoner's dilemma.* Ann Arbor, MI: The University of Michigan Press.

Reeves, B., & Malone, T. (2007, June 11). *Leadership in games and at work: Implications for the enterprise of massive multiplayer online role-playing games* (Seriosity Report). Retrieved from http://www.seriosity.com

Reeves, B., Malone, T., & O'Driscoll, T. (2008). Leadership's online labs. *Harvard Business Review, 86*(5), 59–66.

Svinicki, M. D., & McKeachie, W. J. (2014). *McKeachie's teaching tips: Strategies, research, and theory for college and university teachers* (14th ed.). Belmont, CA: Wadsworth Cengage Learning.

GREEN APPLE GROUP SCRAMBLE GAME
Natalie Coers

Games, Curricular Instructional

Apples to Apples green cards provide the base for this activity to spur conversation toward effective characteristics and traits of ideal group/team members. This activity is adaptable for any size group and adjustable for class time available. If utilizing groups in a class, the activity may also be personalized to help group members understand one another in their early formation.

Learning Outcomes:

Participants will have opportunities to:

- identify traits and characteristics of effective group/team members.
- explain the role of individual traits and characteristics in group/team performance.
- discuss the impact of perceived negative traits and characteristics on group/team dynamics and performance.

Setting Up the Activity:

- Group size: Minimum of 3 participants per group
- Time: 10–20 minutes
- Materials: Apples to Apples green cards, time keeping tool

Instructions:

1. Review instructions for the game (1–3 minutes)

   - The object of this game is to assemble five green cards that best describe an ideal group/team member. Identify a dealer for the game and begin.

- Dealer shuffles and deals five green cards to each player, then places the remaining green cards in the center of the group.
- The player to the right begins by drawing a card from the deck, then discarding the card least applicable as a descriptor of themselves.
- All players take turns around the table, either picking up the top card from the discard pile or drawing a new card off the top of the deck.
- Once a player feels that the five cards in their hand adequately represent an ideal group/team member, that player places their cards on the table.
- All remaining players have one final draw to compose their final hand of traits or characteristics.
- When all players have laid down their cards, each player will share how each of the cards reflects an ideal group/team member.

2. Active game play (7–12 minutes)
3. Debrief (5–10 minutes)

   - In the game play groups, discuss the following questions:
     - What are 5–6 ideal traits or characteristics from your group hands that describe an ideal group/team member?
     - Look through your discard pile. What 2–3 cards stand out as representing perceived negative traits or characteristics of a group/team member? What implications would each trait or characteristic have on a group/team dynamic?
   - Have group(s) report out on the discussion (dependent on the number of groups participating).
   - As a large group: What traits or characteristics are missing that may better represent those of an ideal group/team member?

Facilitator Notes:

- Depending upon the number of participants for the activity, multiple Apples to Apples sets may be needed.
- If you would like to have a more specific discussion of particular traits or characteristics, you may utilize a publishing program to customize or create green Apples to Apples cards.

Resources:
Channon, S. B., Davis, R. C., Goode, N. T., & May, S. A. (2017). What makes a 'good group'? Exploring the characteristics and performance of undergraduate student groups. *Advances in Health Sciences Education, 22*(1), 17–41.

Driskell, T., Driskell, J. E., Burke, C. S., & Salas, E. (2017). Team roles: A review and integration. *Small Group Research*, 48(4), 482–511.

Lencioni, P. (2016). *The ideal team player: How to recognize and cultivate the three essential virtues*. Hoboken, NJ: Jossey-Bass.

Mattel. (n.d.). Apples to apples [Card Game].

Rego, A., Pina e. Cunha, M., & Volkmann Simpson, A. (2018). The perceived impact of leaders' humility on team effectiveness: An empirical study. *Journal of Business Ethics*, 148(1), 205–218.

Saghafian, M., & O'Neill, D. K. (2018). A phenomenological study of teamwork in online and face-to-face student teams. *Higher Education, 75*(1), 57–73.

Schulze, J., & Krumm, S. (2017). The "virtual team player": A review and initial model of knowledge, skills, abilities, and other characteristics for virtual collaboration. *Organizational Psychology Review, 7*(1), 66–95.

THE POWER OF THOUGHTFUL DIRECTIONS
Brittany Devies

Games, Cocurricular Instructional

Teamwork and common purpose are critical elements to the leadership process. This activity aims to challenge participants to fluidly move between the "leader" and "follower" roles with a common purpose of creating shapes together.

Learning Outcomes:

Participants will have opportunities to:

- increase communication skills in providing thoughtful directions to accomplish a common goal.
- use different sensory skills to accomplish the provided challenge.
- use active listening skills and attention to direction to accomplish the given task.
- learn how fluidly a leader can move between a leader role and follower role in the same activity.

Setting Up the Activity:

- Group size: 5–10 participants per group
- Time: 15–45 minutes
- Materials: rope, enough blindfolds for the number of participants present

Instructions:

1. Before the participants begin to assemble, ensure there are no physical barriers to the success of the activity. If indoors, make sure all barriers (like chairs, tables, desks, etc.) are out of the way of the facilitation space. If outdoors, check for barriers such as tree roots or uneven terrain that may be harmful to the participants when blindfolded.

2. Place the circular rope on the ground and instruct participants to gather around the circle. If you are running multiple groups, each group of 5–10 participants should have one circular rope in the center of their circle.

3. As the participants find their spot around the circle, instruct the participants to comfortably secure their blindfolds themselves. Should participants not want to be blindfolded, they are welcome to simply close their eyes.

4. The participants can then reach down and grab the rope with one or both of their hands.

5. Once every participant has secured a spot on the circular piece of rope, the facilitator can begin with the first instruction.

6. To begin the activity, one participant can remove the blindfold and open their eyes to see the rest of the group. The facilitator is welcome to pick the participant that gets to open their eyes.

7. The facilitator will then say a shape (examples listed in facilitator's notes) and tell the group to begin. Only the participant(s) without their blindfold/with their eyes open can speak and offer directions. Encourage the person offering directions to instruct their peers by name when offering directions. This activity can often help to learn and remember peer names as well.

8. Once the group achieves the first shape, ask the participant offering directions to close their eyes/secure their blindfold and ask another participant to open their eyes/take off the blindfold. Once the participants switch roles, offer another shape.

9. Repeat for as many shapes and rotations as time permits.

10. As the facilitator, take note of moments of frustration by both the participant offering directions and their peers following the directions. Also take note of moments of success and other actions/words/nonverbal communications to process in the debrief.

11. Ask the participants to set the rope back down and take off the blindfold. Thank the participants for their willingness to engage in this activity.

12. Debrief:

- What was it like to have to execute directions without being able to see? With having to solely trust one peer to help you succeed?
- What may have come up that was unexpected?
- Was this easier or more difficult than you expected? Why do you feel that way?

Facilitator Notes:

- This activity as it is written involves physical movement. As the facilitator, please accommodate this activity to best meet the needs of the participant. The activity can be adapted to be sitting down, done with everyone's eyes open, or in different physical spaces.
- While the activity is written to have one participant with their eyes open to the group, the facilitator is welcome to have several participants with their eyes open offering directions. This can be useful in cases where participants may not feel comfortable sharing aloud on their own or in seeing how small groups of participants work together.
- Some examples of shapes that have been effective in this activity (in order of perceived difficulty): square, rectangle, house, star, person.

USING A VIDEO GAME FOR LEARNING ETHICAL DECISION MAKING
Virginia L. Byrne

Games, Technology Enhanced

Learners will play a game for learning about ethical decision making, integrity, and personal values. This games-based learning activity provides learners with a real-life simulation of the Nazi Occupation in which they will evaluate the situation and make decisions that have significant consequences for within the game. By practicing ethical reasoning and decision making in the game, participants learn within a realistic context that raises the stakes while still allowing them the freedom to play and tinker with their ideas.

Learning Outcomes:

Participants will have opportunities to:

- consider an ethical dilemma and the values which are at odds.
- articulate how the ethical choices of individuals impact the greater society.

Setting Up the Activity:

- Group size: Depends on the number of licenses for the game. Participants can work in pairs and make decisions together or individually can go through the simulation
- Time: 3 hours with prior reading and writing assignment after game
- Materials: Access to a computer or tablet with the game and internet, headphones, paper, and writing utensil.

Instructions:

1. Prereading on ethical decision making and integrity, for example:

   - Chapter on leading with integrity from *Exploring Leadership* (Komives, Lucas, & McMahon, 2013).
   - Chapter on ethical dilemmas from *Leadership: Theory and Practice* (Northouse, 2019).

2. Participants discuss readings in pairs with questions (5–10 minutes)

   - What is the difference between an ethical dilemma versus moral temptation?
   - What values are in tension during ethical dilemmas? That is, short term versus long term, justice versus mercy, individual versus community, truth versus loyalty.
   - What commonly used principles for ethical decision making (e.g., ends-based thinking, rules-based thinking, and care-based thinking) do you use most often?

3. As a whole class, discuss the small-group questions (5 – 10 minutes)
4. Game Set-up (5 minutes)

   - Explain that learners will practice ethical decision making through a game. Provide an overview of the game. They will have 15 minutes to explore the initial stages of the game. Provide a trigger warning.
   - Distribute tablets or assign participants to computers with the game already loaded. If needed, group participants.

5. Learners play *Attentat 1942* (15 minutes)
6. Discussion (5 minutes)

   - Instruct participants to stop playing and move into their earlier small groups to discuss the following questions:

    ◦ What ethical dilemmas are present in the game so far?

    ◦ What are the ethical tensions facing you and the other main characters?

7. Play (1 hour 15 minutes)

- Ask participants to quickly complete the game. Encourage participants to jot down notes about connections to course content.
- If in a 50-minute course: Ask participants to complete the game for homework or arrange for another class period to play.

8. Facilitator leaders a whole-class discussion with pair & shares (15 minutes)

- Within the game, how did you practice integrity?
  - ◦ What characters stood out to you as practicing integrity?
  - ◦ Who stood out for not practicing integrity?
- Why is ethical decision making essential to leadership?

9. Provide a writing assignment that encourages them to use the content to make meaning of the ethical dilemma in the game. For example, "Reflect on if Operation Arthropoid—Heydrich's assassination—was worth the outcomes. Support your argument with course content." Then, encourage participants to reflect on what they have learned about their own ethical decision-making framework.

10. After participants have completed their assignment, debrief the game with the following questions:

- How did it feel to play this game?
- What course concepts did you see play out in the game?
- Was Operation Arthropoid worth the outcomes?

Facilitator Notes:

- While there are plenty of great games for learning available, Attentat 1942 is a meaningful and engaging game that can aid adult participants in learning about integrity. Attentat 1942 is an interactive narrative video game about the Nazi occupation. The game contains wartime violence; therefore, facilitators should provide a trigger warning to notify their participants of the gravity of the subject matter. The game takes about 1 hour and 30 minutes to complete. Attentat 1942 costs approximately $10.99.

Learn more at https://store.steampowered.com/app/676630/Attentat_1942

- Before introducing a game to participants, play the game or complete the simulation yourself. Enjoy this opportunity to find potential teachable moments within the game. Also use this opportunity to identify any areas that may potentially confuse your participants so that you can address these first.
- Determine how you will pay for and install the program on the tablets or computers.
- Recruit a technologically savvy person to be available in class when you want to implement the game.
- If you choose different reading assignments, remember to update the reading discussion questions in Step 2.

References:

Komives, S., Lucas, N., & McMahon, T. (2013). *Exploring leadership: For college students who want to make a difference* (3rd ed.). San Francisco, CA: Jossey-Bass.

Northouse, P. (2019). *Leadership: Theory and practice* (8th ed.). Thousand Oaks, CA: SAGE.

Resources:

Buy Attentat 1942. (2017, October 31). Retrieved from https://store.steampowered.com/app/676630/Attentat_1942

Gee, J. P. (2003). What video games have to teach us about learning and literacy. *Computers in Entertainment*, 1(1), 1–4.

Prensky, M. (2007). *Digital game-based learning* (Paragon House ed.). St. Paul, MN: Paragon House.

Schrier, K. (2015). EPIC: A framework for using video games in ethics education. *Journal of Moral Education*, 44(4), 393–424.

Shaffer, D. W., Squire, K. R., Halverson, R., & Gee, J. P. (2005). Video games and the future of learning. *Phi Delta Kappan Magazine*, 87(2), 105–111.

FIVE TYPES OF FOLLOWERS AND YOU
Ali Raza

Games, Followership Focused

In this learning activity, participants will have the opportunity to identify the five types of followers as described by Kellerman (2008), synthesize each follower-type by working together in small and large groups, and showcase their findings through a presentation to the large classroom. This learning activity tests participants' understanding of the five types of followers through various learning styles and gives presenters an opportunity to learn from one another and receive feedback from peers. This exercise will further assist in helping participants negotiate a potential elitist view of leadership that is often paired with a conformist view of followership by illustrating the importance of followers (Raffo, 2013).

Learning Outcomes:

Participants will have opportunities to:

- identify terminology and learn about the five types of followership: (a) isolate; (b) bystander; (c) participant; (d) activist; and (e) diehard.
- work together to synthesize learned material in small and large groups and have a better understanding of group dynamics.
- present group findings and receive feedback from their peers and facilitator(s).

Setting Up the Activity:

- Group size: 15–20 participants (small groups of 3–4 participants will be formed)
- Time: 50 minutes
- Material: 5 large sheets of flip chart paper, assorted markers

Instructions:

1. Divide participants into five separate groups of 3–4 people.
2. Once the groups have formed, facilitator will spend time to explain the learning activity offers an opportunity for each group to identify, discuss, and synthesize one of the five types of followers as outlined in the Kellerman (2008) reading. Each group should brainstorm and write thoughts on their follower type on the flip chart paper. (5 minutes)
3. Describe parameters for the activity, including: ground rules, random assignment of follower type,

prompt of questions to consider, usage of flip chart paper in group, length of time, expectation of each group member's participation in the activity, and presentation to the large class, followed by the large-class debrief.

4. Request that each group picks up one flip chart paper and one set of markers.
5. If space allows, encourage groups to spread out and utilize the environment accordingly.
6. Each group will be given time to identify, discuss, and synthesize their follower type verbally with their thoughts written on the flip chart paper. (15 minutes)
7. Once 15 minutes is up, each group will then have time to present their findings. (3–5 minutes)
8. After each group presentation, the large class will have an opportunity to ask questions.
9. Following all presentations, the facilitator will move into the debrief phase of the activity. Questions may include and are not limited to:

- How did your group synthesize your assigned follower type? What examples came up?
- Did your group discuss any of the other follower types? If so, what did that look like?
- What role did each person play in the group? How was each role determined?
- What challenges, if any, did your group have throughout this process?
- Why is it important to understand each type of follower?
- What does followership mean to you?
- What is the relationship between being follower-focused and leadership?

Facilitator Notes:

- Questions may come up following each group's presentation on their respective follower type. The facilitator may choose to address aforementioned questions in the moment or wait until the allocated time for debriefing. The debrief is meant to connect the dots of the five types of followers, raise missing points, and allow participants to think more critically about this topic.
- This activity requires facilitator and participants to have some knowledge of Kellerman (2008) and her text. Number of participants and space limitations may result in adjusting aspects of the activity. This activity is group-work oriented, so it is recommended that the facilitator move around the room and pay attention to the dynamics of each group as well as how each individual contributes. Leave room for silence in the processing of the debrief. Highlight the connection between Kellerman's (2008) five types of followers and the participants' day-to-day

life. Mentally track responses given and participation based on gender and other social identities. Provide an assessment for participants to complete at the end or create a 1-page sheet highlighting the content discussed in the activity. Follow-up with participants in a subsequent class session.

References:

Kellerman, B. (2008). *Followership: How followers are creating change and changing leaders*. Boston, MA: Harvard Business School Press.

Raffo, D. M. (2013). Teaching followership in leadership education. *Journal of Leadership Education*, 12(1), 262–273.

PERFECT STORM
Cara Lucia

Games, Curricular Learning Assessment

In the game "Perfect Storm," players facilitate different motions as part of a large group demonstrating the variety of roles group members fill (game adapted from Burrington, Project Adventure Staff, Project Adventure Inc., Staff, 1995). When players choose to deemphasize the focus on self and engage with others, players are able to see what is possible of a large group (Burber, 1958; Komives, Lucas, & McMahon, 2007; National Invitational Leadership Symposium, 1991). The main purpose of this game is to reflect on the role of leader and follower and demonstrate the impact a large group has in making meaningful change.

Learning Outcomes:

Participants will have opportunities to:

- distinguish between positional leader and follower.
- articulate the difference between self and others as an effective group member regardless of role (leader or follower) in a large group.
- experience creating a storm to demonstrate the impact a large group has in making meaningful change.
- learn about the importance of groups having a common purpose.

Setting Up the Activity:

- Group size: 20 or more
- Time: 20–30 minutes

- Materials: Large enough space for 20+ people to stand

Instructions:

1. Select four players to be storm leaders. One leader will rub their hands together (quiet wind or mist), the next will snap (raindrops) their fingers, the third will clap (heavy rain) their hands loudly and the fourth will stomp (thunder) their feet. The storm leaders are the only players aware that the large group is making a storm. (4 minutes)

2. Inform each leader that they will begin their motion when you tap their shoulder, they will continue this motion until you tap their shoulder for them to stop. (2 minutes)

3. After giving the directions to the storm leaders, you, the facilitator will have the remaining players count off by fours. All of the "ones" will go to the leader rubbing their hands, all of the "twos" will go to the leader snapping their fingers, all of the "threes" will go to the leader clapping their hands and all of the "fours" will go to the leader who is stomping their feet. All of the players will line up facing their leader in a single file line. (4 minutes)

4. Before starting the activity, encourage the players to keep quiet during the activity. Any noises not part of the activity will take away from the ability to create the sound of a storm. (2 minutes)

5. You, the facilitator, will remind all of the players to follow the actions of the leader. Inform the players that they will only move and do the activity of their leader when their leader is completing the movement. (2 minutes)

6. Begin the activity by first tapping the shoulder of the leader who is responsible for rubbing their hands together. Count 5 seconds and tap the shoulder of the leader who is responsible for snapping their fingers. Count another 5 seconds and tap the shoulder of the leader who is responsible for clapping their hands. Count another 5 seconds and tap the shoulder of the leader who is responsible for stomping their feet. As more and more players begin their movement, it will sound like a torrential downpour. Every player should now be following their leader by completing his or her movement. (4 minutes)

7. When you get through tapping each leader, start doing the whole process backwards again to make the room quieter and have the thunder turn into a slight drizzle—the storm is slowly ending. You, the facilitator, will count 5 seconds and tap on the shoulder of the leader stomping their feet. Count another 5 seconds and tap the shoulder of the leader clapping their hands. Count another 5 seconds and tap the shoulder of the leader snapping

their fingers. Count another 5 seconds and tap the shoulder of the leader rubbing their hands, making it sound like the last few moments of a storm. (4 minutes)

8. Debrief with questions:

    •   What do you believe this activity represents (question for the players who were not leaders)? If the group is having a difficult time, ask descriptive questions such as, what did the activity sound like? Once the group has figured it out or is close discuss how the players came together to make the storm (discuss the roles of leader and follower).
    •   How did the players who were not storm leaders feel not knowing initially why they were rubbing hands, snapping, clapping, or stomping? Did you need to know the purpose? Do you think the storm would have been stronger if the leaders had shared the purpose?
    •   What can we accomplish together as a group versus as an individual?

Facilitator Notes:

•   The author of this learning activity used the metaphor of the "perfect storm" to be fitting for the game. However, many other metaphors could be used in its place (e.g., rainmaker, monsoon, raining cats and dogs, torrential downpour). Facilitators should use a metaphor that is relatable to participants. To assess participants' learning the facilitator along with the participants playing the game will reflect on the experience and collectively make meaning of the activity based on the relevancy to the group (e.g., curricular or cocurricular experience).

References:

Buber, M. (1958). *I and thou*. New York, NY: Harper & Row.

Burrington, B., Project Adventure Staff, & Project Adventure Inc. Staff. (1995). *Youth leadership in action: A guide to cooperative games and group activities*. Dubuque, IA: Kendall/Hunt.

Komives, S. R., Lucas, N., & McMahon, T. R. (2013). *Exploring leadership: For college students who want to make a difference* (3rd ed.). San Francisco, CA: Jossey Bass.

National Invitational Leadership Symposium. (1991). *Proceedings from the 1991 National Invitational Leadership Symposium*. College Park, MD: National Clearinghouse for Leadership Programs.

GAME CHANGE MANAGEMENT
Michael Miller

Games, Cocurricular Learning Assessment

Leaders must deal with rapidly changing conditions. For many, making positive change happen in their organizations is central to their definition of leadership. Therefore, leadership educators seek to help learners not only understand the importance of creating change in organizations but more importantly to help them become adaptable with managing changing conditions overall.

Learning Outcomes:

Participants will have opportunities to:

•   "feel" the impact of change in a simulated busy environment.
•   experience ways that changing conditions can sidetrack work toward goals.
•   activate schema to better understand change/change-management theories.
•   better understand how adaptability is an essential leadership skill.

Setting Up the Activity:

•   Group size: This activity can be scaled to work with almost all group sizes; however, 20 or more is best
•   Time: 30–45 minutes
•   Materials: Scratch paper, 8.5" x 11" piece of paper, pens, a prize for the winner (optional), timer for the facilitator, sound amplification (with a larger group)

Instructions:

1. Explain that participants will play a series of tic-tac-toe-games using scratch paper. Briefly remind them of the rules of tic tac toe: in pairs, choosing who will go first, and using a "hash tag" as the playing board, one player marks with an "X," the other with an "O," the winner is the player with three of their marks in a row, across, up and down, or diagonally. (1 minute)
2. Ask participants to create a score sheet by numbering 1 to 5 on their scratch paper. (30 seconds)
3. Inform them that they will be playing in timed rounds and that they must change players after each game, writing their total number of wins for each round on the score sheet next to that round's number. Allow for any questions to make sure participants fully understand. (1 minute)

4. Instruct participants that on facilitator's count of three, participants will begin playing Round 1. Remind participants to note the number games they won on their score sheets. (3 minutes with final warning at 30 seconds)

5. Round 2, instruct participants they will play *silently*. Round begins on the facilitator's count to three. (3 minutes with final warning at 30 seconds) Remind participants to note the number of games they won for Round Two on their score sheet.

6. Ask participants to prepare for Round 3, telling them they will play *with no use of pens*, but may speak. (4 minutes with final warning at 30 seconds) Remind participants to note the number of games they won for Round Three on the score sheet.

7. Ask participants to prepare for Round 4, telling them that they will play *with no use of paper/pens*. Round begins on facilitator's count to three. (5 minutes with final warning at 30 seconds) Remind participants to note the number of games they won for Round 4 on the score sheet.

8. Ask participants to prepare for Round 5 telling them that they will play with pairs playing *back to back*. Round will begin on facilitator's count to three. (5 minutes with final warning at 30 seconds) Remind participants to note the number of games they won for Round 5 on the score sheet.

9. Ask participants to multiply scores for each round by that round's number. Round 1 is multiplied by two, Round 2 by two, et cetera. Participants add multiplied scores to gain a Final Score. (1 minute)

10. Determine the winner by deducing from who has the highest final score. This may be accomplished by asking participants to raise their hand if they score 10 or more, then 15 or more, until the highest score is determined. If desired, award the highest scorer the prize. (2–3 minutes)

Facilitator Notes:

- Participants enjoy the game, but are usually frustrated. Surfacing emotions is important, as having participants feel the impact of change is central to the activity's purpose.

- Facilitators can use the activity to underscore that in leadership: change is constant; advances in technology will serve to increase the rapidity of change in all fields, adaptability and ability to transfer skills are important leader attributes.

- Do not let participants know that the rules change. Facilitator should keep those details from the participants until the beginning of each round. Facilitator may vary the times for each round. Keep the activity moving quickly with a light-hearted, fun approach!

Resources:

Kotter, J., & Cohen, D. (2012). *The heart of change.* Boston, MA: Harvard Business Review Press.

Higher Education Research Institute. (1996). *A social change model of leadership development: Guidebook version III.* College Park, MD: National Clearinghouse for Leadership Programs.

Hughes, B. (2018). How technology is rapidly changing the way things get done across industries. *Entrepreneur.* Retrieved from https://www.entrepreneur.com/article/288025

CHAPTER 11

Arts-Based Learning

Arts-based learning refers to any instructional strategy that uses art as a medium to support knowledge development in subjects other than art (Rieger & Chernomas, 2013). In this approach, active learning is fostered through partaking in or reflectively investigating art (Rieger & Chernomas, 2013). Moreover, arts-based learning facilitates the development of critical thinking skills, creativity, and emotional intelligence (Casey, 2009; Jack, 2012; MacDonnell & MacDonald, 2011; McGarry & Aubeeluck, 2013; Price et al., 2007). When students engaging in arts-based learning, they gain the ability to express and understand ineffable human experiences through its symbolic language (Blomqvist, Pitkala, & Routasalo, 2007; Jack, 2012). Correspondingly, practitioners require these skills to understand the complex nature of human experience (Jack, 2012; Rieger & Chernomas, 2013). It is no surprise that disciplines such as allied health and the medical professions (Lake, Jackson, & Hardman, 2015; Ousager & Johannessen, 2010), literacy and language arts (Dover, 2016), and social work and social care (Hafford-Letchfield et al., 2008) have embraced arts-based learning. As such, various art forms can be used for arts-based learning, including narratives (Rieger & Chernomas, 2013), visual art (Casey, 2009; Price et al., 2007), music (Pavill, 2011), creative writing (MacDonnell & MacDonald, 2011), drama (McGarry & Aubeeluck, 2013), and poetry (Lapum et al., 2011).

ARTS-BASED LEARNING IN LEADERSHIP EDUCATION

Arts-based leadership education is situated within the framework of experiential learning as knowledge creation through the transformation of experience, i.e., "skills transfer," where participants reveal inner thoughts and feelings that may not be accessible through more conventional developmental modes (Kolb, 1984; Taylor & Ladkin, 2009). Its value in leadership education is present in a variety of applications ranging from integration (Sutherland, 2013) and intervention (Romanowska, Larsson, & Theorell, 2013) to

creation (Wicks & Rippin, 2010) and interpretation (Purg & Walravens, 2015); utilizing music (Emiliani & Emiliani, 2012), literature (Loughman & Finley, 2010), and theater (Soumerai & Mazer, 2006), as well as many other art forms (see Katz-Buonincontro, 2015). Respectively, it is most often applied through two approaches: (a) constructivist, where the participant is engaged in the artistic creative process and aware of the direct, personal, sensed experience the material provokes or initiates (e.g., playing or composing music, acting, and creating visual art) (Springborg, 2010); and (b) constructivist-interpretivist, both a projective and reflective approach which emphasizes participants' personal relevance and understanding, i.e., learning in meaningful contexts (e.g., film and television, visual arts, music, and literature) (Willis, 1995).

For a variety of examples of arts-based learning in leadership education ranging from music and podcasts to improvisational theater and the visual arts, see *The Role of Leadership Educators: Transforming Learning* (Guthrie & Jenkins, 2018, pp. 285–298).

References:

Blomqvist, L., Pitkala, K., & Routasalo, P. (2007). Images of loneliness: Using art as an educational method in professional training. *The Journal of Continuing Education in Nursing, 38,* 89–93.

Casey, B. (2009). Arts-based inquiry in nursing education. *Contemporary Nurse, 32*(1–2), 69–82.

Dover, A. G. (2016). Teaching for social justice and the common core: Justice-oriented curriculum for language arts and literacy. *Journal of Adolescent & Adult Literacy, 59*(6), 517–527.

Emiliani, M. L., & Emiliani, M. (2013). Music as a framework to better understand Lean leadership. *Leadership & Organization Development Journal, 34*(5), 407–426.

Guthrie, K. L., & Jenkins, D. M. (2018). *The role of leadership educators: Transforming learning.* Charlotte, NC: Information Age.

Hafford-Letchfield, T., Couchman, W., Harries, B., Downer, J., Jackson, R., Khisa, C., … Douglas, T. (2008, January). *Using arts-based methods to develop service user led learning materials for social work education.* Paper presented at the IRISS International Conference Proceedings, Edinburgh. Retrieved

July 1, 2016, from http://content.iriss.org.uk/pepe2008/files/731_paper.pdf

Jack, K. (2012). "Putting the words 'I am sad', just doesn't quite cut it sometimes": The use of art to promote emotional awareness in nursing students. *Nurse Education Today, 32,* 811–816.

Kolb, D. (1984). *Experiential learning: Experience as the source of learning and development.* Upper Saddle River, NJ: Prentice Hall.

Lake, J., Jackson, L., & Hardman, C. (2015). A fresh perspective on medical education: The lens of the arts. *Medical Education, 49*(8), 759–772.

Lapum, J., Hamzavi, N., Veljkovic, K., Mohamed, Z., Pettinato, A., Silver, S., & Taylor, E. (2011). A performative and poetical narrative of critical social theory in nursing education: An ending and threshold of justice. *Nursing Philosophy, 13,* 27–45.

Loughman, T., & Finley, J. (2010). Beowulf and the teaching of leadership. *Journal of Leadership Education, 9*(1), 155–164.

MacDonnell, J. A., & MacDonald, G. J. (2011). Arts-based critical inquiry in nursing and interdisciplinary professional education: Guided imagery, images, narratives, and poetry. *Journal of Transformative Education, 9,* 203–221.

McGarry, J., & Aubeeluck, A. (2013). A different drum: An arts-based educational program. *Nursing Science Quarterly, 26,* 267–273.

Ousager, J., & Johannessen, H. (2010). Humanities in undergraduate medical education: A literature review. *Academic Medicine, 85*(6), 988–998.

Pavill, B. (2011). Fostering creativity in nursing students: A blending of nursing and the arts. *Holistic Nursing Practice, 25,* 17–25.

Price, S., Arbuthnot, E., Benoit, R., Landry, D., Landry, M., & Butler, L. (2007). The art of nursing: Communication and self-expression. *Nursing Science Quarterly, 20,* 155–160.

Purg, D., & Walravens, A. (2015). Arts and leadership: Vision and practice at the IEDC-BLED school of management. *Journal of Leadership Studies, 9*(1), 42–47.

Rieger, K. L., & Chernomas, W. M. (2013). Arts-based learning: Analysis of the concept for nursing education. *International Journal of Nursing Education Scholarship, 10,* 1–10.

Romanowska, J., Larsson, G., & Theorell, T. (2013). Effects on leaders of an art-based leadership intervention. *Journal of Management Development, 32*(9), 1004–1022.

Soumerai, E. N., & Mazer, R. (2006). Arts-based leadership: Theatrical tributes. *New Directions for Youth Development, 109,* 117–124.

Springborg, C. (2010). Leadership as art—Leaders coming to their senses. *Leadership, 6*(3), 243–258.

Sutherland, I. (2013). Arts-based methods in leadership development: Affording aesthetic workspaces, reflexivity and memories with momentum. *Management Learning, 44*(1), 25–43.

Taylor, S. S., & Ladkin, D. (2009). Understanding arts-based methods in managerial development. *Academy of Management Learning & Education, 8*(1), 55–69.

Wicks, P. G., & Rippin, A. (2010) Art as experience: An inquiry into art and leadership using dolls and doll-making. *Leadership, 6*(3), 259–278.

Willis, J. (1995). Recursive, reflective instructional design model based on constructivist-interpretivist theory. *Educational Technology, 35*(6), 5–23.

THE MIRROR EXERCISE: "FOLLOW THE FOLLOWER"
Chris Esparza

Art, Curricular Instructional

Leadership effectiveness includes the ability to create positive, connective relationships with and between others. In this learning activity, partners build a shared experience by exchanging between "leader" and "follower" roles. One participant leads while the other mirrors (or imitates) the action simultaneously. The pair periodically takes turns leading and following until they finally attempt to move together with both leading and following at the same time.

Learning Outcomes:

Participants will have opportunities to:

- broaden understanding of leadership (and followership) as a fluid, interactional, and shared experience.
- reinforce leadership as a process that involves centering one's attention, presence and connection with others.
- increase understanding of collaboration and synergy as tools for building trust.

Setting Up the Activity:

- Group size: Any size group (even number needed as it is done in pairs)
- Time: 15–20 minutes
- Materials: None

Instructions:

1. Ask participants to form in pairs. Ask each pair to identify a "leader" and a "follower." Ensure pairs are facing each other, unobstructed by other people or objects. (1 minute)
2. Inform participants that this exercise will be played silently. Explain that any movement the leader makes, the follower will imitate as if they are a mirror image. For example, if the leader moves their right hand, the follower will move their left as they face the leader. (1 minute)

3. Announce "go" for participants to begin. The leader starts by creating their own unique movements. The follower's aim is to fully mirror these movements—anything and everything the leader does. (2 minutes)

4. Instruct followers to "just follow what the leader is doing. Reflect as strongly as possible every movement by your partner." Additional coaching might include: "Be as simultaneous as you can." "Focus on your partner 100%. Head to toe. Whole body."

5. After a minute or two, instruct the pairs to switch roles (switch the lead). Call out "switch" and explain that pairs should switch the leader role without resetting the movement. The new leader continues from wherever the previous leader left off.

6. Repeat the process 3–5 times—calling "switch" each time to cue the pairs to switch leader and follower roles again and again.

7. After several switches, instruct pairs to pass the lead back and forth at their own discretion (i.e., without the facilitator or pair calling switch). Partners are to mirror each other's movements without explicitly declaring a leader or a follower. At this point, the pair should rely on their own nonverbal communication to share the leader-follower roles.

8. Ultimately, the goal is for pairs to reach a point where they themselves are unsure who is leading and who is following—a point where they are spontaneously creating movements collaboratively and with no preconceived agenda.

9. Debrief with questions:

   • Were you more comfortable leading or following? Why?
   • What happened as the exercise progressed—particularly after I stopped calling "switch"?
   • What kind of risks did you take together?
   • How did you limit yourself? Did judgment (of self or other) enter at any point?
   • Who was responsible for the communication? Who was responsible for ensuring understanding?
   • What are the characteristics of a good leader?
   • What are the characteristics of a good follower?
   • What does this exercise reveal about the leader-follower relationship and process?

Facilitator Notes:

• This exercise can be used to unpack communication, presence and focus, empathy, and the power of reinforcing what someone is doing. It provides opportunities for participants to explore ways to build a shared experience with others. It requires a non-judgmental approach and centering one's attention to their partner.

• This exercise has many variations and coaching interventions:

   ○ Increasing the ambiguity: One variation is for the facilitator to call switch in increasingly shortened time spans—reaching a point where switch is called every few seconds so as to confuse pairs about who is supposed to be leading and following.

   ○ Increasing the focus: If the facilitator wants to raise the stakes, they can suggest that they will move about the room attempting to detect which partner is the leader and which is the follower. The objective for the pairs is to be so much in sync that the facilitator will not be able to identify the leader. When pairs are in sync, improvisers often refer to this as "following the follower."

   ○ Increasing the difficulty: If it seems that several pairs have started to master shared movement, invite them to heighten and explore their movements together. They can try to step away from each other or move from their spot in the room, they can attempt to turn around, they can incorporate more body parts and/or facial expressions (often pairs start with only their arms); they can attempt to increase their speed—going faster without losing their partner along the way; et cetera.

   ○ Coaching tip—slow it down: One of the most common coaching tips is to suggest that leaders slow down. A key tenet of improvisation is: make your partner look good. In this exercise, encourage participants to take care of one another (helping each other look like expert "mirrors"). If the follower cannot keep up with the leader, it is the leader's responsibility to slow down. Other leaders may inadvertently lose their followers by trying to be clever or introducing outlandish physicality.

   ○ Coaching tip—noticing: When at the point of switching on their own, the facilitator can encourage pairs by suggesting: "Notice if you're the leader … and follow. If you're leading—become the follower. Notice if you're initiating."

Resources:

Alda, A. (2017). *If I understood you, would I have this look on my face?* New York, NY: Random House.

Leonard, K., & Yorton, T. (2015). *Yes, and: How improvisation reverses "no, but" thinking and improves creativity and collaboration.* New York, NY: HarperCollins.

Spolin, V. (1999). *Improvisation for the theater: A handbook of teaching and directing techniques.* Evanston, IL: Northwestern University Press.

THEATER OF BAD LEADERSHIP
Sally R. Watkins

Art, Cocurricular Instructional

This learning activity offers participants the opportunity to connect their learning to lived experiences (hooks, 1994) as they work collaboratively to develop a one-act play. Participants will recall the seven types of bad leadership as defined by Kellerman (2004), develop participant learning artifacts in the form of one-act plays or scenes representative of each type of bad leadership, and finally, act out the scene for their peers. The "audience" is offered the opportunity to articulate their comprehension of Kellerman's (2004) types of bad leadership in a structured debrief of scenes.

Learning Outcomes:

Participants will have opportunities to:

- recall terminology associated with bad leadership and apply the concepts to situations imagined or pulled from personal experiences.
- engage in and observe group development.
- provide critical feedback to their peers.

Setting Up the Activity:

- Group size: Small groups of 3–5
- Time: 30– 60 minutes
- Materials: Facilitator-provided props optional

Instructions:

1. Divide participants into groups of three to five individuals.
2. Explain "Theater of Bad Leadership" (often said in an overly dramatic voice) as an opportunity to be writers, actors, and directors in a one-act play.
3. Prior to assigning each group a type of bad leadership, address any ground rules such as length of scene, use of props, and other parameters you as facilitator would like to include. Optional: To add some complexity, the facilitator may assign roles such as director, writer, and leading role to the individual group members allowing for discussion on positional leadership as well as individual contributions to the leadership process. (3–5 minutes)
4. Assign each group one of the seven types of bad leadership and ask the groups to withhold their specific type of bad leadership from the larger group.

5. If your physical space allows, offer the opportunity for groups to move into different spaces to plan, write, and practice their scene. (10 minutes)
6. Bring the individual groups back together and set the scene for the opening night of Theater of Bad Leadership. Invite the first group to the stage and once they are set call, "Action!"
7. Following each play, allow the audience to guess the type of bad leadership portrayed and let the actors reveal if the audience is correct.
8. Repeat this cycle until all groups have taken the stage.
9. Debrief with questions:

   - How well did the group define your type of bad leadership?
   - How did the group come to consensus when writing your scene?
   - Were the scenes rooted in lived experiences? How so?
   - Did you discuss other types of bad leadership to develop your scene?
   - How did it feel to be "on stage"?
   - Was it challenging to develop a scene without props, incorporating the props, or identifying props?
   - How is the activity representative of the leadership process?

Facilitator Notes:

- The facilitator may choose to debrief this activity between each play and/or following the last show. Facilitator might also offer each small group the opportunity to debrief as a group while on stage with the audience viewing this part of the activity. As noted by Guthrie and Jenkins (2018), debriefing encourages learners' contextualization of their learning via purposeful questioning and intentional reflection subsequent to a learning activity.
- The smaller the acting groups, the easier it is to assess individual contributions to the scene and individual mastery of the concepts.
- To accomplish an individual assessment, the facilitator might ask participants to complete a 1-minute paper on how one or more of the types of bad leadership have shaped their experiences as a leader or follower? The success of their club or organization? In another team setting? This paper could be done at the start of the session to prime participants for scene development or it can be the concluding aspect of the session.

References:
hooks, b. (1994). *Teaching to transgress: Education as the practice of freedom.* New York, NY: Routledge.

Guthrie, K. L., & Jenkins, D. M. (2018). *The role of leadership educators: Transforming* learning. Charlotte, NC: Information Age.

Kellerman, B. (2004). *Bad leadership: What it is, how it happens, why it matters.* Boston, MA: Harvard Business School Press.

LEADERSHIP: CHANGING THE NARRATIVE
Natasha H. Chapman and Naliyah Kaya

Art, Technology Enhanced

This learning activity will promote the critical examination of dominant narratives of leadership using multimedia and classroom discussion. Participants will explore the role socialization has played in the way they understand leadership and consider leadership as a social construction. They will bring to center their own lived experiences to affirm, confirm, critique, or question the narratives about leadership they receive. Participants will interrogate digital images with classmates and collectively coconstruct meaning around leadership.

Learning Outcomes:

Participants will have opportunities to:

- critically examine conventional notions of leadership.
- collectively explore counternarratives of leadership through digital artifacts.

Setting Up the Activity:

- Group size: 10–25 participants.
- Time: 1 hour 15 minutes–1 hour 30 minutes
- Materials: Computer and projector, dry erase board/chalkboard and corresponding writing utensils, videos showing counternarratives of leadership (those that come from the vantage point of those who have been historically marginalized—recommendations are provided in the instruction section), participants personal smartphones, tablets, or laptops

Instructions:

1. Word association (20 minutes)

    - Ask participants to share words or images that come to mind when they think of "leader". Document participant responses in a visual way (i.e., dry erase board, poster paper).
    - Ask participants to share words or images that come to mind when they think of "leadership". Document participant responses in a visual way.
    - Discussion Prompts:
        o What themes are you noticing in your responses to the terms "leader" and "leadership"? Do they reflect the ways you have actually observed or experienced leadership? In what ways do the themes reflect the leaders you know in your life? What experiences have you had that challenge the themes that emerged in this activity?
        o Where do these leadership associations—assumptions, beliefs, or ideas—come from? What social context were you born into that informs your understanding of leadership? Who helped to shape your expectations about leaders and leadership? What did you learn about leadership from social institutions (i.e. school, church, media, organizations, work)? What messages did you receive about leadership? What experiences did you have that challenged or affirmed these messages?

2. Google search (30 minutes)

    - Next, ask participants to Google the terms "leader" and "leadership" on their smartphones or laptops and to describe the images they are seeing. Document their observations in a visual way.
    - Discussion prompts
        o What themes are you noticing in your Google search of the terms "leader" and "leadership"? Do they confirm or contradict your personal word associations with the terms? Do they reflect the ways you have actually observed or experienced leadership? What experiences have you had that challenge the themes that emerged in your search?
        o For whom do these images benefit in our society? Who do they exclude or disadvantage? How is power situated? In what context(s) are the images presented?

3. Counternarrative Examples (40 minutes)

    - Identify one or more videos that challenge conventional notions of leadership (such as those that emerged in earlier activities) to introduce the utility of counternarratives in complicating leadership learning and highlighting leadership as a social construction. Several examples of counternarratives are provided below:

- ○ Radical Monarchs (3:59 minutes): http://radicalmonarchs.org/support-us/
- ○ Video project 562 (4:12 minutes): https://www.youtube.com/watch?v=GIzYzz3rEZU
- ○ Young Women's Freedom Center (8:08 minutes): https://www.youtube.com/watch?v=_9VRjZRLXoc
- ○ Building a Caring America: TEDxMiddlebury (12:25 minutes): https://www.youtube.com/watch?v=ColFFPNgtK4
- ○ This LA Musician Built $1,200 Tiny Houses for the Homeless. Then the City Seized Them (14:03 minutes): https://www.youtube.com/watch?v=n6h7fL22WCE

4. Discussion prompts

- How/is leadership captured in this video? Who are the leaders? Is the form of leadership depicted legitimized? If so, by whom is it legitimized?
- How is power situated? Is there a distinction between leader and follower? If so, what is the role of the follower? Is leadership demonstrated collectively? If so, what is the process for decision making?
- What roles do identity and context play in this video?
- How do these counternarratives challenge, expand, or replicate traditional notions about leadership?
- How have these learning activities changed, expanded, or challenged your definitions and beliefs about leadership?

Facilitator Notes:

- Consider the developmental readiness of participants in group. If participants have already had similar conversations about what leadership is, you may want to begin with the second exercise.
- Speak to your own assumptions and biases about leadership. Acknowledge the lens that you bring to this work and that it is your intent to challenge traditional notions of leadership that perpetuate systems of domination.

Resources:

Radical Monarchs. (2016, February 15). *Radical Monarchs fundraising video* [Video file]. Retrieved from http://radicalmonarchs.org/support-us/

ReasonTV. (2016, December 9). *This LA musician built $1,200 tiny houses for the homeless. Then the city seized them* [Video file]. Retrieved from https://www.youtube.com/watch?v=n6h7fL22WCE

TEDx. (2013, August 18). *Building a caring America: Ai-jen Poo at TEDxMiddlebury* [Video file]. Retrieved from https://www.youtube.com/watch?v=ColFFPNgtK4

TEDx. (2014, July 23). *Changing the way we see Native Americans | Matika Wilbur | TEDxTeachersCollege* [Video file]. Retrieved from https://www.youtube.com/watch?v=GIzYzz3rEZU

Young Womens Freedom Center. (2018, January 18). *Young Women's Freedom Center—Leadership to transform* [Video file]. Retrieved from https://www.youtube.com/watch?v=_9VRjZRLXoc

ENCOURAGING CREATIVE REFLECTION THROUGH JOURNALING
Jessica Chung

Art, Followership Focused

This learning activity offers the opportunity to reflect through an artistic medium that accesses a different processing part of the brain (Taylor, 2015) as well as encourages participants to actively create something uniquely their own and mirrors the artistry of leadership (Ladkin & Taylor, 2010). Through continued encouragement to process in formats and mediums that resonate with participants, we hope to cultivate a confidence in participants' unique artistic voice that parallels their confidence in their unique leadership voice. This conventional reflective practice can be modified to be a one-time activity or an ongoing practice throughout a program or a course.

Learning Outcomes:

Participants will have opportunities to:

- become more aware of their own metacognition styles.
- cultivate a confidence in their artistic voice.
- draw parallels between their artistic journey and leadership journey.

Setting Up the Activity:

- Group size: Any size group
- Time: 5–30 minutes.
- Materials: paper or notebooks that are blank, gridded, or dot patterned (not ruled/lined), pens, markers, and/or colored pencils in various colors and sizes, pad of paper or white board with markers for demonstration

Instructions:

1. Introduce activity by discussing how there will be reflection on a course topic through visual elements. Remind participants that the journaling process is private, is not graded on artistic ability, and is meant to encourage experimentation and potentially doing something new. (1–2 minutes)
2. Start with a header or focus of discussion (for example: "My identities"). Encourage participants to draw this header in an artistic way using bubble letters, fake calligraphy, or colorful cursive. Demonstrate on the pad of paper or white board. Remind participants to slow down, pause, and begin thinking more deeply about the topic as they write the header. (3–5 minutes)
3. As you reflect on a given topic or answer different course questions, encourage participants to continue using a variety of structures to process the material. Select activities that encourage participants to practice higher order thinking skills like analysis (compare/contrast, deconstruction), evaluating (critiquing), or creating (planning, designing, generating) in a visual or spatial way (Anderson, Krathwohl, & Bloom, 2001). Some examples and ideas include:

   - Identities: Draw something to represent you at the core in the middle. Start charting bubbles of the different social identities you hold. The closer or bigger they are, the more salient they are to you and your core identity. Use colors as you wish.
   - Comparison charts: In one column, label your communities. In the second column, identify how your strengths show up. In the third column, identify how you see other strengths show up. Discuss the gaps and overlaps.
   - Word clouds: Draw out the phrases in different styles, colors, sizes as you wish.
   - Key takeaway: After a lecture, take a few minutes to write out a phrase or quote of what you are taking away from discussion. Spend time drawing out the phrase in different styles, in sketches, or highlighting key words in different colors.
   - Draw connections: Write out different concepts or ideas discussed on a blank page. Draw and explain the connections between different concepts to create a web.
   - Ongoing journaling: encourage participants to document their day's events and thoughts in a variety of ways. Instead of a step by step in prose format, encourage participants to tape or glue in tickets, receipts, various mementos of events throughout the day. Experiment with using bullet points or brief agendas and more proselike reflections accompanied by mindmaps, takeaway highlights, and more.

4. Debrief with questions:

   - What was this process like for you?
   - How can this be useful to us in the future? In our leadership development?
   - What did this teach you about your personal preferences?
   - How can we encourage each other to experiment and try new things and be kind to ourselves while we try them as part of art as well as the art of personal leadership?

Facilitator Notes:

- Typically, participants are socialized to reflect linearly and chronologically, typically in written format. We want to push out of the default and experiment with options that may work differently or better for participants' various learning and processing styles which may be less linear, more spatial, or artistic.
- This activity may have been difficult for many reasons, such as: "I'm not artistic," "It took so much longer to do," "I kept looking at other people's paper." How do these limiting stories stifle our abilities?
- The demonstration is an important opportunity to role model vulnerability as you may also be cultivating your artistic skills and do not need to be an artist to engage with the process
- This may be validating for participants who process spatially or visually: "This made so much sense to me," "I never get to do this, I forgot how much I like it," "I didn't realize how much of a difference color would make." Where else are we forgetting to listen to our own preferences? How would we experience the world if we could do so on our own terms? How can we make it easier for others to do the same? How else can we break dominant narrative and limited options?

References:

Anderson, L., Krathwohl, D., & Bloom, B. (2001). *A taxonomy for learning, teaching, and assessing: A revision of Bloom's taxonomy of educational objectives* (Complete ed.). New York, NY: Pearson.

Ladkin, D., & Taylor, S. S. (2010). Leadership as art: Variations on a theme. *Leadership*, 6(3), 235–241.

Taylor, S. S. (2015). Leading to learn. *Journal of Leadership Studies*, 9(1), 52–55.

OOZING LEADERSHIP SLIME
Sally R. Watkins

Art, Curricular Learning Assessment

Incorporating craft in the leadership learning arena offers individuals the opportunity to apply their leadership learning and demonstrate mastery of course content. Specifically, this learning activity offers participants the opportunity to explore their personal identities, leadership roles and lived experiences while engaging in creative play. While typically seen as a fun activity for young children, making slime is enjoyable at any age and adding the purposeful aspects of this learning activity allows for participants to reflect on their leadership learning while having fun.

Learning Outcomes:

Participants will have opportunities to:

• reflect on their leadership journey up to this point.
• identify aspects of their leadership identity.
• articulate specific aspects of their leadership experiences.
• begin to clarify their personal leadership style.

Setting Up the Activity:

• Group size: Suited for small groups (5–10) but can be structured to work with larger groups (can often be constrained by time and cost of materials)
• Time: 45–60 minutes
• Materials: numerous tools and supplies which need to be set up at work tables or stations prior to starting the activity (see instructions for specifics)

Preactivity Set up:

1. Set up slime production work station with the required materials (10 participants):

   • Clear glue (40 ounces)
   • Cool and warm water (20 ounces both cool and warm)
   • Contact lens solution (12 ounce bottle)
   • Baking soda (1 box)
   • Measuring cups and spoons for dry and wet products
   • Mixing bowls and craft sticks for each participant
2. Set up leadership baubles and bits station. Suggested items to use in this activity are:

   • Container for mixing in the bits and bauble as well as storing the slime.
   • Glitter, sequins, foam beads, and water beads

Instructions:

1. Making the clear slime base. Printed instructions for the participants will help to facilitate slime making. When set up for individual work stations with premeasured ingredients the mixing phase is accomplished (5 minutes). Setting the activity up for individuals to stop at a different station for each ingredient. (20 minutes). Instructions to provide participants:

   • Combine 4 oz. of glue, 2 oz. of *cool water*, and 1 tablespoon of contact lens solution in a mixing bowl. Mix very slowly for about a minute.
   • In a separate cup, mix 4 oz. of *warm water* with 1 teaspoon of baking soda. Stir until baking soda completely dissolves.
   • Carefully pour the baking soda mix into glue mixture. Stir very gently for about a minute trying to avoid making bubbles.
   • Let sit undisturbed (5–10 minutes). *This is an important step!*

2. During the slime making process and during the gelling stage (10 minutes), ask participants to reflect on their leadership journey. This can be an individual experience or participants can engage in dialogue around the questions. Guide the process by asking the following questions:

   • Do you identify as a leader or a follower?
   • How do you know you are a leader?
   • How would you define your leadership style?

3. When each participant is finished making the slime, have them sit down and capture the thoughts and ideas that emerged during the guided reflection and dialogue. (Make sure to take the 10 minutes needed for the slime to gel.)
4. Have participants "shop" the bits and baubles station and include items that represent the ideas, thoughts, and concepts that emerged in their reflection. Now, add the items producing unique slime for each participant.

   • Foam beads for leader and/or follower identity.
   • Sequins represent having an elected or appointed leadership position.
   • Glitter for a variety of leadership styles (Include a definition of the style so participants can identify ones relevant to their responses to the reflection questions).

- Water beads grow in the slime, so ask individuals to use them to represent and interest in becoming a better leader.

5. Bring the group together and have participants share their personal slime.
6. Debrief with questions:

- What is present in the slime?
- Which add-in is most significant for them?
- Ask the participants to consider how their slime is similar to others and how it is different?
- What do the similarities and differences mean for the group?

Resource:

Dziengel. A. (2018, March 14). Amazing ice slime: How to make clear slime [Blog post]. Retrieved from https://babbledabbledo.com/how-to-make-clear-slime/

THE EYES HAVE IT: USING IMAGES AS A LEADERSHIP ASSESSMENT TOOL
J. Preston Yarborough and S. Todd Deal

Art, Cocurricular Learning Assessment

Visual Explorer cards (Center for Creative Leadership, 2019) engage learners through vibrant and compelling images designed to spark insight and conversation on leadership-related topics. Learn how to use these cards to assess for individual learning and for performance feedback within project teams. According to Palus and Horth (2014), the creators of this tool, images help engage the right-mode thinking processes in our brains. With the appropriate reflective structure in place, images can help us think more creatively and help us identify options and thoughts that we might not arrive at without such stimulus.

Learning Outcomes:

Participants will have opportunities to:

- explore their current understanding of relevant leadership theories, concepts and/or models.
- engage peers in exploratory leadership conversations.
- use projective strategies for examining group-level strengths and opportunities for improvement.

Setting Up the Activity:

- Group size: Up to 30 people; larger groups may be accommodated with additional cards
- Time: 30–45 minutes
- Materials: Set of Visual Explorer cards or create your own set of images using post cards, magazine images, et cetera (need approximately 70–100 pictures for up to 30 people).

Instructions:

1. Set-up for each method is basically the same.
2. Arrange Visual Explorer cards face up on a large table, or other space. For more than 10 people, position cards so they may be approached from several directions. For example, if you place your cards on a 6′ table, position the table away from any walls so participants can approach the table from both sides.
3. If possible, write the activity directions and prompt so participants can clearly see this information before and during their selection process. The directions and prompt will vary somewhat based on your intent for the exercise. Below, we will provide sample directions and prompts for individual learning, and performance feedback.
4. Participants can be instructed to choose a card and take it back to their seat. But if you have a large group and want to give participants the option to select from any image in the deck, rather than having them choose a card and take it back to their seat, have them "select" a card by taking a picture of it with their phone, thus leaving all the cards on display for everyone participating in the activity.
5. The methods below demonstrate how to use Visual Explorer for assessing/enhancing participant learning as well as generating performance appraisals within participant teams. The instructions below provide a structure for the basic facilitation of a Visual Explorer experience. We have offered recommended phrasing to aid in facilitating this experience. Please note these suggestions are meant for guidance and are by no means absolute.

- Method 1: Individual Learning:
  - Assessing for participants' understanding of a leadership theory or concept.
    * **Intro:** Say "I am interested in learning more about the leadership theories that have influenced your understanding of leadership this semester."
    * **Prompt:** Please select an image that helps you articulate the core principles of a leadership theory, model, or concept you learned this semester. (May choose to

group participants by theory/model/concept.)

  * **Write & Share**: Write about how this theory is represented by the image you selected, then share both your image and why you selected it with the small group. Capture key insights.
  * **Review**: In large group, ask, "What are the key points we need to know to deepen our understanding of this specific leadership theory/model/concept?"

- Method 2: Performance appraisal
  o Helping teams identify strengths and opportunities for improvement
    * **Intro**: Say, "I am interested in learning more about the strengths and the opportunities for improvement within your team. All teams have things they do well and things they can improve, so please do not worry about sharing areas you can improve."
    * **Prompt**: Select one image that symbolizes a strength of your team and select one image that represents an area you believe your team can improve.
    * **Share**: In our small group, share both of your images and why you selected them.
    * **Review**: In large group, ask, "What are key insights you've gained about specific actions your team will take to capitalize on your strengths as well as expand on your areas for improvement?"

Facilitator Notes:

- A deeper debrief of Visual Explorer can be achieve using the STAR model process, an approach that creates a structured dialogue where participants' insights progressively build on one another (Palus & Horth, 2014). The small group sits in a circle and one person at a time shares his/her image(s) according to a four-part pattern:

  o The initial volunteer displays his/her picture to the group. As "owner" of the image, the volunteer describes what s/he sees (e.g., what is happening, significant details, etc.).
  o Next, the owner describes the symbolic connection made between the image and the framing question. "This image represents [insert concept] to me because …"
  o "Putting it in the middle": Owner passes the image to other group members for their commentary. Each member starts by saying, "If I

had selected this image…." These "middle" observations may build on the original owner's comments or they can offer a completely different perspective.
    o After the image has been circulated and then returned to the owner, she or he thanks the group for their input and may (or may not) choose to adapt/adopt the perspectives shared. The steps are then repeated for the image(s) of each member of the group.

- *Varying prompts*: In the learning assessment method, you might find it preferable to identify a specific theory, model, or concept rather than the broader range suggested above. Furthermore, a very powerful reflection process can be created by personalizing the prompt (e.g., "find an image that helps you describe how you've grown as a leader this semester.")
- *Small group discussion size*: How large or small your discussion groups should be can vary. It is reasonable to estimate the average speaking time for each participant to be about 3–5 minutes, especially if you employ the STAR model debrief process. You can estimate groups of three will take approximately 10–15 minutes; a group of 5 would take approximately 20–25 minutes, et cetera.
- *Beyond assessment*: Visual Explorer is a helpful assessment tool but can be used for a wide range of reflection activities. It can also be used to facilitate dialogue, to envision future possibilities, to guide appreciative inquiry, and many other applications (Palus & Horth, 2014).

References:

Center for Creative Leadership. (2019). Leadership Explorer Tools. Retrieved from https://solutions.ccl.org/tools/leadership-explorer-tools

Palus, C., & Horth, D. (2014) *Facilitator's guide for Visual Explorer*. Greensboro, NC: Center for Creative Leadership.

Resources:

Jenkins, D., & Palus, C. (2018, December 27). Enhancing leadership learning and dialogue with visual explorer. *Interface: The Newsletter of the International Leadership Association*. Retrieved from https://intersections.ilamembers.org/member-benefit-access/interface/pause-for-pedagogy/2018ccl

Palus, C. J., & Drath, W. H. (2001). Putting something in the middle: An approach to dialogue. *Reflections*, 3(2), 28–39.

Palus, C. J., & Horth, D. M. (2002). *The leader's edge: Six creative competencies for navigating complex challenges*. San Francisco, CA: Jossey-Bass.

Palus, C. J., & Horth, D. M. (1996). Leading creatively: The art of making sense. *The Journal of Aesthetic Education*, 30(4), 53–68.

Editor and Contributor Bios

Dr. Josie Ahlquist is a research associate and instructor at Florida State University, creating curriculum to build digital literacy and leadership skills for undergraduates up to doctorate level students. Josie also supports institutions, executives and college students as a speaker, consultant, and coach on digital engagement and leadership.

Dr. Anne-Marie Algier is the associate dean of students at the University of Rochester. Anne has over 25 years of practical leadership application experience in roles in campus life including: residential life, student activities, and the office of the dean of students and educational pursuits resulting in a doctorate in educational leadership.

Dr. Sonja Ardoin is a learner, educator, author, and facilitator who is currently serving as an assistant professor in the Student Affairs Administration program at Appalachian State University. Sonja has taught leadership courses to undergraduate and graduate students, directed of an office of student leadership and engagement, contributed to several publications about leadership and leadership learning, and facilitates leadership programs for LeaderShape, Inc.

John Banter is the associate director of the office of leadership and community engagement at Georgia Southern University. He directs leadership programs for undergraduate students, coordinates the leadership course curriculum, teaches leadership courses, and is researching the leadership behavior development of students in formalized student leadership programs through his doctoral dissertation.

Jennifer Batchelder is a doctoral research assistant for the Leadership Learning Research Center at Florida State University where she serves as an instructor for the undergraduate leadership certificate program and contributes to research on leadership programs across the United States and internationally. She received her bachelor's in marketing and master's in student affairs in higher education from Texas State University-San Marcos and has served as a passionate leadership educator in her practitioner roles on Semester at Sea, at Austin College, and at St. Mary's University.

Tamara Bauer is an instructor at Kansas State University for the Staley School of Leadership Studies. Tamara teaches several leadership studies classes ranging from 20 to 150 students and uses experiential learning opportunities, including service-learning, with her students to actively apply leadership concepts to their lives. Her experience focuses on creating asset-based processes to learn about social challenges and apply leadership concepts throughout the process.

Dr. Cameron C. Beatty is an assistant professor of higher education and leadership studies at Florida State University. He has been teaching leadership educations courses for almost 10 years and approaches research on leadership learning and development from critical perspectives.

Brittany Brewster is a doctoral student in the higher education program at Florida State University. Brittany instructs courses for the undergraduate certificate in leadership studies program through the Leadership Learning Research Center. For 5 years, she facilitated co-curricular leadership and community engagement experiences for undergraduate students.

Dr. Jackie Bruce is an associate professor at North Carolina State University. Jackie is the director of graduate programs and teaches undergraduate and graduate courses, both face to face and online, related to leadership, organizational behavior, and qualitative research methods.

Dr. Eric Buschlen is an associate professor of educational leadership at Central Michigan University. Along with teaching leadership courses for over a decade, Eric has published several peer-reviewed articles on how serving others and service-learning experiences enhance a student's leadership identity development.

Virginia L. Byrne is a doctoral candidate in technology, learning and leadership at the University of Maryland, College Park's department of teaching and learning, policy and leadership. Virginia is a leadership and education research and teacher, who specializes in how technology be used for learning, community building, and positive social change.

Dr. Kathleen Callahan is lecturer in leadership studies at Christopher Newport University. Kat has taught leadership at four institutions of higher education over 11 years and currently serves as the past chair of the Leadership Scholarship MIG for the International Leadership Association.

Dr. Natasha H. Chapman is a lecturer for the minor in global engineering leadership in the A. James Clark School of Engineering at the University of Maryland, College Park. Natasha's scholarly interests include critical perspectives in leadership, leadership educator identity, and transforming learning.

Jessica Chung serves as the curriculum and instruction coordinator for the undergraduate leadership minor at the University of Minnesota Twin Cities. Jessica has spent years studying and practicing leadership education and development pedagogies to better serve all students through continually refining course curriculum and instructor training.

Dr. Vivechkanand S. Chunoo is assistant professor of agricultural education at the University of Illinois at Urbana-Champaign. V.'s teaching and research interests involve using cultural relevance and responsiveness in developing leader identity and capacity in first-generation college students, students of historically underrepresented racial and ethnic backgrounds, and students from lower socioeconomic communities.

Dr. Aaron D. Clevenger serves as the dean of international programs and senior international officer at Embry-Riddle Aeronautical University-Daytona Beach. Aaron has conducted extensive research into the use of experiential education and reflection in higher education and is the 2014 winner of the National Society of Experiential Education's Dissertation/Researcher of the Year for his work in experiential education and reflective pedagogy in engineering design competitions.

Dr. Natalie Coers serves as a lecturer of global agricultural leadership development at the University of Florida. She has a passion for connecting leadership education and intercultural development through experiential learning, especially travel and service.

Daniel Collins is a doctoral student at North Carolina State University. Daniel is studying the intersection of transformative leadership and principles of justice and equity while teaching and assisting with undergraduate courses in leadership.

Dr. Jasmine D. Collins is assistant professor of agricultural leadership education at the University of Illinois at Urbana Champaign. Jasmin teaches a number of courses related to leadership theory and practice including leadership ethics and social justice wherein she frequently uses discussion as a pedagogical tool.

Austin Council is a doctoral candidate at the University of Florida. Austin is very passionate about leadership education, particularly among undergraduate students, and his line of research explores the intersection of humility and leadership.

Dr. Amanda Cutchens is a senior academic advisor and the living learning community coordinator for the University of South Florida Honors College. Amanda taught Fundamentals of Leadership and Leadership Theories for 8 years and currently coteaches a study abroad course about social justice and social change in the Honors College.

Dr. S. Todd Deal is senior faculty and higher education practice leader at the Center for Creative Leadership. Todd is emeritus executive director and professor of leadership studies at Georgia Southern University where he and his team designed and created a student leadership and community engagement program that included academic service-learning and a minor in leadership studies.

Brittany Devies is a doctoral student in the higher education program at Florida State University. She works in the Leadership Learning Research Center as an instructor for the Undergraduate Certificate in Leadership Studies program. Her research interests include college women's leadership identity, capacity, and efficacy development and the influence of institutional mission statements and institutional culture on leadership learning.

John Egan is a leadership educator in the office of leadership and community engagement at Georgia Southern University. John coordinates leadership programming, teaches leadership courses, and is a doctoral candidate in educational leadership.

Lisa Endersby is an educational developer with the teaching commons at York University in Toronto, Canada, and also serves as coeditor of Pause for Pedagogy, a regular feature in the ILA Member Connector newsletter. Lisa has served as a project team member at the university, developing and facilitating numerous professional development opportunities for faculty looking to integrate globally networked learning into their leadership development curriculum.

Christopher Ruiz de Esparza is the director of diversity, inclusion, and leadership development at the University of Oregon's School of Law. He was introduced to improvisational theater over 25 years ago, performed with the Stanford Improvisors troupe for 4 years, and has since continued learning and teaching others about the applications of improv's key principles to life and leadership.

Jesse Ford is a doctoral student in the higher education program at Florida State University. His research examines the connections between leadership and multicultural pedagogy, particularly in the experiences of Black males.

Dr. Michael Gleason serves as associate professor of leadership at Wartburg College where he serves as director of the Institute for Leadership Education. He holds the Irving R. Burling Distinguished Professorship of Leadership. Prior to his current role, Michael served as director of the Leadership Institute at Washburn University.

Dr. Elizabeth Goryunova is an assistant professor of leadership and organizational studies at the University of Southern Maine. Elizabeth's scholarship and research are focused on leadership education in a global context as well as infusing gamification in the learning process. Prior to academia, Elizabeth served as president and CEO of the World Trade Center Utah, an organization with a global footprint.

Dr. Justin Greenleaf is an associate professor of leadership studies at Fort Hays State University. Justin teaches primarily undergraduate classes that focus on leadership concepts and behaviors as well as team dynamics.

Dr. Eric Grospitch is vice president for student life at Washburn University. Eric has over 20 years in student affairs at various institutional types primarily with a focus on student and leadership development.

Dr. Kathy L. Guthrie is an associate professor in the higher education program, director of the Leadership Learning Research Center, and coordinator of the Undergraduate Certificate in Leadership Studies at Florida State University. Kathy's research focuses on leadership learning outcomes, environment of leadership and civic education, and technology in leadership education.

Dr. Lindsay J. Hastings is the Clifton Professor in Mentoring Research and Director of Nebraska Human Resources Institute, a 360-student leadership mentoring program at the University of Nebraska. Lindsay has created and/or redesigned over 10 leadership education programs and courses for both K–12 and collegiate audiences in her role on the leadership faculty and has

written extensively on leadership mentoring, service-learning, and professional internships as pedagogical tools in leadership education.

Jason Headrick is a doctoral student and graduate teaching assistant at the University of Nebraska-Lincoln. Jason has incorporated role play and simulation across his courses and believes that students best learn in classrooms that engage their understanding of content through an environment that allows them to learn and tackle real-world issues.

Shelby Hearn is a second-year master's student at Loyola University Chicago and graduate assistant in student organizations and activities at Northwestern University. Shelby has developed an online leadership training platform for student organization leaders, and helps organize the annual Student Organization Symposium, a day of leadership training and development opportunities for incoming student organization officers.

Dr. Beth Hoag is currently the associate director of the Illinois Leadership Center at the University of Illinois at Urbana-Champaign. Beth's primary responsibilities include coordinating research and assessment efforts, designing curriculum, and building academic partnerships.

Dr. Daniel M. Jenkins is chair and associate professor of leadership and organizational studies at the University of Southern Maine. Dan teaches undergraduate and graduate courses in leadership and organizational theory, group dynamics, and research methods. Dan's research focuses on leadership education in face-to-face, blended, and distance learning modalities, pedagogy, course and curriculum design, and assessment and evaluation, as well as critical thinking.

Dr. Eric Kaufman is an associate professor and extension specialist in Virginia Tech's department of agricultural, leadership, and community education. Eric is a past president of the Association of Leadership Educators and has been recognized with national-level awards for distinguished teaching and outstanding educator workshops.

Dr. Naliyah Kaya is an assistant professor of sociology at Montgomery College and facilitates TOTUS spoken word experience at the University of Maryland. As a public sociologist, through artistic projects and assignments, she encourages students to engage in the sociological practice of reflexivity to better understand how external social factors influence and impact them and the ways in which they can utilize agency to address oppression.

Dr. Bobby Kunstman is a leadership educator who has worked in multiple settings in higher education that include noncredit programing, residential life, student union, leadership development, student organization management, volunteer programing, and teaching. When Bobby is not working, he actively engages in social change with volunteer work and in his personal life.

Julie LeBlanc is a doctoral student in the higher education program at Florida State University. She works in the Leadership Learning Research Center as an instructor for the Undergraduate Certificate in Leadership Studies program. She has more than 5 years of experience designing community engagement and leadership education programs and integrates reflective practices in curriculum for undergraduate students.

Dr. Marianne Lorensen is a specialized teaching faculty member in the Leadership Learning Research Center at Florida State University. Marianne wrote her dissertation on the use of service-learning in undergraduate leadership courses and has taught service-learning leadership courses at three universities in the United States.

Brian T. Magee is the associate director of Wilson Commons Student Activities and doctoral candidate at the University of Rochester. For over 10 years Brian has worked and published on aspects of college student leadership development, including currently serving on the Inter-Association Leadership Education Collaborative.

Dr. Amber Manning-Ouellette is an assistant professor of higher education and student affairs at Oklahoma State University. Amber has taught leadership studies courses centered in diversity and women's leadership and continues to research socially just leadership education and college students.

Dr. Cara McFadden is an associate professor in the department of sport management and serves as the faculty fellow for leadership education at Elon University. Cara received her PhD in educational leadership and policy studies from Virginia Tech and has over 15 years of combined experience in higher education. Cara currently serves as president-elect for the NIRSA: Leaders in Collegiate Recreation Board.

Michael Miller is a leadership consultant and speaker represented by SPEAK Educators, the Speakers' Division of Fun Enterprises, Inc. In addition to being responsible for student leadership development at six universities for over 20 years, Michael now serves higher education by working with staff and students to increase their leadership capacity.

Cristian Noriega is a graduate assistant for the student diversity and multicultural affairs office at Loyola University Chicago. Christian works for the Men's and LGBTQIA initiatives and focuses leadership education around recognizing systems of oppression and student identity development.

Dr. Julie E. Owen is an associate professor of leadership studies and coordinator of the leadership major and minor at the school of integrative studies, George Mason University. Julie frequently publishes on the value of critical reflection in leadership learning and is author of the forthcoming book, *Women's Leadership Development in College: Counter-Narratives & Critical Considerations*.

Kirstin C. Phelps is a doctoral candidate in information sciences at the University of Illinois at Urbana-Champaign. Kirstin's research pulls from her decade of experience as a leadership educator, and sits at the intersection of information behavior, leadership, and technology.

Dr. Darren Pierre is a clinical assistant professor in the higher education program at Loyola University Chicago where he teaches courses on student development, leadership in higher education, and oversees the undergraduate leadership minor. Darren has over 15 years of experience as a leadership educator serving in various roles within student activities and leadership programs.

Rachel Pridgen is the director of student involvement and transition programs at North Central College in Naperville, Illinois and doctoral student in higher education administration at Northern Illinois University. Rachel is a Gallup Strengths coach and has worked with strengths based curriculum for over 10 years.

Dr. Kerry L. Priest is an associate professor in the Staley School of Leadership Studies at Kansas State University. Kerry's teaching and scholarship integrates critical perspectives and engaged pedagogies that create the conditions for people to develop leadership through practice.

Ali Raza is a senior program coordinator in campus activities at Colorado State University. Ali is young professional who seeks to integrate leadership learning and education into his multiple roles of advising and supervising students.

Dr. Melissa L. Rocco is an affiliate assistant professor and program manager for leadership studies at the University of Maryland. Melissa's career as a leadership educator includes researching and publishing on leadership learning and identity, teaching in leadership and organizational studies programs, and designing and facilitating cocurricular leadership experiences both within and outside of higher education.

Rian Satterwhite serves as director of the office of service learning and leadership at the University of Nevada, Las Vegas. Rian teaches in the undergraduate leadership certificate program and serves a central role in advancing and tracking service-learning pedagogy across campus, offering professional development and support to faculty and academic units implementing service-learning.

Dr. Corey Seemiller is a faculty member in the organizational leadership program at Wright State University. Corey has taught leadership in curricular and cocurricular settings for more than 20 years and is the author of *The Student Leadership Competencies Guidebook*.

Michaela Shenberger is a higher education doctoral student at Florida State University, serving as the associate director of the Dr. Melvene D. Hardee Center for Leadership and Ethics in Higher Education. Michaela has had a number of opportunities to develop and facilitate leadership education during her time at Florida State University, including both curricular and co-curricular contexts.

Dr. Matthew Sowcik is an assistant professor of leadership education in the department of agricultural education and communications at the University of Florida. Matthew has published numerous articles and book chapters looking at the role humility plays on the leadership process.

Dr. Gayle Spencer is the director of the Illinois Leadership Center, at the University of Illinois at Urbana-Champaign. Gayle also currently teaches Emotional Intelligence and Leading Sustainable Change for the college of engineering at University of Illinois.

Thomas Stanley's career was dedicated to civic leadership development and his life revolved around family, faith and friendship. He started at the Kansas Leadership Center (KLC) as an intern in 2008, and was director of business initiatives when he passed away suddenly in September 2019. Resources Thomas developed during his tenure at KLC are used by teachers and coaches around the world.

Dr. Trisha Teig is a teaching assistant professor in the CWC Women's Leadership Scholars and the Pioneer Leadership program at the University of Denver. Trisha applies critical feminist pedagogy to teaching leadership in experiential classroom environments.

Dr. Sara E. Thompson is a leadership coach and consultant as well as an adjunct faculty at Claremont McKenna College. In her work, Sara focuses on developing the self-awareness and interpersonal skills necessary for individuals and teams to be successful in their personal and professional lives.

Dr. Maritza Torres is the assistant director for LEAD Scholars Academy at the University of Central Florida. Maritza teaches, advises, and facilitates leadership learning and scholarship to undergraduate and graduate students. Maritza's research centers on Latina undergraduate leader identity development, culturally relevant leadership learning and identity based leadership courses. Maritza is a coauthor of *Thinking to Transform: Reflection in Leadership Learning* and has contributed to *Changing the Narrative: Socially Just Leadership Education*.

Dr. Abigaile VanHorn, is the director of curriculum development at the Sigma Chi Leadership Institute. After teaching at the college level for over a decade, she now creates curriculum that promotes leadership and professional development skills for undergraduates across North America. Her background in both academic and student affairs provides her with a unique perspective of leadership theory and practice as it intersects with college student development.

Dr. Jillian M. Volpe White serves as director of strategic planning and assessment in the office of the vice president for student affairs at Florida State University. Jillian has more than 10 years of experience in community engagement and leadership development in curricular, cocurricular, and community contexts. She recently coauthored a book titled *Thinking to Transform: Reflection in Leadership Learning* and the companion manual *Thinking to Transform: Facilitating Reflection in Leadership Learning*.

Dr. Sally R. Watkins is a teaching faculty in leadership studies at Florida State University. Sally enjoys reflecting on her 20 years of professional work in student affairs and time spent teaching at the K–12 level as an art educator to identify ways to incorporate her learning in those arenas into the leadership studies classroom.

Erica Wiborg is a graduate assistant in the Leadership Learning Research Center and a doctoral student in the higher education program at Florida State University. In her role, Erica teaches in the Undergraduate Certificate in Leadership Studies where her courses have been focused on emotionally intelligent leadership, leadership theory, change and transition, social justice, identity, and spirituality.

J. Preston Yarborough is a member of the societal advancement faculty at the Center for Creative Leadership (CCL). Preston has 7 years of experience working in the higher education practice at CCL; before this, he served for 5 years as the assistant director of leadership of the office of leadership and service-learning at the University of North Carolina at Greensboro.

Printed in the USA
CPSIA information can be obtained
at www.ICGtesting.com
LVHW081734141124
796598LV00003B/331